You Say Tomato, I Say Shut Up

• • • •

a love story

• • • •

Annabelle Gurwitch and **Jeff Kahn**

Crown Publishers
New York

ALSO BY ANNABELLE GURWITCH

Fired!: Tales of the Canned, Canceled, Downsized, and Dismissed

Published in the United States by Crown Publishers,
an imprint of the Crown Publishing Group,
a division of Random House, Inc., New York.
www.crownpublishing.com

Crown is a trademark and the Crown colophon is a registered trademark of
Random House, Inc.

Library of Congress Cataloging-in-Publication Data

Gurwitch, Annabelle.
    You say tomato, I say shut up : a love story / Annabelle Gurwitch and
Jeff Kahn. — 1st ed.
        p. cm.
    1. Marriage—United States—Case studies.   2. Man-woman
relationships—United States—Case studies.   3. Gurwitch,
Annabelle—Marriage.   4. Kahn, Jeff—Marriage.   5. Married people—
United States—Biography.   6. Jews—United States—Biography.
7. Parenting—United States—Case studies.   I. Kahn, Jeff.   II. Title.
    HQ536.G86 2010
    306.810973—dc22

                                                                2009029355

ISBN 978-0-307-46377-7

Printed in the United States of America

Design by Donna Sinisgalli

10 9 8 7 6 5 4 3 2 1

First Edition

For our parents, who put up with us when we were kids.
For our kid, who puts up with us now that we're parents.

In loving memory of Dr. Columbus McAlpin, who
saved our son's life, our sanity, and perhaps even our
marriage.

Contents

Introduction

"Marriage is the only war in which you sleep with the enemy."

—CALVIN TRILLIN

He Says

When I was twelve, my sixth-grade English class went on a field trip to see Franco Zeffirelli's film adaptation of Shakespeare's *Romeo and Juliet.* From that moment forward I dreamed that someday I'd meet my own Juliet. I'd marry her and I would love her with the same passion and intensity as Romeo. The fact that their marriage lasted fewer than three days before they both were dead didn't seem to affect my fantasy. Even if they had lived, I don't think their relationship could have survived. Let's face it, being that emotionally aflame, sexually charged, and transcendentally eloquent every single second can really start to grate on a person's nerves. However, if I could find someone to love just a fraction of the way that Montague loved his Capulet, then marrying her would be worth it.

This proved to be a long, futile, and often pathetic search until I met Annabelle. I thought I had finally found my own gorgeous, talented, hyperarticulate Juliet. Unfortunately, much of my romanticism has been lost on Annabelle because she isn't exactly the world's most romantic person and doesn't get overly sentimental unless it's about her cat and certain cuts of beef.

In our relationship I'm the one who remembers and makes plans to celebrate birthdays, anniversaries, and even Valentine's Day. Given her very busy schedule and general forgetfulness, I'm lucky if Annabelle is even in town on my birthday, let alone remembers the actual date. In order to get a present from her, I have to pick out what I want (say, a vintage watch) and then buy it, bring her the receipt, and she'll reimburse me for it. This is why I was taken aback last year when Annabelle bragged about how she'd picked out the perfect Christmas present for me. She kept going on and on about how much I was going to love this gift and how she had really stepped up for me this time. Well, Christmas came and went, so sometime around March I finally asked her about the "perfect present" that I'd never received. She very offhandedly replied that the online company she'd ordered it from said the item was discontinued. That was as close as I've ever been to receiving a gift from Annabelle.

Basically, we have different marital needs. Annabelle craves a probing intellectual discourse of ideas with an academic who's willing to change the cat litter. I yearn for a marriage that is a romantic inspiration, a celebration of passions, and a terrific long-term opportunity to try out some really kinky *Kama Sutra*–type stuff. If you're not married to a person who rocks your world, what's the point? Marriage must go beyond the mundane and reach for the romantic. I don't simply want a convenient shared communal experience, a way to split the bills and grocery shopping. I can take care of myself, thank you very much. I cook, clean, do my laundry, and buy my clothes. It's true that marriage does tend toward the domestic and the pragmatic, but I want to be married for what I don't have, for what is missing in my life, that is, a person who gets who I am and is a really good kisser.

Yes, people love to claim that you and your spouse must be "best friends" in a marriage. Maybe that's true. Annabelle and I go out to dinner, see movies, travel, play tennis, e-mail, tease and kid each other, but at the end of the day, instead of hugging or shaking hands good-bye, as I do with all my other "best friends," I prefer that Annabelle sit on my face.

The only things that Annabelle and I can agree on is all the stuff we don't like: American Airlines, ourselves when we're around our parents, cloying romantic comedy movies about gorgeous wedding planners who help everyone get married but can't find a guy themselves, and when these same characters suddenly start singing and dancing to a clearly choreographed number that's somehow supposed to look spontaneous. We really hate that.

Yet my love for her is like a pilot light that refuses to dim. I love the way she smells, laughs, and the cute little sounds she makes when I snug-up next to her in bed at night. There is something about her that turns me inside out and inspires me. Since we met, she has been my muse. She's my raison d'être in a life filled with chaotic uncertainty, constant insecurity, and very questionable green-lit movies. This is why I married her.

I believe that Annabelle and I, like millions of other people, are standing at a new frontier of marriage. My wife informs me that there are more than three thousand analytical-therapy-inspired self-help books that claim to shed some light on this subject. I have tried to read some of them, but only get agitated and throw them across the room. I like to think of the authors of those books as the Daniel Boones and Davy Crocketts of the new frontier of marriage. And if they are Boones and Crocketts, then you should think of Annabelle and me and our book as the Donner Party. I hope our book will serve as a happy guide for the many people traveling up the same twisting, winding, rocky slopes of marriage as they do their best to avoid the paths we have taken so they won't get stuck with us on some freezing wintry mountain pass. It's in this spirit that we want to make you laugh and perhaps even learn from our profound lack of wisdom and warped perspectives. Because when it comes to being married, Annabelle and I are the Gurus of Wrong. Enjoy!

She Says

Tolstoy once said that it is easier to love all mankind than one man at a time. I don't think he was referring to marriage, but he might as well have been.

I was not the kind of girl who dreamed of growing up, getting married, and settling down. I never played dress-up weddings. I never pushed baby dolls in carriages. I pranced around in a home-made *Star Trek* uniform and had trolls whose hair I brushed until it stood on end, then I set them on fire and tossed them into traffic just to see them get crushed. I was that kind of girl. OK, I did have Barbies, but Babs was neither a wife nor a mother. She lived in a Malibu dream house and if the little accessories that came along with her were any clue, then it would be fair to say that she spent most of her time trying on tight-fitting polyester outfits and packing for overnight trips in teensy bags big enough to hold only tiny panties and a toothbrush. Where was she going? I didn't know, but I was happy she didn't have sweat glands and I liked her freewheeling style. I wanted to be just like her, only in thrift-shop clothing.

So it was a surprise for me even to decide to get married. Twice at this point! As a testament to how much I suck at relationships, when my first marriage broke up, my family took his side. In taking the plunge the second time, I didn't have a plan really—I just hoped to land somewhere between *The Way We Were* and *Who's Afraid of Virginia Woolf?*

Jeff and I reside in a household situated smack in the middle of that hazy divorce-riddled DMZ of the two-working-parents family. Holding a marriage together is getting harder and harder. For the first time since World War II, the number of couples who reach their twenty-fifth anniversaries, a milestone for sure, is declining. Fewer and fewer people are even getting hitched to begin with. In fact, single-headed households now outnumber the married in the United States. Complicating matters is the fragile state of the economy. Thus far, New York has seen a 20 percent increase in divorce filings, while Florida has seen an 18 percent drop-off, presumably because precipitously low property values make it harder for couples to extricate themselves financially from their unions. What does this tell us? Is it just a bad millennium for connubial bliss? More likely, this trend can be explained by studies that refute the accepted but antiquated notion that marriage makes you happier. Luckily, Jeff and I weren't that happy to begin with, so we've soldiered on and bumbled through thirteen years of marriage.

First among our missteps is our ongoing debate over the purpose of marriage itself. While Jeff looks at marriage as an extension of romance, I am a romance refugee. Prior to our union I spent an enormous amount of time on what I believed was a quest for romantic love that I now see as attempts to get laid. When I consider all the time I wasted thinking about getting laid, trying to get laid, and actually getting laid, it's mind-boggling. Not to mention the time I spent trying to get away from the same people I had just lain with once that pheromonal dopamine rush wore off, often immediately after the laying. This experience has made me deeply suspicious of that intoxicating and overemployed emotional state to which Jeff aspires, known as romantic love. I have had fleeting but powerful romances with several works of Russian literature, a pair of Christian Louboutin shoes, and the word *palanquin*. Furthermore, I often believed myself to be in love with scores of men I didn't particularly like and who didn't like me, much less speak the same language. Besides, talk about a revisionist romantic, Jeff might talk a good game about the fun things we do together, but he actually stopped playing tennis with me because he says I'm not competitive enough for him. He forgot that detail, so I win. Who's not competitive enough now? Huh?

At the risk of sounding like a piker, I look at marriage as an expression of our love, yes, but also as a joining together to deal with practical things such as raising children, caring for aging parents, and securing long-term health care insurance. Is there anything that kills an erection quicker than the phrase "long-term health insurance"? However, the horror of these all-too-human experiences is mitigated (somewhat) by sharing and surviving them with someone you deeply love. Look, I sat on a lot of guys' faces, but I wouldn't have picked up for any one of them four times in two months after dental surgery, as I did for my Jeff this past summer.

Jeff and I aren't marriage boosters. I would never dream of telling anyone they should get or stay or stop being married—unless they were attached to the idea that they were going to live "happily ever after." Then I'd tell them they were out of their minds. Wouldn't just "ever after" make more sense—"and they lived ever after"? It's worth noting that contrary to the fairy tales popularized by Disney movies, the centuries-older *Tales of the Arabian Nights* concludes with a far more practical message for children. Those folk tales end with the warning "they lived happily until there came to them the One who destroys all happiness (presumably death)." Much more realistic.

In the end, if Jeff and I do manage to make it to that elusive silver anniversary, this volume will stand as a testament to our love. On the other hand, if we should ever separate, after reading this book, no one will be surprised!

What is it that keeps us together? Is it our son, whom we both madly adore? Our profound soulful connection? The deep empathy that we feel for each other? That Jeff has better health care coverage than I have? Or just plain exhaustion and inertia? Not sure. I often think about the scene from *Goodfellas* when the Robert DeNiro character tells the Lorraine Bracco character to walk down the alley 'cause he's got some great dresses for her. "Go on, go on," he urges her. But sensing the danger in his voice, she turns and runs. I liken our marriage to more of a walk down that alley than a walk down the aisle. What if Lorraine had kept walking? True, she probably would have gotten whacked anyway, but before she died, she just might have lucked into some great dresses.

Jeff says we're the Gurus of Wrong. I think that sounds pretty good—at least we're achieving at something, even failure. Jeff hopes you might learn something. I'm not sure about that, but if you've ever wondered if anyone else is as confused, demoralized, or befuddled about marriage as you, take heart. We are. It's in that spirit I offer our story.

"*Marriage is like* that show *Everybody Loves Raymond,* but it's not funny. All the problems are the same, but instead of all the funny, pithy dialogue, everybody is really pissed off and tense." —Paul Rudd in *Knocked Up*

marriagonomics

The number of marriages in the United States has averaged 2.25–2.4 million every year for the past twenty years, but a third are remarriages. So maybe it's just those serial marriers who are responsible for keeping the number consistent.

forget the seven-year itch

University of Wisconsin researchers have now published findings that suggest the spark actually fizzles within three years: "Folks start getting less happy at the wedding reception" (Professor Larry Bumpass).

familiarity breeds contempt

It's not just anecdotal anymore—less really is more. A paper titled "The Lure of Ambiguity," written by Harvard, MIT, and Boston University scholars, makes it clear that in repeated studies, the more people knew about each other, the less they liked each other.

what i did for love?

75 percent of suicide attempts are due to relationship problems

11 percent of the murders in the United States are killings by intimates

but will we be fit enough to survive marriage?

Charles Darwin came to marriage with some trepidation. Of course he studied it carefully, cataloging the pluses and minuses of the connubial state. His list included the following:

PROS:

Constant companion and friend in old age

Object to be beloved and played with

Better than a dog anyhow

Someone to take care of house

Charms of music and female chitchat

Picture self with a nice, soft wife on a sofa with a good fire

CONS:

Freedom to go where one liked

Not forced to visit relatives

Perhaps quarreling

Expense and anxiety of children

Cannot read in the evenings

Fatness and idleness

Less money for books

• • • • • • • • • • • • • • • • • • •

1

. . . .

Let Us Now Praise Lactose Intolerance

"Kissing is a means of getting two people so close together that they can't see anything wrong with each other."

—RENE YASENEK

Like the universe, every marriage has a beginning, whether it's the "Big Bang," the hand of God, or J-Date. There are places in the world where marriages are still arranged by one's family. We find this practice mind-boggling since we get panicky when our parents pick out a restaurant for us. When, how, why, and where two people first meet and become a couple can often be indicative of what kind of marriage they might someday have. For instance, there are plenty of marriages that begin and end in bars. Our meeting was definitely a precursor to the type of chaotic, unpredictable, and lactose-intolerant married couple we would eventually become.

He Says

It was 1989 and I was a young writer living in New York, working at MTV in their unofficial "Indentured Servitude Writing Program," so when I got a call from the Fox network to write a made-for-TV movie, I leaped at the chance to go to Los Angeles. The good people at Fox were kind enough to put me up at the Oakwood Apartment complex: furnished apartments decorated in late-1970s putrid—shag carpeting, avocado-painted kitchen, and a swimming pool full of hairy Iranians in Speedos. The next thing I know, I'm meeting with the producers Bob and Lou, who are jumping out of their skins to pitch me their "can't miss" movie. They have no plot, no characters, and absolutely no ideas. All they have is a title: *Cooties*. Bob and Lou have come to movie producing from marketing and are convinced that as soon as I come up with a concept, a plot, characters, and dialogue, and then make it really, really funny, they will deliver a veritable Cooties empire of Cooties toys, Cooties video games, a Cooties hotel-restaurant-casino, and a Cooties family theme park. We're all going to become very, very rich from Cooties! Clearly, Bob and Lou are clinically insane, but they're footing the bill, so I go back to the Oakwood to contemplate *Cooties: The Movie*.

A week later, Bob and Lou call to see how the script is going. I excitedly tell them that they "better hurry up and buy those Cooties theme park tickets, because I'm on a roll!" I haven't written a single word. Relieved by my lie that the writing is going so well, Bob and Lou invite me to join them at a Rosh Hashanah party. As a rule, I don't do Jewish New Year parties (they tend to be a little too Jewy for my tastes), but Bob and Lou promise that there will be some cute girls, so I figured why not Jew it up for a night? As soon as I walk into the party, I see her at the stove cooking potato latkes. I'm immediately hit with an overwhelming sensation that I'm looking at my future wife. Armed with the confidence of this prophetic vision, I charge over and commence flirtation with Latke Lady.

Her first name is Annabelle, the perfect name! Her last name is Gurwitch, the worst name. But the Annabelle part is so amazing it obliterates the Gurwitch part. Even better, Annabelle is enchanting, with porcelain skin and hair the colors of autumn in Vermont. She loves Bob Dylan, Isaac Bashevis Singer, and the Tao Te Ching—the holy Trinity of things I also love. We banter, we joke, we laugh, and we sit next to each other during dinner. I'm so enraptured by her I sneak off to call my best friend in New York and tell him I've just met "the one." At the end of the party she writes her name, number, and street address on a napkin for me. This is it, I thought, I'm in! From this point forth, it's Annabelle and Jeff forever. As I walk her to her car she tells me that she has some free time to hang out because her husband is away at art school in Chicago; then she hops into her Honda and drives away. I stand there staggered, all the air in my body sucked out as if Mike Tyson had punched me in the stomach. I need some air, need air! "I'm sorry, her what? Her who?" The woman of my dreams married to some art school student? Was this some kind of High Holiday joke to amuse God on Rosh Hashanah? I hope I made his High Holy Days, because I'm miserable.

Back in New York, I can't stop thinking and talking about Annabelle. My friends literally beg me to shut up. As my career fate would have it, for the next year and a half I shuttle between New York and Los Angeles for work, and I time my red-eye flights so I can be at Farmers Market at the precise moment Annabelle has her morning cappuccino at her favorite café. (I ran into her there once by chance and over the booming noise of my heart pounding in my chest, I was able to make out her saying that she has coffee there almost every day at that time.) While I'm working in LA, I try to see her every chance I get and even dare to write her love letters.

Some see this full-throttle approach to win Annabelle's heart as romantic; others call it stalking and urge me to get professional help. One windy afternoon Annabelle and I find ourselves on Venice Beach and I kiss her. It's the single most romantic moment of my entire life. We end up spending the night together in her apartment because art school husband didn't seem to get home much. I believe we would have had sex that night, but unfortunately, we had eaten pizza for dinner. These were the days before Lactaid tablets, and later the cheese tore at my stomach like thousands of tiny razor-sharp daggers from Wisconsin. It took all my concentration not to fart or pass out from the pain.

The next day we wake up in each other's arms and Annabelle looks me in the eyes and tells me she's very happily married, and we can never do this ever, ever again, *ever.* I tell her she's just fooling herself. How is she going to stay married when we belong together? Annabelle gets very indignant. She wants us to be friends. Suddenly she's very committed to her marriage. I can't believe that after coming so close, I have to spend the rest of my life being friends with the woman of my dreams. Damn cheese!

It's not long before I move permanently to the West Coast and hear that happily married Annabelle is now happily divorced and seeing RJ, a friend of a friend. He's heard all about my obsession with his girlfriend, but isn't concerned, according to my friend, because he's a hot, young Hollywood director with bigger fish to fry. Hearing this has the effect of reducing my ego to the size of a spawning anchovy.

My friend invites me to tag along with him to Annabelle's birthday party. I think that if I go and flirt with other girls at her party, it'll make her so jealous she'll realize she's in love with me, not RJ. My ingenious plan never quite gets off the ground because her party is, by design, wall-to-wall men. Annabelle ignores me and buzzes from guy to guy like a bumblebee in a never-ending garden of man flowers. Fish-frying RJ sits on the sofa like a petulant teenager who's had too much to drink and is looking for a face to punch. Not wanting to be that face, and pissed off at being wholly disregarded by the birthday girl, I leave the party, figuring I'll never see Annabelle again. So I'm shocked when she calls out of the blue a half year later. She and RJ have broken up and she's practically begging me to attend a preview performance of her one-woman show. Yes! Annabelle wants me again. I'm back, baby! During her show I discreetly jot down a few funny lines. This way I'll be able to quote them afterward when I praise her for her fine, fine work. Instead, she's livid with me, accuses me of working on my own scripts during her show, and hangs up on me when I call to defend myself.

I'm completely crushed, which is why I'm astounded when several months after that Annabelle shows up at my door, unannounced, with her incredibly cute new kitten. Annabelle is heading off to New York to act in a play and she desperately needs someone to take care of Stinky. How can she have the nerve to ask me to take care of her kitten after telling me off on the phone and hanging up on me? I look straight at Annabelle and tell her, "Of course Stinky can stay. I'd be happy to have her." Maybe now she will finally see what a great guy I am and give herself to me, body and soul. As it turns out, Stinky is an incredibly loving cat. She follows me everywhere, wants to be petted all the time, desires my undivided attention, and sleeps cuddled next to me every night. Stinky is everything I want from Annabelle, but furrier and happens to poop in a litter box. When Annabelle returns, she doesn't give me her body or her soul, but instead hands me a copy of Søren Kierkegaard's *Leap of Faith*. Does this book mean I should keep leaping in faith for her? I'll never know. It's so tedious to read existential Christian Scandinavian philosophy; I never made it past the inscription "Thanks for taking care of us, Annabelle and Stinky."

I try to accept the fact that Annabelle and I are just not meant to be. Life moves on, my career starts picking up steam, I have lots of friends, I date occasionally, and I see a really good shrink. I am actually fairly content with my life on the day I look out my apartment window and see Annabelle standing by a moving van. She is, I kid you not, moving right next door to me. I'm staggered, thrilled, itchy. This must be fate, a sign from above. I go over to welcome her with a bottle of wine. Later I call to ask her out, but call waiting clicks in before she can answer me. She tells me she'll be right back. Two minutes later she clicks back and says she's almost done with the other call and then she puts me on hold again. I fiddle with a *Seinfeld* script. Floss my teeth. Maybe five minutes later Annabelle's back, saying it's taking longer than she thought, but she'll be right with me. Click. She puts me back on hold. I take a piss and pay my phone, gas, and electric bills. Ten minutes later she's back to say she's in the middle of a major dramathon with her latest ex-boyfriend and asks if I don't mind waiting just a little longer. I start a load of laundry, cook a soy cheese omelet, eat it, rinse off the dishes and dry them. Twenty, maybe thirty minutes later she's still hasn't returned. I hang up and officially abandon any hope for Annabelle. I get rid of my apartment and move as far up into the Hollywood Hills as I can go without actually hitting the HOLLYWOOD sign and hope she'll never find me.

More than a year later I walk into a restaurant and there she is. For some reason, Annabelle seems genuinely, perhaps even *too* happy to see me. "Where did you go?" she asks. "Why did you move? Why didn't you call me?" She gives me her new cell number and wants me to call her so we can catch up. My writing partner at the time informs me that if I call Annabelle after all she's put me through for the last five years, she'll personally kick my ass. Of course I won't call her, I assure my partner. I am fully over Annabelle and whatever strange fried-potato High Holiday Cooties spell she cast over me, I *will not* call her. I mean, come on, I'm not a complete idiot!

On the way home from the restaurant, I call Annabelle and we make a plan to go out, confirming once more that when it comes to very attractive, nutty young women who have conflicted feelings for me, I am a complete and utter idiot. Thank God.

She Says

In my early twenties, my entire ambition in life was to appear in avant-garde adaptations of German expressionistic dramas in un-heated basements in off-off, nowhere-near-Broadway theaters. As it turned out, this goal was not that hard to achieve, particularly if you're not interested in purchasing luxuries like food or furniture. But after ten years of eking out an income in New York City and living in a studio apartment where you could literally be in bed, open the door, and fry an egg at the same time, it was time to con-quer new worlds. The year was 1989 and I moved to a middle-class neighborhood in Los Angeles teeming with aspiring actors, group homes for the mentally disabled, halfway houses, and religious Jews. It's known to locals as the actors' shtetl. It was so filled with mem-bers of the Screen Actors Guild that on any given day you could sit on your stoop going over your lines for an audition, look across the way and see other people sitting on their stoops talking to them-selves, and know that either they were crazy or they were just actors working on their lines, or maybe they were crazy but they were also actors who were working on their lines. My neighbor on one side was George Clooney; and a future porn star lived across the hall. Up-and-coming actors Sandra Bullock and Tate Donovan were shacked up across the street, while the rest of our block was popu-lated by Orthodox Jewish couples whose duplexes were exploding with children. After six months of auditions and working a part-time gig hostessing at an after-hours Euro-trash coke den, I had landed a lucrative gig on TV, so professionally things were on an up-swing. But I didn't have many friends in the city yet so when I was invited to a Rosh Hashanah party, I happily agreed.

Arriving at the house, I settled into the kitchen and began cooking. I don't remember every detail of that particular evening, but I do remember this: Jeff Kahn—funny, sweet—paid a lot of at-tention to me. We shared the same taste in melancholy music and literature, and were both vaguely and pretentiously interested in Eastern philosophy. Did I mention I was married? That's right—I don't think I mentioned this small detail, but why would I? I wasn't on the market.

My then husband was a Church of England, anarchist artist. You know the type: incredibly sweet but exceedingly eccentric. Tall, lanky, blond, choirboyish. Straight, but looked smashing in a dress. Good-natured but given to outbursts of Tourette's-like rants against the evils of "fucking wanker TV idiots" at dinners with the heads of the network I was employed by at the time. Only his posh British accent and dashing good looks kept me from getting fired. We had impulsively decided to get married the night we met, and we actually married within a year from that date so we didn't know each other all that well. Early on, the ex had casually mentioned that his goal in life was to bankrupt himself in pursuit of his art. I assumed this was hyperbole, but only a few months into our marriage, I learned that he meant it literally. By the time I met Jeff, he had moved to Chicago to attend graduate school at the Art Institute and he was well on his way to achieving his stated dream.

I should mention here that due to the aforementioned shambles of a marriage, I was already having an affair with someone and the last thing I was looking for was another complication. That guy was another tortured soul, also married, a Buddhist who was bipolar and addicted to a number of drugs of various varieties. This was ill advised but also highly entertaining. I'd get calls to watch him withdraw from some drug or another, read from an anglicized pocket version of the Tao, and listen to equally spiritually ambiguous music like Sinéad O'Connor and Dead Can Dance. My life was a train wreck when I met Jeff Kahn.

On top of that, Jeff seemed like just the kind of guy I had avoided my whole dating life: nice, totally into me. *Turnoff.* And he was Jewish. Since high school I had stuck to my rule: one Jew per bed is enough!

My family moved to Miami Beach when I was twelve. Not the current hipster South Beach, no, this was strictly the Miami Beach of the past where your alter caca aunt spent her winters at a kosher hotel and my teenage years were spent getting felt up by members of BESHTY, the Temple Beth Shalom youth group. After leaving Miami, I was anxious to expand my horizons: I only dated men of varying religious and cultural backgrounds. I hadn't even seen a circumcised penis in years.

Clearly, Jeff Kahn was "friend" material and possibly only interested in me because I was unavailable. How much more unavailable could I be? I wrote my number down on a napkin. I told him to call and we'd hang out. Between the absent anarchist and the married manic-depressive, I had a little extra friend time.

Not only did Jeff start calling me at odd hours, he would drop by my house unexpectedly. Sometimes I would get a call and he would be circling the house. At eleven-thirty at night. Then he began sending obsessive missives.

I quote: "I came to you a knight in shining armor and offered you my heart and in return you gave me a stick of gum!" He even wrote: "Some enchanted evening, you may see a stranger. You may see a stranger cooking latkes across a crowded room." He was gripped by what I deemed a delusionary fantasy that we belonged together. It was a cross between a Philip Roth novel and a John Hinckley fixation. I had already married one guy who proposed on the night we met; why had I attracted another man who was seized by the same impulse? I wasn't sure whether Jeff was an incurable romantic or whether I should take out restraining orders.

One night he unexpectedly dropped by to drop off a bottle of single malt whiskey when he knew my husband would be in town, a pretext for a getting a look at him. "What's with that guy?" my husband asked in his enticing Cambridge accent. I wasn't kidding when I said, "I have no idea."

Jeff correctly predicted that my marriage would end. I had a succession of boyfriends and yet all the while Jeff kept up his pursuit. I would be out having a morning coffee and he would be sitting at a nearby table. Then there was that birthday party he turned up at. I had no idea why Jeff acted weird and left without saying a word. There were a lot of great guys he could have networked with—wasn't he an aspiring television producer? The play reading I invited him to attend? It was infuriating. Every time I looked up from my pages, I could plainly see that he was writing. Nothing Jeff says will ever convince me that he wasn't working on a script during the entire length of the show. It was so rude! If he was so interested in me, why did he keep doing things I couldn't understand?

Jeff also had something of an acting career going at the time and would excitedly call to say, "Hey, I'm appearing as 'Bell Boy Number Five' on *Blossom* this week." Or, "I'm shooting a movie where I play a character named Nosey. I get to spend three hours a day getting a foot-long nose glued to my forehead; would you like to visit the set?" This, too, was a dating turnoff for me. I really didn't want to date actors anymore. Sleep with them once in a while, sure, but date?

No way. I had had my share of "showmances," including my soap opera costar, who called me my character's name while we were having sex, and my classically trained boyfriend, who insisted I should do his laundry because "Hamlet doesn't do laundry!"* Besides, there's something that turns me off about dating actors. Maybe it stems from my personal experience of knowing how much time they spend looking at themselves in the mirror, primping. I find this kind of vanity in a woman forgivable and something I am completely guilty of, but in a guy, yuk! Vin Diesel is no doubt sitting in a makeup trailer at this very moment checking out shades of blush, right next to Dwayne Johnson, aka The Rock, who's having a little concealer applied. No thanks.

But there was something I liked about Jeff, something that kept drawing me back to him, kind of like the way it's fun to peel a sunburn or how a song gets stuck in your head and you can't stop singing, "You're beautiful, you're beautiful, it's true," even when you really, really want to.

Over the next years, I would run into Jeff and we might go on a date during which time I thought it my moral duty to dissuade him from pursuing me, but at the same time I would irresponsibly find myself making out with him too. Now, I don't pretend this is a respectable way to conduct myself. In fact, it was completely insane. But I was in my twenties, an actress, given to dating men whose most memorable attribute was an interesting accent—the very definition of completely insane.

At a certain point, a truly improbable thing happened. I moved into an apartment building right next door to Jeff. However, while

*A showmance, like an office romance, occurs quite often in show business, where you can find yourself easily confusing your real life with your on-screen life. Which is why it's never a surprise to read that Renee has fallen in love with Jim Carrey, Jack White, Bradley Cooper, or whomever she's working with at the time.

Jeff sees the fact that he happened to live in a very desirable location where rents were reasonable, as the hand of fate working it's way to bring us together, I maintain this is just a very good example of how people like to assign meaning in the random universe. After Jeff disappeared from the neighborhood, I didn't give it another thought.

It was maybe a year later when I ran into him at a café. It was as if a lightbulb went off in my head. Jeff Kahn—what a great guy; didn't he once take good care of my cat? Perhaps it makes sense to date someone who actually seems to like me, who shares my lactose intolerance and sense of humor, and whose sole interest isn't to have me witness the disintegration of his personality. It was during our first date that I confessed something extremely shallow: the one time we had come closest to carnal relations, five years prior, I hesitated only because I had seen the top of his undergarments and was convinced he had on tighty whities. Jeff dropped his pants right then and there in the restaurant and showed me that the Calvins he was wearing, like the ones he had donned on that date five years previously, were, in fact, long briefs. We started dating that very night. Jeff still mourns the fact that this mistaken-undergarment moment set us back years of being together, but I'm convinced that this one snafu is the only reason we're together today. I consider this whole chapter of my life embarrassing and sad, while Jeff refers to those years as our romantic courtship. We'll never agree, but just to put things in perspective, Jeff loves to tell people that he was so smitten with me that he saved the napkin I gave him on the night we met. For the record, it has another girl's phone number on the back.

the single life

In the first decade of the twenty-first century, the *New York Times* reports, the proportion of Americans in every racial and ethnic group who have never married has grown by double digits. Married couples slipped into the minority in the United States in 2006. Census reports found that 49.7 percent, or 55.2 million, of the nation's 111.1 million households in 2005 were made up of married couples—with and without children—just shy of a majority and down from more than 52 percent five years earlier.

location, location, location

What's the best place to get a date? In a survey asking couples where they met:

- 38 percent met at work
- 34 percent met through friends
- 13 percent met at a nightclub
- 2 percent met at church
- 1 percent met because they live in the same neighborhood
- 1 percent of people who meet at gyms end up dating

aging up

In 1900, the median age of people getting married in the United States was twenty-six for men and twenty-two for women. During the period from 1950 to 1960, it fell to twenty-three for men and twenty for women. Since 2005, the median age at marriage has remained at twenty-seven for men and nearly twenty-six for women, an all-time high, according to census data.

the x factor

A nasal spray, Factor X, is being marketed as a product designed to help men pick up women. The Web site features "real life" testimonials:

> "I used to have lots of trouble attracting women. I wondered why other men managed to find women so easily. Factor X changed all that; now I actually choose whom I would like to date. It's a miracle!"
>
> —Pete (name withheld because he doesn't really exist)

The spray delivers what's been called the love hormone: oxytocin. Factor X claims to raise your dopamine level by 500 percent, allowing you to exude charm and raise your confidence level, in turn leading others to trust you and then presumably beg you to undress them.

2

. . . .

A Saab Story ·

"Love is the triumph of imagination over intelligence."

—H. L. MENCKEN

"Marriage: souvenir of love."

—HELEN ROWLAND

Some couples meet, fall in love, and get engaged in a whirlwind of passion and romantic expediency. We call these predivorce engagements. Other couples linger together for years, but never manage to get engaged. We call these people too happy to get married. Our relationship trajectory from dating to engagement was neither too abrupt nor too drawn out, but it wasn't a Goldilocks "just right" either.

He Says

I had only one problem with Annabelle's suddenly liking me after five years: I didn't trust her. I kept waiting for her traditional kiss me–dump me scenario to play out. So this time around I was cautious. I withheld more than I normally did when I'm crazy about a girl and applied the brakes on my customary steamrolling train of emotional needs, so that when the inevitable arrived and Annabelle stopped kissing me long enough to tell me she just wanted us to be friends, I'd be prepared. There was only one slight problem: it never happened. I was as shocked by this as anyone. Annabelle had become the pursuer, the aggressor, the one pushing the relationship agenda, making sure that I was into her as much as she was into me. She was now the one in the insecure emotional driver's seat. I felt like a cornered rat, albeit a really lucky cornered rat.

Honestly, I hadn't had an actual girlfriend since the middle of the second Reagan administration so this was very unfamiliar territory for me. How would I know for sure after all this time that Annabelle and I were really right for each other? I had always felt deeply romantic about her, but what would happen now that we might actually have sex? Since my last committed relationship had ended (during the Iran-Contra affair), I had dated almost every woman in the free world and realized that when it comes to sex, each one presents her own labyrinth of likes and dislikes, do's and don'ts, and don't-you-even-think-about-its. Some don't like oral sex. Some refuse to do certain sexual positions. Some like a finger in their ass; others will turn around and literally punch you in the face if you try. It's not that I'm the Marquis de Sade or anything. I'm more like his kinder, gentler Jewish first cousin, Steven de Sadderstein. So I invented the Perv-O-Meter, a scale that registers how far someone was willing to venture with me into the "realms of the senses." Scoring varied from girl to girl. Amelia, my college girlfriend, was a bisexual, kleptomaniac, and pathological liar, but managed to balance it very nicely by also being a nymphomaniac. She scored a deviant 10 on the Perv-O-Meter. New York Nicole wore a Hudson River's worth of patchouli oil, bathed in lavender, and scented her apartment with strawberry incense twenty-four hours a day. It was like being in a Turkish whorehouse—unfortunately, minus the whore—and scored an aromatic 2. Oklahoma Gracie fucked me in gravelly alleyways outside Chicago's Wrigleyville bars—a painful, yet well worth it, 8.5. So where did Annabelle fit on the Perv-O-Meter? Well, without getting into too many sordid details that will lead our child into years of therapy, Annabelle, although not a bisexual collegiate nymphet, tallied a passionate, inventive, and quite skillful 9. And what's more, as far as I could tell, she hardly ever lied or stole anything.

Another thing I couldn't be sure of was how comfortable or willing I would be to spend the night in someone's company. Let's face it, it's very telling if after being really intimate with someone that you want to stick around to see them in the light of day. For me, having sex with conflicted intentions of becoming serious always went straight to my enlarged, remorse-producing "guiltrious" gland. The by-product was an onset of the PEBs, or Post-Ejaculatory Blues. The PEBs made me restless and self-conscious, rendering it excruciatingly difficult to spend the night. (This is not anything that I'm proud of.) Consequently, I came up with the Cuddle-lator. The Cuddle-lator was the amount of time I stayed in bed after sex before I made up a lame excuse and left. Kayla, the supercute feminist who corrected me if I called any female older than eleven a girl and not a "womyn," scored over forty-five minutes on the Cuddle-lator. Megan, a terrific Chicago actress who lived on top of a jazz club where the thump of the bass shook the walls, got up to almost an hour and a half. Kinky yet kooky Janet, who was training to be a therapist but nevertheless once stalked a good friend months after they broke up, made it to only ten minutes because I was actually afraid of her. Consequently, I was thrilled when Annabelle's Cuddle-lator calculation was off the charts! Not only did I not want to run off in the middle of the night, I had a hard time leaving Annabelle's side in the morning. It was warm and sweet and minus the pangs of guilt, fear, or self-loathing I had felt with others. OK, yes, occasionally I might sneak downstairs and let out a couple hundred farts into her leather sofa so she wouldn't hear them. I figured that was a better plan than letting them loose in the bed and revealing the ghastly flatulence machine I truly am. There'd be plenty of time to cross that bridge to nowhere.

Then, a month or so into our fledgling relationship, I arranged to introduce Annabelle to all my best buddies from college. While they had all heard me nattering on about her for years, they had never actually met her. Unlike my writing partner, a woman who didn't quite trust her, my guy friends didn't trust *me*. They had seen many of my past crushes explode in my face, and here was the mother of all crushes. Let's just say they didn't exactly believe my claim that Annabelle was now into me. Yet when they met her and saw her genuine affection for me, they were overjoyed for both of us. My close pal Rick took me aside after Annabelle had gone off to the bathroom and politely told me, "She's amazing. Don't you dare fuck this up or I will be forced to beat the shit out of you."

Later that night as Annabelle and I were making out in my Saab outside her apartment, she got very serious and declared that she thought we should move in together. She made some very credible arguments for this. We could split the rent on my house, we wouldn't have to waste any more time negotiating whose place we'd be staying over at, and by cohabiting we'd quickly find out how compatible we actually were. She reminded me that Rick had bragged that he had recently gotten engaged and moved in with his girlfriend after less than a month of dating. I respectfully suggested we should take some time for reflection to digest what was happening in order to make coherent decisions and plans. Also, let's face it—I still hadn't farted in front of her. I assured her that Rick would beat me up if I didn't make good on this relationship so she had nothing to worry about. Annabelle backed off a little, but in the way a lioness backs off the prey she's stalking in order to give it an illusion of safety.

About a month after that we took the Saab up to San Francisco because Annabelle wanted me to meet her sister's family in Tiburon, a suburb just over the Golden Gate Bridge. We amused ourselves during the four hundred miles by improvising and acting out a story that had us laughing our heads off all the way to San Francisco. It was the most fun I ever had with someone with my pants on. I imagined that this kind of spontaneous creativity and inspired intimate amusement was to be a lasting cornerstone of our relationship and looked forward to every second of it. (We never did anything like that again.)

Our good time stopped very short when we found ourselves lost in San Fran looking for, of all things, the Golden Gate Bridge. Annabelle insisted she knew where she was going, but we just kept getting more and more lost, leading us not to Tiburon, but to our first major fight. I asked if she knew which street led to it, and she said that she didn't go by street names, but by landmarks and some kind of internalized homing sense. I told her that her method was actually quite stupid. The longer it took to find it, the more frustrated and defensive she became. And soon we were squaring off at each other. My sarcasm was "unhelpful and rude." Her ineptitude was "astonishing and pathetic." We finally called her sister's husband for some directions that used actual street names and intersections. However, by the time we found the Golden Gate Bridge and got to Tiburon, we were more than an hour and a half late and not speaking to each other.

I had no idea that her sister had made a grand Shabbat dinner in my honor. I also had no idea that Lisa was not only Annabelle's older, very successful sister, but also Northern California's reigning queen of Judaism. I pretty much detest organized religion so when Lisa directed her seven-year-old son to chant the Kiddush wine prayer, I began to get itchy. The kid performed what seemed to be the entire Old Testament before we were allowed a sip of wine. Keeping me from wine when I needed it most was grating, but when I looked over at Annabelle, I saw she knew exactly what I was thinking and was feeling the same thing herself. Suddenly the fight about being lost melted away.

On the way back to LA, I felt very close and loving toward Annabelle. Things really were going incredibly well with us. I told her that I had thought it over and was ready for us to move in together. But she had changed her mind. Annabelle had given moving in some thought as well and now felt strongly that we shouldn't live together until we were officially engaged. Engaged? Annabelle turned very serious and told me she wanted "more." You mean "more" than the sweet, blissful, joyous, worry-free, sexually mind-blowing love we were currently enjoying? If I couldn't make a commitment to "wanting more" right then and there, she continued, I should get out. Get out? It took me five years to get in! I wanted to enjoy the scenery a little. Annabelle was not moved. Rick, my friend who had threatened violence if I screwed up with her, was about to send out wedding invites and here I was hesitating about becoming engaged.

It took almost two months to find the right ring for Annabelle. I rationalized that the time it took to find the ideal engagement ring would make me feel better about rushing things, which was true, but not as crucial as the fear that if I gave Annabelle a ring she didn't like, she'd reassess our entire relationship and find me unsuitable to be her lifelong mate. It's not that she's superficial or materialistic; she's just very particular and extremely judgmental.

Ironically, by the time I was about to propose, my buddy Rick and his fiancée had already broken up, moved out, and called off the engagement. I carried the ring in my pocket for a day and a half, waiting for the right moment to pop the question. Then it hit me what to do: Annabelle never, to this day, gets into a car without checking herself out in the vanity mirror. So I taped the heart-shaped ring box to the vanity mirror. It was set. All Annabelle had to do was get into the car, pull down the visor, look at herself, and bang—we'd be engaged! Here it was, the moment I had been waiting for since I saw *Romeo and Juliet* in sixth grade. My heart was pounding as Annabelle got into the car, buckled her safety belt, and did *not* check herself out. I couldn't believe it! Now what? Drive off and leave the ring taped there? I had to think quickly. "Do you have a zit?" I asked, pretending to see one. Annabelle freaked out. "Where!?" "There, on your chin." Still she did not look in the vanity mirror. "You know how cruel it is to point out that I have a zit, like that?" Annabelle was getting really pissed off and my perfect proposal was going to hell, and fast. "Maybe it's just a shadow, I don't know; take a look for yourself." Finally, Annabelle pulled down the vanity mirror and examined her chin. Amazingly, she was now so concerned about her nonexistent zit that she didn't see the engagement ring box taped haphazardly right in the middle of the mirror. "I don't see it!" She meant the zit. "It's green," I said of the zit, but meaning the ring box. "It's green and in the shape of a fucking heart!" "What are you talking about? I don't see anything!" she screamed. This was now spiraling out of control. If my proposal went any worse, we'd end up breaking up instead of engaged. Finally, Annabelle noticed it. "What the hell's that?" She seemed completely mystified and annoyed by the whole thing. As she untaped the box, I scrambled outside to her side of the Saab, got on my knee, and asked her to marry me. For the first time that I could recall (and the last time), Annabelle was speechless as she processed what was happening. She started to laugh/cry and as we were hugging and kissing half in and half out of my Saab, I think Annabelle choked out a "Thank God I love my ring." Which I took as a yes.

Later that night I confessed about the fart couch that I had been visiting on an almost nightly basis for the previous five months. She told me I was being ridiculous and that I could fart in front of her and even in bed if I had to. And thus, it began . . . Annabelle having no idea at the time that permitting me to let it rip in front of her was akin to opening up Pandora's box, only with lots and lots of gas.

But before we moved in together, Annabelle, without saying a word to me about it, quietly got rid of the fart couch.

She Says

I had only one problem with suddenly liking Jeff after all these years: I didn't trust me either. Sure, I thought I had fallen in love with Jeff, but even so I was worried about my poor judgment and fickle nature. Then something unexpected happened that further sealed my conviction. The night I met Jeff's college buddies I fell in love with them too. Friends since school, they were all great guys—smart, charming, funny, and fiercely protective of Jeff. They immediately won me over. Sometimes it helps to see things through someone else's eyes. Jeff was no longer just this random guy who had waged a kooky, corny poetry campaign to win me over—that might have been enough to get me in bed in the past—now I saw him as a devoted and loyal friend who had earned himself devoted and loyal friends. I loved them for loving Jeff, I loved Jeff for loving them, and I wanted him to love me as much as he loved them. I knew I had to make this work.

While Jeff was busy measuring our compatibility on his sexual barometer, I was working on what I thought was important: convincing him that I was serious about us. I wanted to do something big and bold, but I'm not good at that kind of thing so I reasoned that I'd make a small gesture, and what says I'm a caring, responsible individual more than buying your beloved an oven mitt? This attempt at trustworthiness produced unexpected results, which actually led to my high score on the Perv-O-Meter. You see, Jeff's participation in improv groups during and after college has left an indelible stamp on his personality, whereby socks, cutlery—inanimate objects of any kind—have personalities, nicknames, and voices to go with them. The oven mitt happened to be in the shape of a lobster claw, and on Jeff's hand that claw morphed into a character that came to be known as Lobster Boy. Lobster Boy started making regular tantric appearances in our bedroom, and it was the most fun I had ever had with my pants off.

Jeff seemed pretty happy too, and after only a month of me actively not breaking up with him and applying continuous pressure directly to his penis, Jeff no longer doubted my sincerity. It had proved much easier than I had anticipated. Then I needed to determine if Jeff could survive my own system of relationship measurement, which I call Annabelle's Derang-O-Meter. Could Jeff stand prolonged exposure to my particular brand of crazy on a long-term basis?

I'd like to note for the record that there have been many accomplished and fascinating women throughout history who certainly rate mention on the Derang-O-Meter. If the scale runs from 1 to 10, then here are some examples:

Catherine the Great, crazy for power, slept with horse: solid 7
Joan of Arc, crazy for God: a memorable 8.5
Sylvia Plath, crazy for being crazy, but a brilliant scribe: a nicely baked 9
Divas: Courtney Love, Britney Spears, Sarah Palin—all perfect 10s

Initially, I exposed Jeff to some garden-variety actress crazy. I read for a TV pilot he wrote and was producing. When I didn't get the part, I spent two days in bed weeping nonstop, and then cut out of town for a weekend Zen retreat, even though we had made elaborate and expensive plans together. Perhaps Jeff's checkered dating history came into play here. He seemed inured to female flakiness, and was just happy I hadn't stolen his credit card to pay for my trip.

Jeff's next glimpse was brought about by my scheduling the visit to meet my very stable older sister and her very wholesome and respectable family in Northern California. I feel I should try to explain the story that Jeff so enjoyed on the drive. It involves all of the things I would learn that Jeff loves: silliness, humiliating job stories, chance meetings, vegetables, and sex. I was a bottomless dancer who lived in a pumpkin patch, while he was a waiter at a greasy spoon along the highway. We met unexpectedly in the patch. Sex ensued. In the patch, so to speak. (I had no idea I would be expected to keep up this kind of thing for the rest of our lives.)

In defense of my "pathetic" sense of direction, let me just say that finding the entry to the Golden Gate Bridge is much like getting rich in America today: you might see it looming in the distance, but it's a lot harder to get there than you think. Upon arriving at Lisa's house, I instantly surmised that I had made a serious error in judgment. My sister's family practices Judaism as though they're training for a competition in extreme Judaica, and here I was inviting someone who abhors organized religions to a veritable Jewapalooza. But our mutual disdain was the first time we realized how much we enjoy disparaging things, which quickly turned into one of our favorite activities and the closest thing either of us has to a hobby. Our shared suffering brought us even closer, although, ironically, bonding over suffering is even more Jewish than celebrating the Sabbath.

That occasion predated my biggest crazy of all: I announced that not only should we move in together, but I'd move in only if we got engaged. Jeff mistakenly remembers this as two separate discussions in the Saab, but he's wrong. I am certain that both of these issues were brought up in one fell swoop in the Saab, where so many important events in our life occurred, which, to be honest, makes me seem even kookier than Jeff's recollection.

I think I produced some pretty cogent arguments recommending this course of action. There was the financial incentive and the added bonus that moving in would increase Jeff's chances of scoring more morning sex and accruing a never-ending reserve of cuddle time.*

The thing was, I was positively freaked out at the prospect of combining households without some assurance that this wasn't a temporary arrangement. I had begun to worry that my unavailability was central to Jeff's attraction to me, and that he might dump me once we moved in. I'd not only be heartbroken, but also homeless, which is my worst nightmare.

I grew up in a home where it was not uncommon to wake up and discover that overnight our circumstances had significantly changed. This resulted in several moves across the country. When I was five, my father's Rolls-Royce with the luxurious mahogany pulldown dinner trays was suddenly replaced by a Ford station wagon into which everything we owned had been crammed, and we found ourselves moving across the country to stay with relatives until we got on our feet again. Since that time I have stubbornly clung to locations as magical talismans.

---

*I happen to have an abnormally low body temperature, so cuddling is fine but mainly I want the warmth. I'm not picky; mammal or electric blanket, it's all the same to me.

After being evicted from my NYU dorm room for a series of infractions that included not being enrolled in the school anymore, I moved exactly one block over and lived in three different buildings within a two-block radius over the next six years.

Once in Los Angeles, I settled into a studio apartment and I subsequently resided in four other units all in that same actors' shtetl building. Each move was precipitated by a different event in my life. First: divorced, needed new starting-over space. Second: acquisition of more money, moved into two-bedroom unit. Third: downsizing to save cash, moved back into one bedroom. Fourth: started therapy, determined to change entire life, but had courage only to move across the hall. Fifth: OK, no big reason, except for the desire to climb fewer stairs. After seven years in that building, I finally worked up the courage to relocate to another part of town and start anew, but when the deal for a cute guesthouse I had procured fell through the week before I was to move in, I ended up placing all of my belongings in storage and checking into a residential hotel in the heart of Hollywood. The deep shag carpeting was always suspiciously damp and flea infested, and my neighbors were junkies, hookers, and would-be screenwriters.* I couldn't stand being in there for more than an hour at a time. I was so distraught that I began dating a man whose apartment was the mirror image of the place I had just left. Those were the circumstances that predated my inadvertently moving into the apartment next door to Jeff's old place. After that debacle, I vowed that if I ever moved again, it was going to be permanent or at least based on a relationship that offered a blueprint of permanence in the way that marriage offers that illusion.

*The Highland Gardens Hotel famously boasts that Janis Joplin and Jefferson Airplane once lived there, meaning that you could probably get a contact high from inhaling old carpet threads. If it sounds a lot like the Oakwood Apartments, where Jeff worked on *Cooties,* it's because these joints all look the same!

I don't know which was more ridiculous, my demand or that Jeff went out and bought me a ring. Jeff's retelling of our engagement story is exactly as it happened except that I'll never fathom why he thought his plan was a good idea. No woman likes to be told that she has a pimple on her chin. No man does either. There's a billion-dollar skin care and cosmetic industry entirely devoted to selling products to ensure that no one on a date ever has to be told that he or she has a pimple. You know perfectly well when you have a blemish, and you carefully conceal it before you go out. That's one of the unspoken rules of the early stages of dating: the obligation—no, requirement—to cover up one's imperfections. That's why I was mortified to think that I had missed a zit. Jeff may not have farted in front of me, but I was still going to bed with my makeup on. Plus, this was an important night. Jeff neglects to mention that we were headed to visit friends whose number included an ex-boyfriend of mine. As everyone knows, one of the most pressurized of all social occasions is the encounter with your ex.* You need to look great, but not just great, so *great* that even though you no longer covet his attention, and he no longer carries a torch for you, your mere presence reminds him that he missed out on something *great,* and by the way, you're doing just *great* now too, thank you, better than you ever were with him. That message is communicated without even speaking, just by seeing you, the version of you that doesn't have a gigantic green pimple on your face! That's why I was so freaked out.

At this juncture, all prescriptions recommended by dating and relationship books disintegrated into dust: wait two days until you

---

*Once, wrestling with a terrible flu, I was on the subway home from a doctor's appointment, stuffing a Snickers bar into my mouth and reading the *National Enquirer,* when I ran into a high school boyfriend. I immediately switched to a doctor closer to my apartment. Lesson learned!

call him back, don't ask him to move in, let him think he's making all the important moves. These guides don't always take into account the particular mental and emotional quirks of your beloved, because at the time we got engaged and decided to move in together, I think I was scoring a textbook 10 on the Derang-O-Meter.

Our engagement also proves the old adage that there's someone for everyone. The caveat is that the "someone" isn't necessarily someone who is perfect. It's someone whose eccentricities complement your eccentricities and then, fingers crossed, over the years you don't outcrazy each other, because as nutty as I was, Jeff still wanted to be with me. So who's really the crazy one? Him or me? I think we all know who that is: Jeff.

And for the record, Jeff's close friend Rick is married and has three beautiful children with that same girlfriend he moved in with, got engaged to, and broke up with. They have been married for twelve years, only one year less than we have.

I really do love the ring he picked out for me.

If I knew then what I know now, I never would have given that couch away. I would have had it incinerated.

"Forty percent of women say they have hurled footwear at a man."

—Y. Kaufman, *How to Survive Your Marriage*

don't ask, don't tell, don't want to know

CNN reports that although personal boundaries and privacy expectations differ from couple to couple, most people seem to agree that being exposed to the following behaviors stretches acceptable norms: farting, burping, plucking eyebrows, using the toilet, weighing oneself, clipping toenails, shaving, popping pimples, and blowing "snot rockets."

too old to care?

A 2009 study from the University of Chicago tells us that marrying at an older age makes marriage last longer, but why? "Marriages that take place at a very late age may actually be more unstable than those contracted in the early or mid-twenties but individuals, having become more cynical or just practical, settle for poorer matches that are far from optimal."

worried about long-term commitment?
marry like the stars!

Pamela Anderson and Kid Rock lasted only three months in marriage, but that union beats her hookup with Rick Salomon, to whom she was married for only two months. Robin Givens was married to Mike Tyson for eight months, which was a long run compared with her betrothal to her tennis pro, which lasted all of eight hours. Married at ten a.m., they had irreconcilable differences by four p.m. That knot stayed tied longer than screen legend Valentino's liaison with Jean Acker: they were shacked up for only six hours.

you're not gaining a spouse, you're adding to your girth

University of North Carolina researchers have shown that young marrieds experience a six-to-nine-pound weight gain over their single and even co-habitating peers.

looking for love in all the right places

With more than 20 million people looking for love online once a month, 120,000 marriages a year are now attributed to Internet dating hookups. One of the most successful, at least by their own reports, J-Date claims to have helped 21,000 couples find love in 2008 alone.

• • • • • • • • • • • • • • • •

3

. . . .

A Tale of Two Kitties

"Never go to bed mad. Stay up and fight."

—PHYLLIS DILLER

Dating is one thing, and seeing your beloved trim his or her nasal hair for the first time is quite the other. Cohabitating couples see up close and personal for the first time what the next few decades of communal living might have in store for them. Living together before getting married is like a fight between two heavyweights in the opening rounds. You're trying to read each other's strengths, weaknesses, and strategies before you're comfortable enough to really start pummeling each other. It could also be likened to the musical trajectory of The Beatles. Just when you think you have a handle on what they're doing with "I Want to Hold Your Hand," they hit you with "Let It Be." Moving in together is in many ways a *Magical Mystery Tour.*

He Says

Long before Annabelle was packing her bags to move into my hip little house in the Hollywood Hills, I was known by my friends as the unofficial president of "Roommates Without Borders." All were welcome at Chez Jeff. There was always someone—friends, friends of friends, and sometimes even a celebrity or two—sharing a home with me. Joan Cusack was my college roommate, and years later her brother John crashed at my apartment between girlfriends, houses, and movie roles. He had let me crash at his house back in 1988, so it seemed only fair. When I first moved to New York, I slept on Ben Stiller's foldout couch. After that I shared a cozy one-bedroom with my oldest friend, Peter, whom I met in summer camp in 1972. When Peter's girlfriend moved in, the three of us slept in the same teeny-tiny bedroom. When people ask if that was ever uncomfortable for me, I tell them the God's honest truth, that if I wanted to masturbate, I'd just get up and do it in the bathroom. Perhaps the revolving-door roommate situation was a residual effect of going to summer camp for eight years and how much I enjoyed sharing a cabin with ten other boys: all that camaraderie, the late-night dirty jokes, panty raids, and circle jerks. Another reason for communal living was necessity, namely splitting the rent. But even after I had more money, I still insisted on having roommates. In short order, in Los Angeles, the residents at the Pension de Kahn were my friends: Rick; Diana; Victoria; Rick's friend Larry Brandenburg; an actress named Kimmie, who dreamed of becoming an extra in the movies until her first day as an extra sent her packing back to Indiana; a cute German girl I met at a café—she never paid me a dime in rent but cooked dinner every night; and last, my first college roommate, Evan, who moved in from Chicago following his divorce.

So how hard could it be to live with me in a terrific three-bedroom house in the Hollywood Hills? I wasn't the type of single guy who watched football games sitting on a blow-up plastic chair with a can of Coors, fisting a bag of pretzels. No, I was the type of single guy who watched football games on a vintage Stickley chair with a glass of French rosé, chopsticking Thai noodles and tofu. I was renting a very sleek midcentury home, which I had furnished with several pieces of arts and crafts furniture, and a trendy-at-that-time Indonesian teakwood dining room table set. I even owned an upscale espresso machine. However, Annabelle still insisted that I reupholster my Ethan Allen sofa so it wouldn't look so "Ethan Allen-y," and that I take down my beloved framed *Elvis Costello Trust* album poster and in its place put up a jumbo-sized painting of a female's backside standing in front of a bathtub, the work of her ex-husband. I happily acquiesced, believing that by letting her redo and redistribute the decor, I was genuinely making room to share the house with her. As further reassurance that *mi casa* was her *casa,* I agreed to the purchase of an immense, cavernous armoire that swallowed all the electronic devices to placate Annabelle's desire that "watching TV wouldn't be the dominant activity of our lives," overlooking the inconvenient truth that *making* TV was *the* dominant activity of both our lives.

Annabelle's other precohabitating concern was that although she was moving in, I wasn't asking Evan to move out. Besides being one of my best friends, he is good-natured, hilarious, and perhaps the only person I know who farts more than I do. I thought it only fitting that he was my first and now would be my last roommate; consequently, I didn't want to kick him out without giving him time to find a suitable place for himself. I thought it only fair to do so.

Within days of Annabelle's arrival, I became very much aware that she demanded solitude and had the housekeeping habits of a feral animal. In addition to those observations, I noticed that she could be impatient, quick-tempered, slightly belligerent—even bellicose—and wouldn't hesitate to mix it up whenever she didn't get her way. This behavior concerned me slightly, but I chalked it up to post-moving stress disorder and believed that once Annabelle had acclimated herself to new digs, she'd mellow out. (This was the last time I ever entertained that notion; Annabelle does not do mellow.)

One morning I saw her making mincemeat of my beloved espresso machine while trying to concoct cappuccino, and when I offered her some friendly advice on how to properly use it, she promptly tore my head clean off. She was an "adult" who knew very well how to make coffee and I didn't have to "micromanage" every little thing she did. It was the first time I had heard that word and I hated it just as much then as I do now.

I was familiar with the side of Annabelle that could knock the world on its ass—she could captivate, charm, and wow everyone she met—but now I saw her come home and completely crumble after a bad audition. It would take a ton of her energy and mine as well to get her back on her feet. And Annabelle had this thing about "boundaries." She went on and on about the importance of "establishing clear and defined boundaries." She fumed if a friend of mine called after eleven at night. If I had the audacity to try to get into her pants during what she deemed the "no-sex times" of the day or night, or the "no-sex zones" of the house, Annabelle would read me the riot act. If I wanted to talk to her in the morning before I went to work, I had to wait until she had her third cup of coffee before she would be civil. If I needed to tell her something when she was in her office, I had to knock, and then when she decided that knocking was too disturbing to her sense of boundaries, I was told to slip a note under the door and wait for her to respond. My once sweet fiancée had transformed into Rulella, the Queen of Rules.

Not only were there all these rules to deal with, there was also a variety of other issues concerning Annabelle and our newly shared space. To me, Harvey, the guy who managed the house I was renting, was my own little fix-it guy trying to keep things in order and see to it that everything in the house ran smoothly. To her, he was always around and in her way. Then there was the matter of my next-door neighbor Rudmila. I hardly ever even spoke to her. All I could pick out from her absurdly thick accent was that she was of Serbian origin. However, in very little time, Rudmila and Annabelle were embroiled in some kind of turf war over the ring volume of Annabelle's telephone. The house didn't have air-conditioning, so we kept the windows open for the hillside breeze. Yes, the phone occasionally rang during the day, no louder than any other phone in the world, but according to Rudmila, it sounded as if we were blasting dynamite, mixing concrete, and building a tower to the moon. I was usually off working at my office in Beverly Hills and unfortunately missed Rudmila's bloodcurdling shrieks of "Turn your phone down!" coming from inside her house.

Another thing that irked Annabelle was that not only was Evan still living with us, but I also still kept my own open-door policy for friends to stop by whenever they wanted, day or night. Weren't they there for me when I was pining after Annabelle not all that long ago? The life I had constructed without Annabelle had suited me well, and for all intents and purposes, I'd thrived in it. What's more, I had been able to keep my espresso machine immaculate!

I secretly feared that maybe the whole moving-in-together thing might not have been the best idea. At the same time, I was in love with Annabelle, and it was wonderful to wake up beside her every day and hold her in my arms before she'd push me away to go get her coffee. I just had to find some way to balance all that was good about living with her with all that was troubling. And the thing that tipped the scales for the better was Annabelle's cat Stinky. The very same one Annabelle left me to care for as a kitten when she was away doing a play in New York. Stinky was still the champion of cat cuteness, affection, and nonstop lovability. Maybe Annabelle wasn't perfect, but Stinky was.

Late one night the three of us were in bed, all warm, cozy, and purring. I woke up thirsty and went downstairs for some water. In the darkened kitchen, I was dumbstruck by what was at Stinky's food bowl: the ragged, knotted fluff of some strange cat crunching away at seafood Friskies. I thought I was seeing things. How did this cat even get in the house? I took a small step to get a closer look, but the black puff of ratty fur fled off in speedy terror. I searched the whole house to find it, but it had simply vanished. Was it a ghost cat? Was I losing my mind?

The next morning I told Annabelle of the spooky feline apparition, and she offhandedly disclosed that it wasn't a phantom kitty at all, but her other cat, Esme (perhaps the worst name ever for a cat). Annabelle had two cats? Since when? And why hadn't I ever seen her before? Annabelle told the sad tale of Esme's socializing problem that had sent her to live most of her life inside a closet. She had thought Stinky needed a companion, but even as a kitten, Esme was just too skittish about everything to interact with anyone. Obviously, this cat has some issues. Annabelle feared that this really shy cat was even further traumatized by the move to the new house. I had always fancied myself a major cat person and I boldly predicted that I could get Esme (God, I hate that name) out of the closet and into our house proper.

After breakfast I hunted in all the house closets in search of the mysterious feline. The extensive exploration had me using flashlights, opening tins of tuna for dietary enticement, making clicking come-hither sounds as well as meowing as if it were some sort of feline sonar detection. Finally, I found her in the back of the deepest, darkest, and hardest to reach closet in the entire house. I set down a fishy can of tuna, which in Catlandia is as enticing as foie gras to gourmets and shooting speedballs to junkies. Yet all it did was back her up even deeper. I cooed at her and made sure she knew I meant her no harm. This just led her to push up farther against the back wall as if she were trying to thrust herself through to the other side. Then I reached my hand out to gently give her a loving, reassuring pet. Although she neither hissed nor scratched at me, when the tip of my outstretched finger touched her outermost wisp of fur, she somehow, contradicting many established rules of physics, managed to diminish herself so compactly in the far corner that she virtually disappeared. At that instant she let out a choked, garbled, sickening meow that I swear was additionally accompanied by a copious (for a cat) amount of drool. Annabelle's *other* kitty was not just "shy" and "traumatized," she was a drooling, freaked-out, significantly emotionally disturbed mess of a mammal. She was hopelessly afraid of any form of contact or interaction—human, cat, or otherwise—hence I rechristened Esme "Fraidy Cat." The nickname stuck like feathers on hot tar from that moment forth.

Annabelle agreed that Fraidy was perhaps the most pathetic pet ever, but felt bad for her and hoped that someday she might miraculously recover her wits and start behaving more like a normal cat and not one who needed a kitty straitjacket. All we could do in the meantime was pray she didn't starve herself to death in the closet, leaving us to fish out her stiff, furry corpse.

Living with Annabelle, I was quickly learning, was a Tale of Two Kitties. Sure, she could be confident, well groomed, and extremely charming, like Stinky. Yet she could also be neurotic, insecure, and tentatively fearful, like Fraidy Cat. I would have to find a way to effectively contend with Annabelle's Fraidy if I was to have a shot at getting to her Stinky.

Sure, we had lots of laughs and morning sex, but at the same time, Annabelle was calling me at work every hour on the hour with another complaint from the home front and how it was making her miserable and impossible for her to concentrate on her work. It could be said of our budding communal experience: "It was the best of times, it was the worst of times."

She Says

After becoming the latest participant in Casa Kahn's open immigration experiment, I began to notice aspects of Jeff's behavior that gave me pause too. A Tale of Two Kitties? Please! It was a *Comedy of Errors* over at Kahn House.

In truth, things like decorating aren't that important to me; it wasn't as if I insisted that we adopt the oppressively shabby-chic interior decor that everyone in Los Angeles was slouching around in at the time. Yes, Jeff had some furniture that didn't require assembly, but what was on his walls I can only describe as "early dorm room." I found it startling that he would consider a poster of a band to be living room worthy. What would be next? Would our wedding reception be a kegger? Jeff suspected that he was being asked to hang a portrait of me painted by my ex-husband, that I was the nude woman with the well-formed posterior in the large canvas, but anyone who has ever seen me naked knows that my behind never looked as good as the one in the painting. Ultimately, Jeff can't resist a great ass, so the canvas went up.

I did made a mistake in insisting that we purchase our armoire. What seemed attractive in the store looks so different out of its retail environment, so clunky, so like something we could go over Niagara Falls in together. It still occupies center stage in our living room: a squat barrel-shaped, brightly painted albatross that holds our big old TV. But given its coffinlike shape, and the state of our retirement accounts, it's possible that when the time comes, Jeff and I could be buried in the fucking thing.

These things were all just small potatoes, really, because I was being confronted with the fact that I had put enormous pressure on our cohabitation by insisting that we were going to get married. Having been divorced once, I didn't want to make a mistake a second time, so I began to look at every aspect and little habit of Jeff's through the lens of *forever*. Is this the penis I want to wake up to forever? Will I love his smell forever? How did I not notice that ear hair? How much more of *that* is in our future? How about that funny little sound he makes when he swallows? Is he sneezing to get my attention? I mean how can a sneeze be so loud? Will he ever once put the toilet paper roll on the dispenser, or am I going to be doing this for the next who knows how many years? Because life expectancy has increased by ten years in our lifetime, till death do us part can loom like a freaking eternity, so it might not be a bad question to ask yourself, *"Can I live with this forever?"*

An example of this was something I termed the Curse of the Socks, not the Red Sox, which I quickly learned is Jeff's favorite team, but the athletic socks. Jeff always wore socks, even during sex, but it didn't occur to me until after I moved in that I had never really gotten a good look at his feet. Sure, we had taken some showers together, but these were "dating showers," candlelit, romantic, watery sexual-trysts where a brief glimpse of feet might be had—not cohabitating in the cold light of day actual washing-to-get-clean showers. Now that we were living together and potentially sharing a home, *forever,* this struck me as troubling, maybe a little sophomoric, and moreover, what was under those socks? Webbed feet? An extra toe? Was he going to wear those tube socks *forever*? I went on a campaign to de-sock him. Actually, I just deployed that old standby strategy, which works almost every time for almost every problem with almost every man: "No more sex unless you [*fill in the blank*]." In this case, insert "take your socks off." It turns out that there was nary a web nor an excess number of toes, but what I didn't realize was that he had been wearing socks for so many years that leg hair no longer grew under the sock encasement zone, giving his legs a surprisingly smooth surface that, unexposed to sunlight, perhaps since birth, lent his pale bare calves and feet an almost spectral appearance. It was also possible that even Jeff had forgotten what was under there, because now, sans socks, I was being grazed by toenails that were kept just a tad too long and were too hastily trimmed. "Get those suckers back on!" I demanded. Let this serve as a warning to all women who have ever looked at a potential mate like an old house and thought: good bones—he's a fixer-upper. Some things you just need to accept as is.

Meanwhile, Jeff and I had significantly different ideas about sharing our home life. Namely, I needed large quantities of coffee and quiet to piece my personality together on a daily basis, while Jeff thrived on constant human contact. It's not something I'm proud of. I'm cranky in the morning, mildly annoyed in the afternoon, and just plain exhausted at the end of the day. At the time, I was actressing, which, contrary to popular belief, is not at all glamorous. You're on your feet all day trying to satisfy picky people, hoping they might become regular customers. It's like waitressing, with moderately better lighting. Plus, what Jeff perceived of as melancholia, I preferred to characterize as contemplativeness. It's not that I was hoping to build an actual fence around myself like some people would like to see on, say, the U.S. border with Mexico. What I had in mind for us was more like the Canadian border, where a distracted guard might check your passport but not bother to pop your trunk. I imagined this would all work itself out when we were both home at the same time because I could always take a long and restorative bath, my long-standing go-to retreat, and then regroup in our spare bedroom. However, within days of my moving in, Jeff announced that Evan would be staying on indefinitely, and faster than you could say, "But the only bathtub in the house is the one attached to the spare bedroom," he had a new girlfriend, Heather, sharing our home as well. Suddenly I was living with three people.

Unlike Jeff, I was used to living alone. In college, my first roommate contracted a mysterious disease and had to be removed from our dorm room on a stretcher. Next roomie lasted only a few months with me before ditching school to join a bus-and-truck-traveling children's theater troupe. My third and last roommate borrowed my clothes and makeup without asking and just plain scared me.* Ex-husband and I lived together less than a year before he moved to Chicago to attend graduate school.

But that was only the tip of the iceberg. Harvey, a Hobbit who was employed as the manager/caretaker of our home by the owners, who lived in San Francisco, was perpetually hanging about the place. OK, he wasn't really a Middle Earth Tolkien character, but he was about four foot something with a furry furtive manner and was in the habit of turning up unannounced and burrowing into the house for hours at a time. On a typical day I might come downstairs in my pajamas and find Harvey in the kitchen tinkering with the plumbing or puttering around in the garage. Once I thought I saw him hunched over a pile of our firewood, whittling a sharp stick. According to Jeff, he and the Hobbit had long coexisted in peace, but as soon as I moved in, an alternating passive-aggressive streak marked all of our contact. When we'd complain about the army of ants who were conducting a military occupation

*She now fronts a hard-core band and is known in the underground music scene for her pain- and rage-filled lyrics.

of the kitchen, he would produce an obscure city ruling exempting landlords from responsibility for insects smaller than an inch, but when we'd inquire about some ordinary landlord responsibility such as, say, painting the peeling exterior of the house, he'd scowl at us and hiss and demand we do it ourselves—didn't we have any pride in our home? Then the next day, as if nothing had happened, I'd find him downstairs doing some bidding from those precious nameless, faceless owners in "the north country."

Meanwhile, living right next door to us was Rudmila, a stylish if faded Serbian version of a Gabor sister if the Gabors had had their blood supply replaced with liquid steel. Rudmila was glamorous, but also one tough broad. It wouldn't have been hard to imagine that she had at one time greeted her Bosnian and Croat neighbors with a hatchet in her hands. Ironically, although she was incensed by the sound of my telephone ringing in the middle of the day, from the middle of our house we were awakened by the clickety-clack of her high heels and her piercing screams to her little yippety-yappety dogs, Precious and Honey, to do their business on her brick patio every day at four a.m. When her phone calls failed to produce results, she simply yelled at our house when she was annoyed. Then she came up with a truly brilliant strategy: she began bringing over homemade food on her complaint runs. She'd stand in the street, hurling grievances and invectives in our direction, and then leave really fattening but tempting culinary concoctions on the front doorstep: heart-stopping dishes such as an apple turnover oozing with butter lathered in heavy cream, or lamb dumplings wrapped in bacon smothered in lard gravy. Either she was going to get us evicted or have us carried out in body bags.*

---

*In hindsight, it occurs to me she might have surmised that because I was an actress, if I ate her food, I'd gain so much weight that my phone would stop ringing. Really, she was very clever.

Nothing she did bothered Jeff much and really, why would it? First of all, Jeff had a steady gig, so every day he would disappear into the Saab and drive across town to his well-appointed office, while I would find myself at home, making small talk with Evan and Heather, bumping into the Hobbit, or being assaulted by Rudmila's shrieking complaints. All the while, having removed all traces of food from the kitchen, the ants were now on a Bataan Death March across our counters. By moving in with Jeff, I had become a supporting cast member in the Jeff Kahn Variety Hour, a show playing 24/7.

But as I soon discovered, Jeff has little regard for any concept of personal space. To him, my bending down to place a dish in the dishwasher seemed to be the perfect occasion to put his hand down the back of my pants and touch my ass. Tying my shoe? An invitation to slip his palm under my skirt. The guy had some sort of nudity radar. I would take my clothes off even for a second, and he'd be in front of me cheering as if he'd scored box seats at Fenway Park. I suppose the shuttling back and forth between our respective homes had mitigated this tendency, but now he was everywhere I turned. Door closed? No matter, he'd think nothing of walking into the office when I was rehearsing or writing some of the inane journal entries I was given to in my thirties. "Why do I still define myself based on what other people think of me?" "I am worth it!" "My only competition is me!" or some other positive-thinking crap I was forever trying to hypnotize myself with and that demanded my undivided attention. On the phone? Not a deterrent. Jeff would jump in my lap! Jeff also had suggestions for how everything should be done in the house. He corrected my baristing technique, assessed my bed-making skill, and commented on my admittedly massive consumption of beef, pushing me to try his assorted faux meats: tofu wedges that tasted like rubber bands soaked in liquid smoke. If I hadn't spit them out, I'd still be chewing on them today.

I started to see Jeff as a kind of virus, multiplying and absorbing everything around it; like the Andromeda Strain, he just spread. The years of living with roommates had made it OK with Jeff for strangers to drop by, friends to move in, acquaintances to phone until one a.m.—it was as if Jeff had a sign around his neck: ALWAYS OPEN FOR BUSINESS. I have always been the diametric opposite. Even when I was ten, my mother needlepointed my sister and me little greetings for our bedroom doors. Lisa's read COME ON IN, while my sign announced DO NOT DISTURB.

It was just not in my nature to share so much. I've never been a supporter of the don't ask–don't tell policy for the military, but in a relationship it makes sense—hence the popular phrase "too much information." Maybe I did neglect to mention that I had a second cat that happened to live in my closet; was it really that important?

There happens to be a perfectly logical explanation for the two-cat situation. Since the first day I acquired Stinky, she has been a flirt who sits on everyone's lap. Long and lean, she is the feline incarnation of supermodel Naomi Campbell if she successfully completed an anger management course. Esme, on the other hand, was a cat I rescued from the streets. She came into my life with dirty matted hair, a persistent drool, and a paranoia that made her shun all society, and that's how she remained for her entire little life. Her husky gravelly meow made her the Brenda Vaccaro of cats, with the wild wasted look of Amy Winehouse after a long night, or for that matter, Ms. Winehouse at any time of the day. I had thought Esme could become a beta companion for alpha Stinky, but Stinky lorded it over that psychotic foundling. She basically kept her prisoner in the closet—Esme came out to eat only late at night when number one cat had gone to bed. I reject Jeff's perception that these two cats were somehow embodying my two natures. I saw rescuing the frizzy neurotic ball of drool from the streets as an act of kindness and generosity. Could I be expected to toss out a cat because she wouldn't be my best friend? What kind of person does that? Anyway, those two cats were never seen together, so the only two kitties as far as I could see were Stinky and Jeff.

That's right. Perhaps the most startling revelation upon moving in with him was that Jeff kept up a constant stream-of-consciousness dialogue with himself. In cat language. Some guys hum, some snore, some unconsciously tap their feet, some masturbate with alarming frequency and ferocity. Jeff meows. Jeff wasn't just a visitor to Catlandia, he was a citizen. Maybe its president. From the first tentative meow he'd make upon rising in the morning, he'd keep it up, right until bedtime, when I'd hear little mewing sounds punctuated by staccato meeps, one for each step he climbed to our bedroom. It never ends. If you've ever heard that recording of cats singing "Silent Night," and you chuckled, you know you really need to hear it only once. Any more than one time and the words *cloying* and *grating* start to form in your head, and then the phrase "OK, I get it" might escape your lips. I had never experienced anything quite like Jeff's meowing. Even with actual cats.

It really could have been the end for us. I would lie awake imagining Evan, Heather, Harvey, and Rudmila sitting around a plate of apple strudel, consoling Jeff over our breakup but assuring him he'd find someone who would fit in better. Kind of a suburban kitchen table version of the scene in the 1932 movie *Freaks:* "One of us, one of us!"

Our saving grace appeared in the form of a blue old-model Mercury Sable. One night the car turned up parked directly opposite Rudmila's garage, making it difficult to navigate her own late-model Cadillac out of its port. The car was still there a week later. We might have commiserated with her if she hadn't become obsessed with the idea that this junker belonged to us. "No," we assured her, "we have a Saab, not a Sable or whatever the hell it is." She called the Hobbit; the Hobbit called us. Every day. Several times a day. Neither one would accept the fact that we had absolutely no knowledge of the provenance of the offending vehicle. A month passed. Finally, early one Sunday morning, we received a call from the owner of the house, who identified himself only as "the owner of the house." I am still convinced that it was Harvey. The next thing I know, Jeff is standing outside our house yelling to Rudmila, something to the effect that "it's not our fucking car, and the next time your Slobodan Milošević high heels and yapping dogs keep us awake, I'm going to call the World Court in The Hague and have you deported!" This was a little much because she had committed no crimes against humanity that we knew of, but Jeff had sided with me. Something had shifted. Even the ants relented. (OK, that was only because it rained, so the ants' disappearance was totally unrelated.) Jeff and I had become the "us" in "one of us."

I suppose what happened next was inevitable. Not long after the showdown, we were on a hike in the hills behind the house; we'd gotten separated and it was getting dark. I called out to Jeff so we could return home before our local coyotes, cougars, and transient alcoholics came out. He answered my call with a plaintive mew, and without thinking, I mewed right back. Oh. My. God. The next thing I knew I was meowing around the house too. I had seen the two kitties and the kitties were us.

It's not as if Jeff and I were combining our lives and by doing so we were bringing out the best and brightest qualities in each other. On the contrary, we were mixing up our worst and our weirdest, but all signs were indicating that our boundaries had been changed forever. Maybe we were like Georgia and Russia. Sometimes Georgia is part of Russia. Sometimes Georgia is an independent state. And sometimes they go to war and fight like hell with each other.

"*If you want* to sacrifice the admiration of many men for the criticism of one, go ahead and get married." —Katharine Hepburn

let's do the numbers

Average cost of weddings in the United States: $26,327

Average cost of divorce in the United States: $27,500

Average cost of a round of marriage therapy: $3,000–$4,000

Most expensive wedding to date: Vanisha Mittal and her fiancé Amit Bhatia, 2004. The wedding was held at Vaux le Vicomte, a seventeenth-century French chateau. Twelve chartered Boeing jets flew 1,500 guests from India for five days of festivities in France. Five thousand bottles of Mouton Rothschild 1986 were consumed, and pop star Kylie Minogue entertained the throngs before a makeshift castle. Cost: $55 million.

Most expensive wedding singer: Peter Shalson and bride Pauline paid £2 million to Elton John to sing at their 2002 nuptials.

most commonly played songs at weddings

"Unforgettable" (Nat King Cole)

"Can't Help Falling in Love" (Elvis Presley)

"It Had to Be You" (Harry Connick Jr.)

considered uncouth to play at the ceremony

"King of Pain" (Sting)

"All Apologies" (Nirvana)

"You Oughta Know" (Alanis Morissette)

singularly happy

A Pew survey finds that 79 percent of Americans say a woman can lead a complete and happy life if she chooses to remain single. The comparable figure for men was 67 percent.

male bonding

How well men fare in marriage has been linked to genetics by researchers from the Karolinska Institute in Stockholm in 2008. Their study suggests that if a man has more of the "bonding gene"—a gene modulating the hormone vasopressin—in the brain, he is more likely to want to stick with his partner. Women married to men carrying the "poorer bonding" form of the gene also reported "lower scores on levels of marital quality than women married to men not carrying this variant."

4

. . . .

28 Days Later

"Marriage is a great institution, but I'm not ready for an institution."

—MAE WEST

One of Western culture's early marriage boosters, Martin Luther, wrote, "There is no more lovely, friendly, and charming relationship, communion, or company than a good marriage." Of course, why wouldn't he think so? Who wouldn't want to be married to Luther's wife, Katrina? She cooked, cleaned, home-schooled six children, massaged his feet, nursed him through Ménière's disease, excruciating constipation, and kidney and bladder stones, among his miserable maladies. Centuries later the concept of marriage has evolved from a means to secure property, status, and sexual access into a binding legal contract that we expect to also include romantic love and mutually assured foot massages. People still believe in marriage and many vow to stay together "till death do us part." We suspect that this is why the first month of marriage can be either the blissful honeymooning delight of two people secure in their belief that they have made the right decision or the tortuous slow-motion odyssey of a couple simultaneously reaching the same conclusion: "Oh my God, what have we done?!"

She Says

ELOPE *V.:* to go away suddenly without telling anyone, especially in order to get married without the knowledge or consent of parents or guardians.

WEDDING *N.:* a marriage ceremony usually with its accompanying festivities.

When I married the anarchist, we eloped. I wore a vintage green dress and sobbed the entire time. The minister who performed the ceremony pronounced them "tears of joy"; I think they were more likely tears of "I suspect this is a mistake." I have long since filed that particular memory under "things you do in your twenties."* Now here I was marrying a nice Jewish guy. I had been transformed into someone else entirely. Someone who wanted at least a semblance of normalcy. Someone who wanted to include her family in this important life decision. That could mean only one thing: I had turned into someone who was going to plan a wedding. Clearly, at our age, we didn't need our parents' consent, but I did see the value in publicly marking the occasion. Besides, traffic is so bad in Los Angeles that if you want to see your friends who live outside a five-mile radius, you have to provide food and entertainment, and if someone's saying some vows, you have a much better chance of getting people to show up.

---

*Like many people who elope, particularly on the spur of the moment, I suspect my ex and I probably never would have married if we'd actually had to plan a wedding and stand up and recite vows in front of people we loved.

Fifty billion dollars is the amount the Iraqi government is estimated to have received in the first three years after the invasion to rebuild its nation. It is also estimated to be how much money people around the globe spend on weddings every year. By my estimation, it's a ridiculous waste of money on both accounts. If you were to amortize the cost of Liza Minnelli's extravagant wedding to David Gest, it works out to $29,000 for each day they were married. And that doesn't include the cost of their divorce! I guess Liza can afford it, but three and a half million dollars buys an awful lot of mascara.

I figured that Jeff and I could come up with a celebration that expressed both our style and our sensibility and that didn't cost a fortune but was more memorable than a fourteenth-century affair where after exchanging a couple of goats you were considered hitched in the eyes of the community. Jeff seemed game to go for all the wedding-related festivities.

We even embraced the shower and bachelor party tradition. Jeff didn't have strippers at his party, but for my shower my girlfriends had arranged for not one but two male strippers, Chance and Thunder. Together they were known as Chunder. The duo had been hired to entertain our all-female gathering, but it was clear once they began their spirited disrobing that they only had eyes for each other. Perfectly buffed and impossibly smooth, they resembled plastic action figures, twin Ken dolls clad in matching red and black satin thongs, a look that not a single woman I know finds appealing, though plenty of gay men find irresistible. It was a hilariously horrifying evening, and though it was totally unnerving, I was doing everything to start this marriage on the right path, which in America means someone's got to get a lap dance, damn it!

Jeff and I managed to plan the wedding without killing each other, something of a feat for any couple. We discovered we shared common ground in our aversion to overly formal pretensions, so we agreed that we didn't want our guests facing the chicken-or-fish question and happily arranged a cornucopia of delicious salads and pastas. Neither of us wanted to haggle over whether cousin So-and-stein would want to sit with cousin So-and-berg, so we planned a buffet instead. Neither of us wanted to see photographs of ourselves shoveling wedding cake into each other's mouths, so we cleverly ordered a French croquembouche. OK, we might have missed the mark on the croquembouche. Right now, pastry balls stacked into towering pyramids are decaying in landfills all over the country, because truth be told, no one really eats those things. Are you supposed to use a fork? Pick them off with your hands? They're stickier than they look, and not at all soft, as you might have expected, incorrectly assuming they were going to be like doughnut holes with crème fillings. Even if your caterer tells you it's a "crème puff tower," the name actually translates into "crunch in the mouth." Because it just doesn't seem right to crunch on a cake, you end up just putting it on your plate and staring at it. But don't put two on the plate, because they'll look suspiciously like testicles. Are they a metaphor for the groom's balls? Someone will think they're very clever and suggest that. Don't order the croquembouche unless you're French, you're getting married in France, and everyone coming to the wedding is French. If for some unfathomable reason I ever get married again, I'll get the damn wedding cake.

Jeff and I signed a Jewish marriage contract, a ketubah, promising to cherish each other in the "way that Jewish men and women had cherished each other through the ages." This probably doesn't refer to King Solomon, who reportedly had seven hundred wives and three hundred concubines, but much of the document was written in Hebrew so we really have no idea what we agreed to.

Our wedding was truly a dazzling day and while we didn't

have sex the night we got married, one out of three couples doesn't either. I can't remember why. Bloated? Tired? Bloated and tired? Anyway, we planned to make up for that on our very, very relaxing honeymoon. Our first stop was a two-night stay at the San Ysidro Ranch in swanky Montecito and then we were to head to the Napa Valley. Sociological surveys consistently tell us that money can't buy you happiness. The data suggest that once you meet your essential needs, you are not happier than when you didn't have as much money. Maybe, but the people questioned in these surveys never stayed at San Ysidro.

If you've ever been to a luxury hotel in Vegas, think the opposite. Where Vegas is chrome and glass, San Ysidro is wood and stone. While Vegas plays high-stakes roulette, San Ysidro putts lazy croquet. Ginormous skyscrapers light up the Vegas strip; little adobe private bungalows dot the San Ysidro hillside.

JFK and Jackie honeymooned there, Vivien Leigh and Laurence Olivier exchanged rings in the garden, Winston Churchill nursed a brandy at the ranch, and not much has changed since those days. Once in a while you might hear a horse neigh from the adjoining paths, or see someone strolling across the grounds, but for the most part, the ranch is very, very quiet. The kind of quiet only the superrich can afford. So quiet you can almost hear the sound of your money slipping away if you listen very closely. I don't believe in heaven, but if I did, I imagine it would be something like the San Ysidro Ranch, if the Supreme Being has vaguely equestrian taste.

The staff at the ranch keeps up all kinds of quaint touches, including spelling out your last name in little wooden letters by the entryway to your cottage to announce that you are in residence. Always the comedy guy, Jeff quickly rearranged the letters before the attendants had a chance to change the name from the previous occupants, the Lictmans. I have to admit, after I got over the initial embarrassment, it was funny to hear the attendants address us as Mr. and Mrs. Clitman for the duration of our stay.

Our first day we hiked long wooded trails, swam in the pool, and I got spa treatments at day's end. Afterward we retreated to the bungalow to sink into thick down comforters, fluffy pillows, and white sheets, whiter than you are ever going to get your own sheets—it was like being enveloped in clouds. We so exceeded our budget on dinner that first night that the next day we were foraging the free apples in baskets at the front desk and the mixed nuts and berries by the bar to save some money for Napa. We were lounging on an overstuffed chaise, searching for dried cranberries that had gotten wedged inside the deep folds and talking about our next destination, when my mother phoned. My grandmother had dropped dead. What? Only days before she had been dancing at our wedding. Apparently, she had an advanced form of leukemia that had gone undetected. Frances had checked into the hospital and by the next morning she was dead. And just like that, with a trunk full of unopened wedding gifts, we drove back to Los Angeles.

What do Wilmington, Delaware, and the Napa Valley have in common? Both are located on the North American continent and the primary language spoken is English, but the similarities end there. Napa was where we were scheduled to go, but Wilmington was where my grandmother lived, the place she'd be buried, and where we were now headed. Though many people know Delaware as the first state of the union, that place where their company was incorporated, or where Joe Biden is from and where he returned to every single night he served in the Senate, let's face it, you just never hear people say, "So we spent our honeymoon in Wilmington and it was glorious!" In Napa we were going to sample wines; eat gourmand food. Our trip couldn't have turned out more different.

My grandmother's funeral was as unpretentious as she had been. Frances wanted to be a nurse but her family couldn't afford to send her to college, so instead she worked as a bookkeeper, married my grandfather, raised two daughters, saw her husband through Alzheimer's, and hadn't stopped working until not long before she died. Frances always smelled like Johnson & Johnson Baby Magic Lotion. She was a bit of a taskmaster, but she never voiced any discontent about her circumstances. She probably hadn't been feeling all that well at our wedding, but didn't want to be a bother. My grandmother was gone, but on her little bedroom desk was a note she had written to me before she went to the hospital. In the thank-you note, she tells us what a wonderful time she had at the wedding. Ever the realist, she didn't wish us a lifetime of joy; in her sober understated way she wrote that she simply wished us "many years of happiness together."

As we shoveled dirt on my grandmother's coffin, my mother offhandedly let it slip that she had a brain tumor sitting at the base of her skull and that she might well be following her own mother into the ground soon. It had been discovered right before the wedding and she hadn't wanted to spoil it for us, but now she felt she should tell us because she needed to have it out right away. Napa would have to wait. Next stop, Jackson Memorial Hospital in Miami.

On day one in Napa, we were going to taste Syrah at Jade Mountain Winery; instead, Jeff flew home to Los Angeles while I downed espressos bought from a street vendor selling café con leche outside the hospital where my mother was scheduled for surgery.* Jackson, by the way, is considered one of the best places in the country if you need your head cut open. Located as it is in a high-crime area of downtown Miami, they've had a ton of experience

*You can get a great café con leche on any street in Miami; thank God for that!

with gunshot wounds to the head. My mother was the only patient during her stay in the ICU who didn't have a police escort and wasn't handcuffed to the bed. Instead of our sharing the salmon tartare dinner we'd planned, Jeff's and my only contact was when I called to let him know that my mother's neurosurgeon, Dr. Heroes (really), was able to pluck the tumor out of her head, like "picking a daisy," he said.

There was a television series called *The Surreal Life*. I never saw it, but I'm certain I can beat it. As my mom was recovering in the ICU, her head having just been sewn up, I looked up at the television that was on above her bed. On the tube, an old episode of *Seinfeld* was on. It was an episode in which a character played by me falls into one of Larry David's "comas of unknown origin." There I was sitting by my inert mother's bedside and in a bed above her was my image in virtually the same position. Now that's the real surreal life.

The next day in Napa we had planned to check out the sparkling wine at Domaine Chandon. Instead, I was stone cold sober while my mom had the benefit of some really strong drugs, which meant she didn't have to deal with the hospital staff's attitude. The nurses' bedside manner ranged all the way from surly to downright unhelpful, so I volunteered to spend the night with my mother to make sure they didn't forget she was there. As I lay down on my makeshift bed, a deflated physical therapy mat on the dirty floor, I comforted myself by remembering the facial I had gotten at the San Ysidro Ranch and tried to think positively. The sheets I was now wrapped in were so rough, you might say they had an exfoliating quality to them. The last thing I saw before I collapsed into an exhausted sleep was my mother's sagging behind peeking out from the opening in her hospital gown, a sight that can only put one in mind of the march toward the grave.

Amazingly, my mother was back on her feet (if unsteadily) only a day later, and I flew home to my new husband. When I landed back in Los Angeles, Jeff suggested that we should try to get back to our honeymoon. But I had no time to waste on frivolous pursuits like honeymooning. Earlier in the year my gynecologist had informed me that a small growth on my uterus had gone citrus. What had been an innocuous plum for years had suddenly grown and was now a grapefruit.* Chances were that this fibroid was benign, but we wouldn't know for sure until it was removed. I had been advised months before our wedding that there was no need to take action until I wanted to get pregnant. I phoned the doctor the day I got home and scheduled the procedure. Fuck it. I called Jeff from the doctor's office to let him know I was going in the following week. "Jeff, there's no time to waste. We'd better get on with our lives before another person drops dead. And if I expire on the operating table, you can use the wedding invitation list for my funeral."

Merriam-Webster's dictionary reports the etymology of *honeymoon* as coming from "the idea that the first month of marriage is the sweetest" and notes that the custom dates back to the sixteenth century, but it wasn't until the late nineteenth century that couples other than royalty took a wedding holiday. That most Americans expect to go on some sort of spree is no doubt a function of the rise of the middle class and the adoption of some of the expectations and luxuries formerly afforded only by the upper class. It also served a useful purpose. Some couples, even my own parents, married in the 1950s, had a very old-fashioned courtship conducted mainly through long-distance correspondence. My parents had

---

*When doctors inform you that your tumor is a danger to you, why do they label it as if it were a citrus fruit, usually a grapefruit? Maybe it's because if the tumor is the size of an orange, it would sound manageable; whereas a grapefruit implies a certain heft. If it is watermelon sized, it would be obvious to everyone. (You get seventy-two thousand Google hits on "tumor the size of a grapefruit.")

met on only four occasions before they were betrothed, so having a short interval to get to know each other or at least find out each other's middle names before settling into a daily life made sense. But for Jeff and me, the whole notion began to look absurd. I was just too damn old. I had been busy with my career, my narcissism, and important things like "finding out who I really was" but now I knew who I was: an ordinary human female who had grown a tumor instead of a baby because she had waited too long to get pregnant and whose parents and grandparents who might have made great babysitters were now falling like flies.

We had been married on May 12 and only twenty-eight days later I was transformed into a zombie. We may have been at the beginning of our marriage, but we were also in the middle of our lives; the only difference was that now we had a large stack of perfectly useless Waterford crystal bowls.

He Says

Nothing says to God, or the universe, or life "bring it on" more than getting married. "It" all began with the wedding planning, which led Annabelle and me to lots of really excellent premarital squabbles, most of which she seems to have totally forgotten. This may be because Annabelle's brain is a little like TiVo. Her DVR memory chip has only so much space to store and save our countless arguments and disagreements before it starts deleting some in order to make room for new ones. Annabelle has never quite learned how to properly program the TiVo, and her brain works in the same fashion: what it selects to delete or save seems to be completely ad hoc. This is thoroughly exasperating given that I never know which of our arguments she'll bring up forever and ever and which will fade away as if they never happened, like the minor opera we had about whether her friend, a rabbi, should conduct the wedding ceremony.

OK, first of all, why a rabbi? Wouldn't that be hypocritical for two seriously nonobservant Jews? Here's another Annabelle factoid: she claims to be an atheist, but she's a complete sucker for religious ceremonies—chanting, choral singing, holidays, meditation retreats, and a hundred other varieties of quasi-spiritual performances. God she can do without, but not rituals. I, on the other hand, dislike rituals as much as I do religions, but I'm perfectly open to believing in God. Between all of our vast contradictions and because we are both of Jewish origins, having a rabbi began to seem like something of a happy compromise. This was especially true when compared to the other LA, So-Cal, PC, New-Agey marriage officiating alternatives. Neither of us wanted to be married by a surfing shaman; by some one-time minor child star from a minor 1980s sitcom turned feminist fertility goddess; or by a burned-out ex–Grateful Dead groupie who, following the death of Jerry Garcia, went on a vision quest, read Joseph Campbell, and obtained his license to wed couples online.

If having a rabbi was in, Annabelle's friend Rabbi Mel, who, although very nice, sensitive, and intelligent, also happened to be her sometime shrink, was out, at least for me. As her therapist, Mel knew things, secret things, maybe even bad things about Annabelle and subsequently now about me too—things I didn't want to think about his knowing while I was standing next to her in front of him under the chuppah with everyone I ever knew watching. So, I found someone who seemed like a suitable substitute rabbi whose only drawback, as Annabelle pointed out, was his insistence on playing guitar and singing during the wedding (which we strictly forbade him to do).

Another Annabelle TiVo memory deletion is how she fought me tooth and nail about hiring strippers for my bachelor party. It's hysterical to me that she can't even recollect how freakin' adamant she was against my having strippers at my bachelor party. According to her, guys who paid for strippers to come to their bachelor parties were cliché and immature, and for someone like myself who was nearly thirty-four, it was just flat-out disgusting and sad. (What's more, she gave me an ultimatum: from then on in, I was no longer allowed to look at another girl's pussy live and in person.) I'm willing to cop to the fact that before we started seriously dating, I'd go out to a strip club occasionally, maybe once or twice a year. It was usually during a stretch of time when I hadn't had sex in a while and the thought of a live vagina in such proximity filled me with childlike hope and wonder. It's not as if I was a regular customer at Jumbo's Clown Room, Star Strip, Crazy Girls, Seventh Veil, or The Body Shop on Sunset Boulevard. Or that I ever developed enough of a rapport with a gorgeous stripper to learn her name (Taylor) or how she lived in North Hollywood with her cute younger sister and costripper (Eva) or that they both wanted to be actors someday and had selfish boyfriends who were in struggling rock bands. What can I say? I like looking at and talking to naked women even if I can't touch them. And, yes, if need be, I would throw single dollar bills in their dance pit to entice them to give me a closer view. However, having a stripper give me my ceremonial wedding lap dance was a real deal breaker for Annabelle. Years later I can say with complete sincerity that my stripperless bachelor party is memorable for one thing and one thing only: it was not, in any way, shape, or form, memorable. My best man organized the party. My best man was my writing partner, who is a woman. Here is my advice to all men getting married: do not have a woman plan your bachelor party. Nothing against women, but women and bachelor parties are incongruous. It's like having Rush Limbaugh coordinate the Democratic convention or Joseph Goebbels arrange your daughter's bat mitzvah. The idea of the bash was to have all my closest friends roast me; but without the fuel of slutty strippers stripping everywhere and an anything-goes *Hangover* attitude, the roast came off forced and contrived. The event was so infinitely lame that several of my friends left right after the sad roast because they had wisely made other plans. Meanwhile, two nights later at her bachelorette party, Annabelle had not one but two strippers! She claims that she didn't know about them and that none of the girls even liked them, but you should see the photos from the party. Those girls were having the time of their lives, including Annabelle. Some couples actually think it's sweet to remarry after many years together; I'd like to skip the second wedding and instead have a second shot at a bachelor party and this time do it with at least a half dozen strippers!

Our wedding planning hostilities came to a boil over the subject of floral arrangements. Not that she remembers, but Annabelle wanted them desperately and was ready to spend what I felt was an outrageous amount, particularly when we were going to get married outside, in Santa Barbara in the springtime, in the middle of a fuckin' *garden!* We would have all the flowers, trees, and foliage we would ever need for the grand sum of *free.* Adding expensive floral arrangements seemed to be the very essence of overkill, like Robin Williams inviting Jim Carrey to join him onstage to do some improv comedy. After several clashes and nasty phone calls on the subject, we compromised on our little "War of the Roses," put aside our other differences, and braced ourselves for the coming tidal wave that comprises our families.

Besides having the wedding reflect our own particular tastes and ceremonial philosophies, the other positive aspect about planning our own wedding was that we didn't have to listen or deal with our parents over every little detail. The wisdom of this became glaringly apparent during the rehearsal dinner. My father, Bob Kahn, offered to pay for that and hosted our families and closest friends. For almost a half century my dad has been a divorce lawyer. That's divorce, more divorce, and nothing but divorce. He's seen the absolutely worst, most desperate, and despicable side of humanity and he's loved every minute of it. It's not that he's antimarriage, he's just prodivorce. Divorce conveniently affirms his passionate belief that people are huge assholes on a daily, almost minute-to-minute basis. When I called to tell him that Annabelle and I had gotten engaged, after what seemed like a full minute of complete silence, my father stated with an almost Dick Cheney–esque emotional disconnect, "You know, half of marriages end in divorce."

Besides his intrinsic cynicism, Bob Kahn's other most pronounced personality trait is that he's a total ham. He loves to be the center of attention, be it in a courtroom in front of a judge or in a rehearsal dinner hall filled with friends and relatives, most of whom were from Annabelle's side and were meeting him and me for the very first time. I held my breath as he delivered a speech whose main thrust was that I, his son, was "weird." Although he doesn't even know what TiVo is, I gathered by the ample evidence presented in his speech that my dad's DVR memory machine had been carefully cataloging my behavior since infancy and it had been overwhelmingly "weird, different, and very, very strange." What I had rather naively seen as my being sensitive, unique, and intellectually curious was, according to my dad, just "Jeff being a weirdo." As his speech continued, my embarrassment swelled into a fervent desire to vacate my body. I really did think I might actually faint when I looked over at Annabelle's relatives, whom I had barely met, and they seemed to think my dad's speech was hysterical and, for all they knew, completely true. Great. Now I was going to be "weird Jeff" to yet more people. If I ever get married again, however doubtful, improbable, perhaps impossible that may be, I will be paying for the rehearsal dinner.

The wedding day itself stumbled out of the gate when our rabbi, who had told us with absolute certainty that he had one and only one rule when it came to our wedding, "Do not under *any* condition be late," was a no-show. He had warned us that nothing sends a wrong message more than when any member of the wedding party is not where he or she is supposed to be at the appointed time. So Annabelle and I made sure to arrive safely early and then quickly slid into a state of sheer panic when the time for the wedding came and went and the rabbi was MIA. Annabelle and I had to down shots of vodka to help us squelch the foreboding. Was this a sign? Perhaps even a portent of things to come? We called his cell phone, his temple, his home, but got nothing and no one. We didn't know where he was, whether he was on his way, whether he had forgotten or gotten lost, or whether after giving it some more thought, he had decided that Annabelle and I were a terrible match and he was going to have no part of it. Plus, I started feeling very guilty. If I had consented to letting Rabbi Mel do it, we would have been married by now.

Although we were freaking out, our guests seemed just fine. This wasn't some hushed indoor church wedding; it was outside in the warm California sunshine, surrounded by the beauteous Santa Barbara landscape. I saw several members of Annabelle's family happily coming up to my dad to congratulate him on his "My Son Is Weird" speech as if it were Martin Luther King's "I Have a Dream." Plus, many of our friends are in the entertainment business and most of them in comedy. Comedians abhor a vacuum, however brief, that they can't fill with their jokes and sarcastic comic observations, so it was a fortuitous opportunity for them to try out their latest material on their peers, guests, and unsuspecting strangers. Our wedding was turning into an impromptu rehearsal for several future HBO and Comedy Central specials.

An hour and a half after we were supposed to be standing under the chuppah and saying our vows, the rabbi finally pulled up in his red Miata convertible, the most unrabbinical of automobiles, without even an ironic apology after all his dire warnings about being late to your own wedding. And to top off his banana split of hypocrisy with the perfect insincere cherry, he gave the most clichéd of tardy excuses: the Los Angeles traffic was bad.

However, from that moment forward, the rest of our wedding was simply spectacular and, to this very instant, the best day and night of my entire life.

The next morning, as Annabelle eloquently described it, we were resting off the bacchanalian nuptial festivities at the über-opulent San Ysidro Ranch resort before heading up to Napa for our honeymoon when we got the news of her grandmother's death. From all accounts, Grandma flew back to Delaware and promptly died. Our honeymoon was over before it had even begun.

We flew to Wilmington for the funeral, Annabelle crying the whole way while I, palms sweating profusely, drank Jack Daniel's straight from the bottle in a futile effort to quash my shockingly bad and equally annoying fear of flying. The only thing that interrupted Annabelle's constant stream of tears, nose blowing, and low-pitched wailing was my inebriated inquiries to the increasingly irritated flight attendants: "Did you hear that? What was that noise? That doesn't sound right, does it?"

We made it to Delaware, alive, exhausted, and with me still slightly drunk, to join Annabelle's family for two days of mourning, smoked fish, and other decidedly nonhoneymoonish activities.

The highlight of the event, for me, came when Annabelle's Queen of Judaism sister, Lisa, deduced from my last name, Kahn, that I was Kohanim, a so-called direct descendant of Moses's brother Aaron and the ancient Hebrew line of temple high priests, who, according to Jewish tradition, cannot be in the presence of death.

Armed with my last name and the laws of the Almighty, Lisa had me immediately escorted out of the graveyard by two large Orthodox guys who I presumed worked for the Jewish Burial Police. I spent the entire next hour and a half banished from my new wife in her time of need, hanging out instead with the funeral limo drivers in their time of lunch.

The rest of our sad excursion to Wilmington was spent looking for a decent espresso and any food that wasn't a smoked, cured, or salted fish, namely, any kind of a fresh vegetable. We found none, and flew back to LA with dry mouths, completely constipated.

It was also during the time when I was banished from the graveyard that Annabelle was informed that her mother had a brain tumor that needed to be removed right away. Instead of retreating into a honeymoon cocoon for what was left of our time in Napa, Annabelle had to turn around and fly to Miami to help take care of her mother. The day she left town, my car was broken into. Several of the wedding gift certificates were wrenched from the glove compartment along with my driver's license and a couple of my credit cards. When I vented about the loss of property, the smashed car window, and feelings of being violated, Annabelle accused me of being selfish, materialistic, and superficial. How could I care more about a few measly gifts and personal effects than I did about her, the recent loss of her grandmother, and now her brain-tumored mother?

At this point, I have to admit, I didn't know what had hit me. I spent the time Annabelle was in Miami feeling numb and lost and replaying the happy memories of the wedding in my head. I figured what had happened was that I hadn't actually married into the Gurwitch family but Death itself. I had definitely not signed on for this, but what could I do? I was married, right? Her problems were my problems and mine hers. We were married, what every self-centered, party-going, club-hopping, dating, dancing, drinking, sex-obsessed single person in the world was striving so hard to achieve. This was what all the fuss was about. No wonder everyone in the world, gay or straight, wants to get hitched. Oh what fun, what joy, what giddy and blithe excitement!

Annabelle's mother survived her surgery and had the good fortune of a great prognosis for a full recovery. Annabelle returned from her nursing duties both physically and emotionally depleted. Thankfully, she was also irritable and very anxious. All this death and near death had made her positively consumed with thoughts of birth and life. She was now very worried that becoming pregnant might be problematic because of that uterine fibroid tumor. I had known about this fibroid, but assumed that having a baby was something we were going to think about after all the worry-free excitement and bliss of our wedding and honeymoon had worn off, in a year or two. But after all she had been through since we'd married, a new reality dawned on her: she wasn't some twenty-year-old bride, but a thirty-five-year-old woman whose time for frivolity and fun had been replaced by fibroids and biological clocks.

I am well aware that many single people see marriage as the answer to or the end of their relationship troubles and the beginning of their happily-ever-after. I never considered myself one of these singles because I thought I was more like those self-involved pouty romantics listening to the Cure, searching for passionate, erotic love while shunning sunny happiness like leprosy or Disneyland. Yet I never imagined that the beginning of my marriage would make me long for any kind of break in the weather. I was beginning to understand why marriage "experts" like to say that if a couple gets through the first year of marriage they stand a good chance of making it. They all seem to agree that year one is the most difficult. (After thirteen years of marriage, I would tend to agree with them, except that they left out years two through twelve.) Perhaps this is why weddings and honeymoons are so vital. They serve as the buffer, a euphoric boot camp, if you will, between the illusion of marriage and the reality of it. But Annabelle and I weren't going to get that lovely little respite, because over the course of the twenty-eight days since we'd said our vows, we had jumped right over "to have and to hold" and landed smack in the middle of "till death do us part."

generation S for selfish?

Only one in three couples says raising children is an important part of marriage.

A recent Pew survey says children used to rank as the highest source of personal fulfillment for their parents, but having kids has dropped to one of the least-cited factors in a successful marriage, after "mutual happiness."

in sickness or in health?

A lousy marriage might literally make you sick. Marriage has traditionally been thought to prolong life and promote health; new research from Brigham Young University has shown that that's true only if you have a *good* marriage. Marital strife can raise your risk for heart disease.

and baby makes . . . us miserable

Twenty-five separate studies establish that marital quality drops substantially after parenthood. The married research team at Berkeley, Carolyn and Philip Cowan, announced the findings in 2009. Their investigation found that the drop in marital satisfaction was almost entirely accounted for by the couples who slid into being parents, disagreed over it, or were ambivalent about it. Couples who planned or equally welcomed the conception were likely to maintain or even increase their marital satisfaction after the child was born.

5

. . . .

Hungry Like the Wolf

"Marriage is about raising children, that's the purpose of the institution."
—RUSH LIMBAUGH, "FAMILY VALUES ADVOCATE,"
MARRIED THREE TIMES, NO KIDS

Deciding to have a baby can be one of the most important and exciting decisions for a couple. For many, trying to procreate brings them even closer together. Ha! Not us. We couldn't even agree on who wanted one in the first place. Having a baby was another opportunity for us to plumb the depths of marital mayhem and strife. Good times!

He Says

Annabelle wanted to have a baby. She wanted one, she wanted one from me, and she wanted one now! If I showed any resistance to this, she cleverly ascribed her newfound baby lust to me because of how baby friendly I was around my friends' children. It was one of the things that finally made me attractive to her.

Yes, it was true that I loved making my friends' little tykes giggle until they spit up. But the thing I loved most of all about them was that they weren't mine. I admired my friends for having babies in the same way I admire Picasso's *Guernica,* Washington's surprise Christmas attack on Trenton, or how anyone can put together anything from IKEA. Just knowing I could never accomplish any of these things in my lifetime makes them all the more impressive. And so it was with my married friends and their offspring. They seemed so responsible, selfless, and mature—so not me. Life for them was no longer a string of temporary arrangements, transitional relationships, casual sex, and cheap adolescent thrills. Had these friends with infants lost their minds? But Annabelle put it to me hard: if I truly loved her, shouldn't I take that step out of Adolescentville and stride with her into adult parenthood? Check and mated and off to Cedars-Sinai to take out the grapefruit fibroid.

But first, the night before her surgery, I took Polaroids of Annabelle's pristine, never-been-operated-on body in the buff. Her pussy was so perfect and pretty, I couldn't believe they were going to cut into it. I spent the next three nights sleeping on Annabelle's hospital room floor while she weaned herself off the morphine drip and peed into a bag. Recognizing how nervous she was about the surgery and recovery, I did my best to pretend I wasn't scared shitless. Here we had just got married and already we'd had to deal with death, disease, and surgery. If this had been a movie script I'd written, everyone who read it would laugh in my face and tell me, "This could never happen. Now go and rewrite it and be sure you make it more believable and realistic."

I remember thinking that if I was able to help Annabelle get through all this, weather the storm, as it were, then she would never doubt how committed I was to her and our marriage. (God, was I naive back then or what? A mere babe in the great marital woods.) I accepted the operation as a necessity and therefore inevitable, so there was nothing more to do than to try to keep up a

brave front, make her as comfortable as possible, and perhaps steal
a couple of her Vicodin.

To celebrate Annabelle's release, we spent a ridiculously expensive night at the Four Seasons Hotel. It was too soon to have sex,
but Annabelle wanted to show me her surgical scar. She worried it
would turn me off. I assured her nothing could turn me off when it
came to her pussy. She undid her robe and presented it: large, thick
black stitches going diagonally across, jutting in and out. I tried to
think of something comforting and loving to say, but all that came
out was "Oh my God, my wife has a Franken-gina!"

With her uterine tumor safely removed from the picture,
Annabelle thought it was time for us to get down to the business of
making her pregnant. I imagined getting a neurotic, high-strung, and
overly anxious person like Annabelle pregnant could take months,
even years, and by that time, I might actually be ready for fatherhood.
Then a little problem arose less than a month into our sexual
Olympics—Annabelle was pregnant. Oh, come on! What kind of
luck is that?!

After the initial disappointment of being cheated out of all
those years of fucking passed, a wave of euphoria hit me. Annabelle
and I had decided to do something together, and wonder of won-
ders, we did it! We're having a baby! Maybe this having a baby
thing was actually going to bring us closer. Maybe during Annabelle's
pregnancy we would spend the time planning how we were going
to be this whole new kind of family. Having a baby would reflect
our cool, hip, "enlightened" postmodern personalities and world-
views. Or I could get a job writing a TV show in Austin, Texas, and
we would spend the next seven months apart. I was hesitant about
taking the gig; I was already employed with my writing partner at
a production company, and I had seen myself playing the part of
the dutiful husband massaging his wife's tired swollen feet and

lying to her about how awesome she looked even when her butt tripled in size. But Annabelle absolutely insisted I go. She knew that the business reality of being the head writer of a show in production was vastly superior to gambling that one of my own scripts would ever see the light of day. She said I'd be an idiot to pass on such a great opportunity, and so somewhat against my better judgment, I accepted.

I remember shopping with her to stock up the house the day before I was to leave and it just didn't feel real that I'd be gone for so long during such a crucial period in our lives. We made heartfelt promises to travel back and forth as much as we could, and just to make matters even more complicated, we also decided that before our child was born, we should buy a new house. We rationalized that doing two completely different things in two completely different parts of the country was all part of our experiment in having a cool, nontraditional family.

The climatic seasons in LA are as follows: summer, more summer, two weeks of light rain, and then summer again. With this in mind, I mocked those who warned me that Texas was way hotter. Within seconds of exiting the Austin airport, I realized I might have slightly underestimated my idea of heat. Central Texas in the throes of summer is 100 degrees during the day and 101 at night, and it has 1,000 percent humidity. This makes Los Angeles feel like Green Bay in February. After visiting for just one miserably hot night in Austin, Annabelle, dripping with sweat and anger, got back on a plane to LA and told me she would never come to Texas again for any reason.

This left me working on a show that was run on a shoestring budget and shot guerrilla indie film style, which meant that writing and filming went on around the clock. My working hours consisted of whenever I managed to wake up until whenever I lost consciousness. No one on the show was nice to me, every meal was some kind of meat barbecued and drowned in cheese—a lactose-intolerant vegetarian's dream come true—and worst of all, Austin is a college town teeming with the prettiest, longest-legged gals in Texas, who all seemed to be in an extremely fierce competition with one another over who could wear the shortest, sexiest miniskirt. It was the ultimate tease for a thirty-five-year-old married man without the slightest chance of having sex for months.

During my long, hot, sexless, miserable months in Austin, Annabelle was back home busily searching for a new house in between morning sickness vomiting and bouts of frequent constipation. She was also informed that her uterine surgery prevented her from giving birth vaginally, and she would have to have a cesarean section. (*Vaginally* is the least sexy of words that refer to all things vagina.) As for us, we resorted to the only behavior appropriate for a postmodern married couple in such a tense and unpredictable situation: we bitched, griped, and moaned at each other daily by phone. This quickly escalated into a contest of who was having a worse time of it, which in turn led to more frustration, miscommunication, yelling, and phone receiver banging.

The nadir of our phone conversation confrontations, or "conphontations," came the day the *New York Times* review of my series *Austin Stories* came out. It was a rave. Finally, I had some long-overdue satisfaction for all the hard work and outrageous hours. I imagined that with a strong review from such a prestigious paper there was now a possibility the show might get an order for a second, even a third season. Although I truly hated Texas (and its inferno weather as well as its pork-grilling, gun-toting, pickup-driving, execution-happy citizens), I thought if the show got picked up, the best thing to do was to get a nice apartment in Austin. This way, when I had to be there shooting, Annabelle and our baby would be more comfortable when they came to visit. When I relayed this merely speculative sentiment to Annabelle, it was as if I had invited her to a medieval witch burning and she was the witch. She exploded in a Krakatoa-like volcanic rage, calling me all sorts of things, most beginning with *fucking* and ending in *idiot*!

My getting a place in Austin turned out to be one of the stupidest things I ever proposed. Despite the positive reviews, the executives at MTV hated the show, they despised me for writing it, and even the cast and crew detested me. I returned home to an unsympathetic wife now seven months pregnant. (I never forgave myself and vowed never to make such future plans, however vague, again.) Reunited in the same city, Annabelle and I would finally have the opportunity to find common ground and get back to creating our twenty-first-century household. Together we were going to move into the new house Annabelle had found for us, study the latest baby research, get the nursery ready, and choose the perfect pediatrician. But the week I returned, Annabelle began having prelabor contractions and was ordered on bed rest. And to make sure the baby stayed inside, she was given a medication that gave her intense and perpetual intestinal gas. So I was sent out into the world while Annabelle was quarantined in the bed. Once again we were forced to go about lives apart from each other. We were fast becoming a contemporary John and Abigail Adams, minus, of course, their acute intellectual brilliance and profound selflessness.

I took over the pediatrician search and got an instant tutorial on the tangential effect show business has on a whole community. Even the baby docs act like stars in Los Angeles. Big egos, fancy Beverly Hills offices, and a Hollywood medical swagger that oozes "I take care of the Banderas/Griffith kids, so I may not even have time for your baby." I especially disliked the cultlike guru aura that surrounded Annabelle's choice of pediatrician, Dr. Paul Fleiss. He's the father of the infamous Heidi Fleiss and he has a slew of rules for new parents, the biggest one being no male circumcision. He won't work with you if you circumcise your son. I attended an open house where he spoke to a group of parents-to-be for forty-five minutes, mainly on the subject of the foreskin. He also insists on breast-feeding until the child is eleven, but for the most part, for Fleiss it's all foreskin all the time. Some of these newly expectant parents were moved to tears by Dr. Fleiss's passionate advocacy of the penis flap. Yet all I could think of while he talked was: this is Heidi Fleiss's father, and she's a whore-pimp-madam-drug-addict-alcoholic-felon-of-a-train-wreck. Given how his own daughter turned out, perhaps he doesn't deserve his cult status or to take care of my baby, foreskin or not.

Although Annabelle relented on Fleiss, she did like some of the things he had advocated, especially his theory about never giving a baby a pacifier. I was of the let's-wait-and-see school of what works for us and our baby. I thought that because we had never been parents, it would be better to get some empirical experience under our belts. This touched a raw nerve in Annabelle. She had collected books and articles and had scanned research online for several minutes on the subject of pacifiers and forbidding them was the only way. I was not only unqualified to have an opinion, but was also once again an "idiot" for not understanding the more profound ramifications. My play-it-by-ear pacifier approach was to Annabelle akin to devil worship, or worse, voting Republican. At one point during our dispute, I feared she might actually leave me over this matter, but fortuitously, she couldn't get out of bed. This having a baby wasn't transforming us into enlightened beings freed from the antiquated notions of the vox populi, emancipated from the mistakes, ignorance, and shackles of procreations past; instead, it was more like an iron curtain coming down between us. Leaving us to argue who represented freedom and liberty (me) and who was dogmatic oppression and tyranny (her).

One night we lay at opposite sides of the bed, Annabelle belching, I engrossed in a nature program where a snow wolf chased a snow rabbit halfway across the snow-covered Arctic tundra before killing it and bringing it back to his mate and their wolf cub. The "wife" of the hunter wolf took the bloody rabbit out of his mouth and she and the cub eagerly sauntered away to eat it, leaving father wolf exhausted, alone, and hungry. Annabelle had, and I'm not exaggerating, tears streaming down her face watching how the mother wolf took care of her cub. "What about the papa wolf?" I exclaimed. "He did all the work and got nothing. What kind of mate wants her spouse to die of starvation? Shouldn't she give him at least the bunny tail to nibble on?" Annabelle thought that was absolutely ridiculous. It was a biological imperative for a mother, any mother, to sustain herself and her offspring. I was getting very upset. "I thought we were going to be different. I thought we were going to be a progressive, forward-thinking couple having a baby together." Annabelle turned toward me with what seemed to be her incisor teeth dripping with saliva and growled, "Together? You don't know what the hell you're talking about! I'm pregnant, I can't move, and I'm starving! Go to Hard Times Pizza and get me two slices with sausage, pepperoni, and ham!"

A few weeks later, after returning from yet another Annabelle pizza run, she informed me it was time to have the baby. This came as a bit of a surprise because her C-section wasn't scheduled for another two weeks. I was working on a script deadline with my writing partner, so I *casually* asked if it was *possible* she could keep it in there a little longer? She serenely informed me that if I really wanted to keep it in longer, I could shove it up my ass and keep it in *there* for as long as I wanted.

On the way to the hospital, a wave of dizzy, light-headed existential nausea came over me. In my mind I was screaming, "Not ready for this! Not ready for this!" My brain was racing. What were we thinking of, having a baby? Annabelle and I, parents? We could barely manage our own lives. How would we be able to care for some helpless pod creature? How were we going to do all the extra cooking and laundry and buy the diapers, groceries, and baby food? How were we going to be up all night when he cried and couldn't sleep? Shouldn't we have been talking about all this instead of arguing about the philosophical ramifications of paci-fucking-fiers? And how could I be the wolf daddy bringing home the rabbit and just watch them eat it? I happen to adore *lapin à la dijonnaise*.

By the time we got to the hospital, I could hardly catch my breath. For God's sake, all I wanted to do was have sex without a condom for a little while; now we were moments from bringing a new life into the world!

Once inside the hospital, Annabelle was prepped and ready for surgery. Then suddenly, there he was! I started snapping photos: bloody Annabelle stomach, bloody baby, and incandescent blue umbilical cord.

I felt as if I were hallucinating. It was way too quiet in there. The baby wasn't crying. One of the interns moved our infant's arms up and down and said, "Breathe, Ezra, breathe." Yes, I was definitely hallucinating.

Then, finally, baby Ezra began to cry. Involuntary tears started streaming down my face as I kept repeating "Oh my God" over and over. I cut the umbilical cord, and Ezra was wheeled away into an examination room. I stumbled over to Annabelle. "Is everything OK? Is the baby all right?" she asked as they were sewing her gut back up. At that instant I knew Annabelle had been right about the wolf mom and cub getting the food. I knew I'd do anything to sustain the new life brought into the world, even chase a rabbit all over Los Angeles, in my car, during rush hour, if I had to. Annabelle was right and I was a jerk for even thinking otherwise. Trying to be a hip, enlightened, postmodern couple having a baby was just as preposterous a myth as flying unicorns, fire-breathing dragons, or "The insurgency is in its last throes." They may all sound good, but no matter how strongly you believe they are real, they're not and never will be.

She Says

Funny, I thought having a baby was Jeff's idea. Sticky, whiny, mess-making machines with runny noses. It's not that I don't like kids; I've just always felt the same about having children as I do about communism and monogamy: sounds good in the abstract. I've never been one of those women who feel compelled to make a baby with all the men they sleep with; that's like wanting to bring home a souvenir from every town you drive through. But then Jeff came into the picture.

Yes, I may have offhandedly dropped the hint that if we ever wanted to consider having a family, we should get going right at that very instant, but from the time Jeff and I were seriously dating, I was under the impression that he had already packed his own bags and was looking to hitch a ride out of Adolescentville and into a new life as an adult male.

In recent years, Adolescentvilles have cropped up inside many of America's metropolises, but the Los Angeles enclave is its capital. Los Angeles is populated by man-boy Peter Pans sporting backward-facing baseball caps; driving late-model, gas-guzzling convertibles; and serially dating very young women with thong-line tattoos, superlarge sunglasses, and demo DVDs of their latest appearance on a reality show. Gertrude Stein astutely observed of California that there's "no there there." I believe that there actually may be a "there" there, but you can't get "there" from here if your "here" isn't in your twenties and bankrolled by a massive amount of cash. Clearly, Jeff and I had been "here" long enough to know that we didn't belong "there." Jeff was already renting a family-friendly house and his pursuit of me gave every indication of a desire for a long-term relationship, and to my eyes, Jeff Kahn appeared to be Mr. Baby.

Jeff has always had nicknames for everyone and everything, and kids are the perfect audience for his antics. His preternatural silliness makes him a pied piper to little sneechers, snoochers, yon-dermans, and herkimer children (his nicknames) who unfailingly giggle and jump into his arms. There is an undeniable effect that a man who is good with children has on women of childbearing age. This phenomenon, noted in numerous women's top ten turn-on lists, was not lost on me, and Jeff's kid appeal had the effect of kicking my eggs into high gear. If he didn't really want to have kids, as he claims, then it was irresponsible of him to expose me to his baby wrangling. Add to this the undeniable fact that we weren't getting any younger. Young in appearance, maybe, but saddled with aging body parts, our generation has had to accept the fact that you can't Botox your uterus. Couples we knew were trolling for surrogate carriers. I had girlfriends who were spending a good part of their days evaluating egg donors with impressive degrees and the odd combination of skills, such as "I speak six languages and make my own deodorant." That's the real explanation for why we were on an express ride to parenthood.

At the onset of my pregnancy, I didn't have a clue about the kind of family we would make together. Like Jeff, I entertained a fantasy of us as a globe-trotting, baby-toting artsy duo, but in terms of actual delineation of duties and plans . . . not so much. Not having had a picture of myself as a mother, my only plan was to be the opposite of my own mother, who had had the audacity to try to transcend her 1950s working-class upbringing in hopes of attaining a 1960s suburban lifestyle. She had worked at the onset, and then spent the rest of her pregnancies lounging in a peignoir, smoking, and stocking up on baby formula. My mother says she never really thought about having children; she just did what was expected of her, and following our births, the majority of important familial decisions were delegated to my father. To her credit, my mother had indoctrinated me in the kind of feminist rhetoric she had been denied, repeatedly assuring me from the time I was a little girl that I could have it all, so now that I was going maternal, I was determined that I would prove her right. I was going to distinguish myself from the women of her generation. I was going to be an engaged, educated mother, a successful businesswoman with a baby on my boob and my day planner packed in the outside pocket of my Kate Spade diaper bag. But before we could craft our new family plan together, Jeff was off to work in Texas. So much for all of our togetherness.

My first plan of action was to enroll in the same Los Angeles prenatal yoga class that Madonna and Cindy Crawford had attended. That class is led by a Sikh whose claim to have weathered a twenty-four-hour labor by continuous consumption of raw liver has made her an icon among the famously knocked-up of Hollywood. It's true that birthing can be something of a competitive sport, and at the beginning of each session, each expectant mom would announce her intentions: "I'm having my baby vaaaginally" or "I'm having my baby vaginally at home with a midwife." "I'm having a vaginal birth at home in a bathtub with Tibetan monks chanting kabalistic incantations, and Madonna is my midwife" is what I wanted to say, but instead I admitted that I'd be at Cedars-Sinai having a planned cesarean and I was really looking forward to the awesome drugs, which meant that I made not a single friend among the super politically correct breeders in that class. In what was to become a pattern, Jeff teased me mercilessly about my attendance. The class was relaxing and full of just the kind of motherhood tips I was seeking, but my husband is suspicious of anything being embraced by what he perceives as the trendy liberal elite class. Cognitive behavioral parenting techniques, attachment parenting, and the newly fashionable but-practiced-for-millenniums family bed were all things Jeff deemed too popular with the PC crowd to be practiced by the soon to be created Gurkahn family. I knew that anyone who talks about saving the environment while residing in a ten-thousand-square-foot home, people who drive Priuses,* and everything written by Deepak Chopra were fodder for Jeff's cynicism, but I was beginning to be annoyed that every suggestion I made was met with the same disaffection. Jeff would reject breathing if he could, just because everyone else is doing it. For the record, the mothers in that class ended up having statistically the same rate of C-sections (approximately one in three) as the rest of the population in the United States. Meanwhile Jeff kept laughing at me and asked me to join him in Texas.

Of Austin in the summer I can only say it was like being in an oven. I was already an oven cooking up a baby. Now I was an oven in an oven. Jeff still refuses to acknowledge that he suggested we *move* to Texas, not just get an apartment down there.

Scientific research tells us much about the different ways that the male and female auditory systems work. Studies indicate that men listen with one hemisphere of the brain, while women listen

*I drive a Prius.

with both.* Scientists are befuddled by the implications of this difference, but anecdotal evidence suggests that men simply don't hear what we are saying. However, no evidence can explain why men can't hear themselves. Like, Jeff insisting that he merely suggested a rental in Austin. Someone should research that phenomenon. Jeff also forgets that I grew up in the South, where I learned that every day south of the Mason-Dixon Line is a bad hair day for a Jewish girl. Whenever I return, my head channels Barbra Streisand in *A Star Is Born*. Though I enjoy my meat barbecued, fried, battered, and buttered, I have no desire to live there again. As if that weren't enough, Jeff had been sending photographs home in which he appeared extremely chummy with the support staff of the TV series: those supershiny, supple girls in tiny tube tops and good-ass pants. I was already trying to wrap my head around the fact that my boobs were exploding out of my body and my ass was expanding so fast it was like a Starbucks franchise. On every corner of my ass there was another branch of ass opening up. I was freaking about how my life was going to change, so now I was supposed to pick up and move to a place where everybody my husband works with is an MTV beach-house bunny and I know no one? No, thank you.

One lucky break for me was that one of Jeff's numerous former roommates, Eric, was moving to Los Angeles and needed a place to stay. I found myself uncharacteristically thrilled to have company. In what was one of the high points of Eric's stay, Jeff asked him to take me out for a really big steak for my birthday. Other patrons looked stunned and slightly disgusted at the speed and efficiency with which I dispatched that meal, which quickly

---

*This finding received wide attention in a 2001 study published by Indiana School of Medicine's Dr. Michael Phillips.

was absorbed into the hugeness that was my posterior. I had no way of knowing that that dinner would be one of my last meals out of the house for months.

Meanwhile, we had pressing issues in Los Angeles. Our lease on the Hobbit house was running out, so even if we couldn't decide which configuration we'd be sleeping in, it was imperative that we find a new home. So there I was, knocked up, wearing Sea-Bands, puking my guts out at work on a TV series where I was hiding my pregnancy behind huge mixing bowls, and now I needed to buy a house. I was finding that "having it all" in reality just means doing it all. Before Jeff arrived back on the coast, I had picked out a home; arranged a mortgage; had it painted, reroofed, rewired, the floors refinished; and taken care of the insurances and inspections we were required to have. It's true, the house I bought may or may not be sitting on top of a newly discovered earthquake fault, but I did get us a roof over our heads.*

Jeff devotes all of one line to a description of the period of time during which I was ordered to bed. This is probably due to the fact that he wasn't the one who was reduced to lying on one side of his body for six weeks straight with strict instructions to rise only to go to the bathroom. The prospect of bed rest had sounded like fun, and it was, for maybe the first forty-five minutes. At that point, I would have preferred my mother's pregnancy, which, lubricated as it was with coffee and the odd martini, had progressed completely uneventfully. I had numerous ambitious goals for my bed rest: make photo albums of our wedding, learn conversational Pashto, earn an online degree in animal husbandry; sadly, I accomplished

---

*Jeff really dislikes this characterization of him as someone who can't handle anything to do with home improvement. "But you can't change a lightbulb," I often remind him. "I can too; I just can't get the fixtures back on afterward" is his standard answer. I rest my case.

nothing.* For the record, I did read entire chapters, if not entire books, on pregnancy, but by that time I could barely string a sentence together, much less read, because the side effects of the anti-contraction medication included anxiety, palpitations, and violent burping. The only horrible side effect it didn't have was to make me fat and that's only because I was already a big fat pregnant lady!

This may be the ultimate explanation as to why Jeff and I are still married today. That another human witnessed me in this condition and can still look me in the eye, much less find me desirable, is unfathomable. Perhaps the CIA will one day try "bed rest" in lieu of water-boarding and the other forms of torture they've employed, because after six weeks of being unable to move from my side, I would gladly have confessed to being a high-ranking member of the Taliban, the second gunman on the grassy knoll, and John Wilkes Booth's getaway driver.

It was during the bed rest that I discovered that watching nature shows while pregnant could produce a hormone-induced weeping identity crisis. I would find myself sobbing into my copy of *What to Expect When You're Expecting*, torn between whom to root for, the bunnies or the wolves, but by the middle of the programs all I could think was "I'm starving." That's how I knew I had truly gone maternal; any latent sentimentality had been transformed into survival instinct, and I was sure I would rip that rabbit limb from limb if my cub was hungry. Was Jeff even present? Did the papa wolf need to eat? Who cared? Jeff was right—my baby was my future now and I was hungry like the wolf.

It was in this ravenous state, and maybe because of it, that Jeff and I held the great pacifier debate. I had agreed with Jeff's assessment of Fleiss, even though his office was within walking distance

*Our wedding photos are *still* in boxes.

of our home, the holy grail of geographical desirability in Los Angeles, but I wasn't about to give in on the pacifier. Jeff championed flexibility and said don't make plans in advance, but I was not going to be like my mother, damn it; I was the decider. I was only adamant about a few things. Unlike my own mother, it would be the boob over bottle, the binky would be banned, and I was thinking it would be nice to have our baby sleep in our bed. Meanwhile, Jeff was under the impression that numerous chores were left to him, when in reality, the only things left for him to do were to see the few doctors I hadn't yet visited and to keep my supply line of sausage pizzas unimpeded while I endured the last stages of the pregnancy in my new incarnation as a beached belching whale.* This seems to be the perfect time to debunk that canard that has crept into the lexicon of contemporary procreation: "We're having a baby" or "We're pregnant." This phrase reflects the delusional gender-equalizing development that has betrayed us by improperly depicting reality. "Jeff," I unattractively bleated, "*we* aren't having a baby; *I* am having a baby and would be thrilled if you plan to stick around, and if 'we' were pregnant, both of us would have been here the whole fucking time and neither of us would be ambulatory, but one of us wasn't, and one of us is, so you're going to get me a pizza, and I'm going to decide if our baby gets a pacifier! And make that *extra* cheese!"

During the last few weeks of the pregnancy we went to the hospital three times. Each time I was given more medication, and told to wait it out. By now I had so little brainpower, I just lay

---

*According to the *Wall Street Journal,* men's domestic role has changed little in the last twenty years, though women's working hours outside the home have increased significantly, which means either we're all living in filth or, as the report suggests, the ladies are picking up the slack, so why should the prenatal preparedness be any different?

there on my side, counting the seconds of every minute and then starting all over again, in between burping, bitching, and moaning to my husband. Jeff describes the moment I informed him "it was time" as though I were actively conspiring to stand between him and his work. I don't need to remind any woman who has given birth that you just can't hold in a baby, like gas, which I was also holding in at that moment. I was so stunned by Jeff's response that I turned around and sat in the bathtub for an hour.* So I sat in the tub, contemplating how I knew it was going to be: me working full-time, the baby on my boob while I assembled the nursery furniture we'd ordered from IKEA, searching for Jeff's hidden cache of pacifiers. But by the time I emerged, it was the middle of the night and I thought we should wait a little longer to give the doctor some more time to sleep, so Jeff did, in fact, have time to finish the assignment he was working on. But as they wheeled me into the delivery room, having been up for twenty-four hours and in bed for three months, I wasn't terrified, I was freaked out: "I'm not cut out for this . . . trolls . . . hair on fire!" I cried. Suddenly I realized that I may have been hungry like the wolf, but Jeff had done his best. Jeff had been in an equivalent of the Arctic tundra, surviving show business purgatory in Austin, hunting down bucks not bunnies, and I was a jerk for not recognizing how much he had contributed in his own way. But had I known beforehand what we were in for next, I might have skipped the whole thing and bought expensive moisturizers instead.

*I wasn't in the agonizing labor contractions that probably would have made me punch Jeff as I called a cab; they were those pesky preterm labor contractions. We had been told that the next time they increased, it would be time to deliver the baby. If you've ever tried to wear three pairs of Spanx at once and still considered breathing an essential activity, well, it was kinda like that. For the record, at 36½ weeks, our baby was not considered a preemie.

"The majority of divorces occur in the first year after the birth of a child."

—Rutgers University, 2005

Women who "self-silenced" during conflict with their spouses, compared with women who did not, had four times the risk of dying, according to findings published in 2007 in the journal *Psychosomatic Medicine*.

reflections of love

Couples begin to look alike for many reasons including diet, environment, and general predisposition (or in Los Angeles if they frequent the same plastic surgeon), but psychologist Robert Zajonc and colleagues have published a study indicating that as couples empathize with each other, they copy each other's facial expressions and thus actually develop similar facial features.

"When choosing a long-term partner . . . you will inevitably be choosing a particular set of unsolvable problems that you'll be grappling with for the next ten, twenty, or fifty years."

—Psychologist Dan Wile, *After the Honeymoon*

in sickness and in health

Parents with chronically ill children are at significant risk for experiencing marital distress. Blame often becomes an issue. The time constraints alone of caring for a chronically ill child are very challenging to any marriage. The normal "escape" outlets—such as a simple evening alone—also are limited; simple fatigue becomes a big problem.

—"Chronically Ill Child Can Doom a Marriage," *USA Today*

6

. . . .

The Years of Living Sleeplessly

"Life is divided into the horrible and the miserable."

—WOODY ALLEN

On the day of our wedding, we recited vows to each other that included these lines from a translation of the Tao Te Ching: "Can you coax your mind from its wandering and keep to the original oneness? Can you step back from your own mind and thus understand all things? Can you deal with the most vital matters by letting events take their course?" And the answer would be no. However, we didn't realize how *no* the answer was until the day our son was born.

He Says

I had an overwhelming sense of awe, terror, and dread when our baby son, Ezra, was scooped out of his mother's gut and taken into an examination room where a doctor with a thick Dutch accent and the bedside manner of Donald Rumsfeld told me that he had no anus.

"No, what? Shut up . . ." I scrutinize him: Is this doctor serious

98

or is he just seriously fucking with me? Everyone knows the Dutch are known for speed skating, legalized pot, prostitution, and even very tasty Gouda cheese, but comedy? I'm sort of a wiseass myself so I say to him, "Well, he's just been born, so maybe his anus is really, really tiny and you just can't see it." Van Rumsfeld looks at me as if I'd just drunk his last Heineken. He's not joking. He never jokes. He's Dutch. I immediately check Ezra's rear for openings and find the smoothest, most hole-free ass in the history of assholes. I'm stunned, confused, and as usual, I'm angry. "Where's his hole?! I cannot take him without a hole!" I cry out, as if my son were a pair of Diesel jeans without a zipper.

Annabelle was so delirious from all the C-section drugs that after I told her he had no anus, she was laughing hysterically. She joked to the nurse that she couldn't believe Jeff Kahn's son doesn't have a butthole because "that's my husband's favorite part of the body." Ha, ha, ha, Annabelle's so witty when she's hopped on painkillers. OK, it is true everyone knows that I am somewhat obsessed with that end of the body and if given a choice between watching Shakespeare's *King Lear,* a great episode of *Seinfeld,* or *Up the Butt Girls 23,* I can't lie and tell you *Lear* or *Seinfeld.* It's nothing I'm proud of. So was this all some kind of karmic payback? Was I being told, "Hey, you like ass so much, Kahn, OK, here—deal with it 24/7. Not so much fun, huh? Next time do yourself a favor and fixate on Shakespearean tragedy, schmuck."

Less than two hours after the birth, Annabelle and I are in her hospital room listening to Doc Van Dutch inform us that having no anus is the tip of the birth defect iceberg. Little Ezra has what is called VACTERL, an acronym in which the letters *V, A, C, T, E, R,* and *L* each stand for one or more birth defects. This can be one, all, or several different combinations of: having no anus; stricture or fusing of the esophagus and trachea; heart problems; kidney abnormalities; vertebral anomalies; and even limb defects, such as not enough toes or fingers. As far as we knew at that point, Ezra was definitely anus free, he had an esophageal stricture (too small to let food into his stomach), holes in his heart, and a possible conjoined or horse-shaped kidney.

I'd love to claim that my response to all this was to be a stoic, brave husband and that I was a beacon of hope, optimism, and stability to my wife, family, and friends, but what I did was weep. I cried because I felt lost, overwhelmed, and ill equipped and unprepared to deal with any of this. I cried because I knew that the life I had been living up to this moment was gone and over forever. And I continued to cry for hours until a hospital administrative liaison was summoned to warn me that if didn't stop crying, I'd be personally escorted out of the hospital. Finally, my writing partner, who came to the hospital for moral support and is no fan of hysterical, overly emotional males, especially when it is her writing partner, slapped me right across the face. She ordered me to get hold of myself so I could be strong for Annabelle, who was coming down from the postsurgery drugs and quickly beginning to lose it as well. It was definitely not one of my strongest moments. Thank goodness I never had to sail across the world with Magellan, storm the beaches of Normandy, or interview Tom Cruise about Scientology.

In order to survive, our baby needed surgery immediately to make him a feeding tube and a colostomy. My hand was trembling as I filled out surgical consent forms when I heard the nurse tell me, "You're lucky." I'm lucky? Hey, screw you, lady, I thought to myself. "You're getting Big Mac," she continued. "I'm getting a Big Mac?" "No, Dr. Columbus McAlpin, Big Mac, is going to be your baby's surgeon. He's the head of pediatric surgery. The entire hospital parts like the Red Sea in front of him." At that moment, I saw a short, squat, black doctor in blue scrubs, with a furry beard, advancing down the hallway toward me. Every nurse, doctor, resident, and orderly politely moved out of his path. He had a big smile on his face when he shook my hand and a gentle, assured glint in his eyes. "Hey, I'm Columbus McAlpin." Perhaps it was the feel of his steady hand or the subtly raspy, jazz trumpeter lilt to his voice, but it was the first time since Ezra exited Annabelle's womb that I didn't feel as if the whole world was coming crashing down on top of me. This was the first of many occasions that Big Mac would subside my worries and lift my sagging spirits.

In the neonatal intensive care unit later that night, I find I can't stop staring at our kid. So that's my baby down there in that incubator, hooked up to heart and oxygen monitors, wires and IV lines going into and out of his body. A feeding tube protrudes from his tiny stomach, an oversized plastic colostomy bag farcically droops over his little diaper. A black string runs from his mouth down his throat out the feeding tube hole and back into his mouth again. I have no idea what that's for. Ezra simultaneously looks like a newborn infant and a tired old man. It's at that moment that a part of me leaves my body, looks back at where I'm standing, and waves good-bye. He says he's off to Iceland, a land where everyone is either drunk or fucking or both, and would I care to join him? I really wanted to go to Iceland. Beautiful, icy . . . distant Iceland . . . But for some reason my feet felt nailed to the floor. I couldn't move a muscle. No, I didn't want to stick around and deal with what lay ahead for Annabelle and me and Ezra, but I equally didn't want to miss it.

Our lives quickly turned into complete shit, literally and figuratively. After three weeks in the hospital, the nurses bundled up tiny Ezra, handed him to us, and wished us luck. Annabelle asked if there was some kind of "no anus" class for new parents like us, and the nurses just laughed. "Anus class, you two are funny." And then they walked away. We were on our own. From here on out, we'd have to wing it.

When Annabelle was pregnant, we purchased diapers and bottles; now we were faced with colostomy-bag changing and pouring milk through tubes into his stomach every four hours. Modern medicine is often quite miraculous, yet when it comes to colostomy bags, it's downright medieval. It's a tortuous device that must have been created during the Spanish Inquisition. I made several frustrated, futile, and foolish attempts to master those fuckers until I had to tell Annabelle that there are some things I was never, beyond a shadow of a doubt, going to learn: the French language, calculus, and how to change a colostomy bag. Fortunately, although Annabelle has never been able to master our home security system, she was quite capable of handling the C-bag changing.

It would be nice to report that Annabelle and I were able to give Ezra the twenty-four-hour focus and attention he needed daily to be kept alive. But we also had to do all that postmodern family stuff, such as both of us having to work and make money to make ends meet. So to help us with the round-the-clock routine of colostomy bags and feeding tubes, there was a never-ending parade of nannies and nurses, day and night, who marched in and out of our lives. Some were helpful. Some were helpless, such as the one who actually said she couldn't feed Ezra through his feeding tube because it grossed her out too much. One nanny, a tiny Brazilian lady with a really witchy, voodoo vibe about her, drove Annabelle batty because she refused to let her hold Ezra or even let her into the bedroom to kiss him good night when she was taking care of him. But we were afraid to fire the witch because she was the only one at that time who could get him to stop crying long enough to fall asleep.

Eventually, the witch flew away and was replaced by a smiley, patchouli-scented New-Agey nanny who told us, "Everything happens for a reason," including, I guess, her mysteriously quitting after less than a half a month. She gave way to a born-again night nurse who was certain that God doesn't give anyone anything they can't handle. Lovely little sentiments that nevertheless left me feeling cynical, angry, and in dire need of alcohol. If everything in the universe happens for a reason, how do you explain or justify plagues, genocide, or why people think Dane Cook is funny? Seriously. Dane Cook—good-looking guy, not funny at all. And as far as God giving you what you can handle ... God, of all omnipotent deities, should know that if I can't handle my computer crashing, Los Angeles traffic congestion, and restaurants that don't serve egg white omelets, how in his name could I handle having a child without an anus? The lack of sleep, juggling work, the endless revolving door of nurses and nannies and the mountains of money they were costing us, plus the sheer physical and psychological effort it took to take care of baby Ezra, were really taking a toll on our marriage. There was no sleep, at all, ever. We had been transformed from insecure, neurotic, self-involved, artistic but kindly individuals into snarling, seething, self-involved emotional vampires out for each other's blood. Annabelle, not exactly a temple of stability to begin with, started to become even more unhinged. First, she sought out anyone who would listen to her. After exhausting her friends, our doctors, neighbors, and passing strangers she met on the street, she turned to the Internet and found a site devoted to kids born with VACTERL. Yes, there is actually a Web site and a monthly newsletter devoted to anusless kids and their parents. She started e-mailing members, hoping to bond over their common experiences and trade tidbits on how best to deal with these birth defects. Not satisfied with online chats, Annabelle sniffed out local parent support groups and begged me to attend one with her. She guaranteed it would change my perspective. She was right; listening to these mothers talk about their babies did change my perspective. Each story was more tragic than the next: babies born with hearts outside their ribs, blind, brain damaged, lungs that could barely breathe. It was otherworldly: a child with lobster hands, a fused-legged mermaid girl, a half boy/half lamb, and a baby born without a head. Without a head—how is that possible? By the time it got around to my turn to speak, all I could say was how my heart went out to all of them and how lucky I now felt that we, in comparison, had it so easy. I mean, can lobster child ever learn to use a fork? Does mermaid girl have to live in water? Does lamb boy grow his own wool? What in the holy hell do you feed a headless baby? We screamed at each other in the parking lot. I told Annabelle I would never go to another one of her support groups, and she shouted back that this just reinforced her feeling that I refused to accept and deal with what had happened to Ezra. I yelled back that I accepted what happened and was dealing with it in my own way by working all day, staying up all night, and not dropping dead.

During these surreal couple of years, we were at the hospital so often it was as if we had stepped through a portal into an alternate reality. In this reality we lived among cheery Disney murals donated by Jeffrey Katzenberg, bald leukemia kids walking around with their chemo drips, and nurses whom we'd see so often that they'd greet us as if we were their old friends from high school. There was no way we could have negotiated this neon-lit medical universe without Dr. McAlpin. He performed four of Ezra's major surgical procedures. He also did more than a dozen esophageal dilatations. It's not like Ezra was his only patient. He literally had hundreds if not thousands of kids to tend to. How did he manage to be so omnipresent? How many Big Macs were there? Above all, it was astonishing that he constantly remained the Rock of Gibraltar for so many of us scared and uncertain parents.

Meanwhile, Annabelle and I took turns sleeping next to Ezra's bed on a tiny hospital cot last used by Papillon on Devil's Island. We had the pleasure of being awakened every five minutes by nurses taking Ezra's vitals. But I'll never forget the sheer and utter euphoria, the absolute joy and jubilation, of seeing a tiny spec of turd swimming in his diaper for the first time.

In those long days and nights in the hospital with Ezra, it seemed as if no matter how much espresso I drank, I would never be fully awake again. Once while walking in the corridor that connects the two Cedars-Sinai towers, I caught a glimpse of myself in a large window. Who was that burned-out guy with bloodshot eyes and an expensive haircut trying to fool into believing he wasn't scared out of his freakin' mind? I stared at myself. Was it really me? Was this really our life now? I still loved Annabelle, but everything had changed so much, so quickly and dramatically, I wasn't sure our marriage would survive. We couldn't agree on anything. Annabelle wanted to go to support groups, have parties at our house for kids from all over the country who also had VACTERL, and insisted on taking Ezra to every physical therapist in LA. I just wanted to keep working so we could keep paying other people to change his colostomy bags.

Everything that we ever thought was wrong with us, our careers, our relationship, and now our child, started to collide, creating explosions of blame, finger pointing, and score keeping. It was a time of emotional button pushing, and Annabelle and I treated each other to a barrage the likes of which hadn't been seen since Aaron Burr and Alexander Hamilton and would not be seen again until Rosie O'Donnell and Donald Trump. I'm sure a large part of this marital sniping was a release from all the stresses we were under. Because we couldn't treat the doctors and nurses badly, or take our frustrations out on our friends, family, the people we worked with, or those who worked for us, we were left with just each other. We became each other's psychological punching bags. It left us both with invisible internal scars just as all of Ezra's surgeries left external physical ones.

I began to fantasize about what life might be like to be a divorced, single dad of a kid who had a man-made anus. However, fantasizing about divorce and actually getting divorced are two very different things. Like porn and sex. Porn sex might look genuine when it's free on the Internet, but it doesn't exist in reality. Every porn video ends the exact same way, with the guy cumming all over the girl's face and she loves it. She can't get enough of it! I wonder what percentage of marital sexual couples finish in this manner? None-percent, that's how many. At least I had enough perspective to realize that. Subsequently, instead of divorcing, Annabelle and I went to therapists, both together and separately. I started downing antidepressants, going to yoga twice a week, and picking up a newfound appreciation for the wines of the Rhône Valley.

In all honesty, it was the most unimaginable and difficult crisis of my life. I was in the thick of "for better or worse"; and although I might have sucked at it, I wasn't going to quit.

If there's one thing I can do well, it's being scrappy. I don't give up. Whenever I play basketball, I'm this little five-foot-six gnat of energy using quickness and tenacity against much bigger and taller players. I had relied on my never-quit can-do scrappiness in my quest to win Annabelle's heart for more than five years. As a writer working in Hollywood, I had definitely seen my fair share of rejection and failure, but I stayed in the game, and no matter what happened, good or bad, I kept plugging away. And that's exactly what I intended to do as a father and a husband.

I tried adopting a noncynical optimism that Ezra was going to be all right. It frustrated me that I could not get Annabelle to put a more upbeat spin on things or stop her from her obsession that Ezra might have a horrible undiagnosed VACTERL-related spinal column condition. Ezra seemed fine to me. He was even showing signs of having remarkable eye-hand coordination and I began to father-fantasize about his bucking the odds of his defects and becoming a professional baseball player. About how he'd one day hold the World Series trophy over his head and say, "This is for my dad. He has been my inspiration ever since I was a little kid, even though he never learned how to change a colostomy bag." But Annabelle was adamant about getting Ezra an MRI of his spine, and sure enough, he had that fucking birth defect too and it needed to be repaired as soon as possible. It was a complicated and scary three-and-a-half-hour surgery, but Ezra made it through with flying colors and got his cutest scar to boot. Annabelle's inquiries and insistence on the MRI had saved him and our family an immeasurable amount of pain and unhappiness. I am eternally grateful to her for being a huge pain in the ass and for making damn sure she got her way when it came to Ezra's spine.

Unbelievably though, when Ezra turned four, our doctors determined that Ezra possesses not a larger horseshoe-shaped kidney but just one solitary kidney that's undersized, cystic, and sitting in an exposed position below his rib cage. This meant that Ezra must maintain a low-protein diet, take sodium bicarbonate tablets twice a day to aid in processing toxins, and because his ribs do not protect it, the kid will never be able to join the rodeo, the Marines, or the World Wrestling Federation. (So something good has come of it.) In more disheartening news, the pediatric nephrologist who was monitoring Ezra's kidney predicted at this time that it would lose its ability to function and begin to fail in his teenage years.

I respectfully chose to disagree. I thought, "Well, how can she be totally sure?" He was so young; maybe it would grow stronger and function more normally as he grew older. Annabelle considered me just another victim of magical thinking. I was only trying to stay as optimistic as possible and to instill that attitude into Ezra whenever I could. Annabelle denies being a pessimist, but she's absolutely certain that Los Angeles will be hit with an apocalyptic earthquake in the next few years and has stocked her car with every provision imaginable: extra pairs of clothes, shoes, jugs of water, reams of toilet paper, tins of tuna, packages of dried figs, oatmeal bars, several radios, flashlights, an emergency surgical equipment kit, and an inflatable raft. Come the inevitable catastrophe Annabelle's covered, sadly she'll have to go it alone, because her car is so crammed that no one else will fit in. I wanted little Ezra to be able to live as normal a life as possible, to feel good about himself and not fear the future, whatever it might hold for him.

Perhaps this is the twenty milligrams of Celexa talking, but it does in some crazy way make sense that Annabelle and I would have a child with these unusual types of birth defects. Just about everything in our lives is a little off. Our house is much smaller than it appears to be from the outside. Annabelle's butt is much bigger than it looks when disguised in clothing. She's told me many a time that my hair is far grayer than it appears to me in the mirror. Doors don't close all the way and they squeak every time they're opened no matter how much WD-40 we apply; the drain in the tub doesn't quite close so it can never properly fill, leaving the bather scrambling to keep adding water; Ezra's bedroom floor has a slant that causes his desk drawers to be constantly open; and we can't get the outdoor floodlights to shut off during the day, even though they are on light-sensitive timers, so by the time we actually need them at night they've burned out. Plus the refrigerator door won't properly seal; none of our eclectic furniture matches; my brand-new computer chirps like a cricket; our backyard tree grew into our neighbor's yard, breaking the Spanish garage roof tiles and costing us more than a grand to fix; and we never get it together enough to send out Christmas/New Year's cards until well into spring, if at all. Annabelle stuck our adorable, sweet-as-pie cat with the smelly name of Stinky and our superhandsome, seemingly normal standard-issue kid has all these quirky anomalies inside of him.

When the shit hits the fan, so to speak, Annabelle has been the one who does all the research and consults with the experts, while I adopt a wait-and-see approach and when the ball is passed to me, such as giving Ezra one of my kidneys, I'll be sure to take it right to the hoop. Call it Zen acceptance, or some strange faithless sense of faith, but I believed that maybe by the time Ezra became a teenager there could be a cure even more effective than a transplant. Things do change and, unlike the Middle East and the traffic in Los Angeles, sometimes they can even get better.

She Says

Jeff insists that I made a comment about his fascination with all things anal on the day our son was born. I have no memory of this, but I did say, "No anus? What happens if he's gay?" "We'll be making him one," our doctor informed us. "Great," I answered. "My son was born in Los Angeles and they're already making him an asshole!"

I missed out on Jeff's hospital weepalooza because I was otherwise occupied with morphing into a character from a Russian novel. Anna Karenina couldn't hold a candle to my moroseness. From my hospital bed, I phoned our friends and family, and instantly the cheerful muffin baskets we'd received with cards saying "We can't wait to meet him!" were replaced by somber flower arrangements bearing notes announcing "Our prayers are with you." I didn't have a train to throw myself under, but I was able to heave myself into a wheelchair and take up residence in front of Ezra's little isolette. With all of his appliances and the black silk sleep mask they had placed over his eyes, Ezra looked like a sickly baby rock star.

The next day Jeff and I made our first trip together into the neonatal unit. Oddly enough, the staff greeted us with confused looks. Finally, the nurses drew me aside, "We really wonder what it is you do exactly," and they showed me the form Jeff had filled out when we arrived at the hospital. Where the form asked "father and mother's occupations," he had written "divorce attorney" and "balloonologist." Jeff's father, Bob, is the divorce lawyer in the family, of course, and his mother had at one point owned a novelty store that specialized in party-themed balloons. It truly hadn't occurred to Jeff that they meant *us*. We were the parents now. Jeff had failed our first test as parents and I had something to tease him about until the day we die. I got my comeuppance not long afterward when we were informed that our baby's esophagus was too small to aspirate his fluids. This meant that breast-feeding was out and the dreaded pacifier was actually prescribed to satisfy his need to suck. Ezra would also be required to sleep in a crib on a slant so that when he was fed through his tube, gravity would help the formula slide down easier. Thus ended the family bed idea, too. A parent for one day and the only real plans I had made were out, and Jeff, who had correctly predicted the pointlessness of my planning, now had something he could tease me about, too. All of my postmodern, enlightened motherhood posturing was instantly wiped away. I just wanted my kid to live.

People joke that children don't come with owner's manuals, but ours did; we were just too idiotic to understand it. When we got home from the hospital, we were afraid to be left alone with him. That's when we entered the Kafkaesque labyrinth of home health care workers. It wasn't just that the nurses were often incompetent; sometimes they didn't even show up. Sometimes they felt the need to wake me up at three a.m. to inform me they were only staying the rest of the night if I paid them extra money under the table. One lasted less than fifteen minutes. Though her name has been forgotten, I will never forget her long fingernails—really, they were something akin to paring knives. Imperiously she strode into our home, and then took one look at Ezra and announced, "This isn't for me," wrapped her talons around her handbag, and disappeared forever. And she billed us later. I'm going out on a limb here, but anecdotal experience tells me that the home health care worker sector attracts more religious fanatics than other professions. Not only did we now have our friends and family praying for us, we also had baby nurses of all denominations exhorting the Almighty: Jehovah's Witnesses, Catholics, Protestants, and a Seventh-Day Adventist. How desperate were we? We even hired a Christian Scientist who didn't believe in medical intervention.* One of the only things Jeff and I found common ground on at this time was that we accepted their prayers. We were just too tired to refuse. After the initial crew we graduated into more-secular nanny types, but it seems as if there was some sort of tacit requirement to

---

*One benefit to hiring Seventh-Day Adventists is that they don't celebrate New Year's, Christmas, or even birthdays, so they'll work on most holidays. We didn't even mind the pamphlets we'd find around the house, and we cried when she left to go on a mission.

be a little eccentric to even want to take on the challenges of a baby like Ezra. I have fond memories of my favorite, Penelope. A salt-of-the-earth British lass who was "daylighting" as a nanny while in the evening she pursued her true life ambition, which was to become a bartender and make a living on a traveling darts team. Sure, we might come home and she'd be sleeping off a hangover while Ezra was in her care, but she could whip a colostomy bag on faster than you could say "'enry 'iggins" or "Another pint, please, mate!" Penny was my favorite because not one of our family members was able to deal with Ezra when his clothes were off and all his appliances were out in the open, but Penny was completely unfazed. Or she was too drunk to care.

We were just completely ill prepared for parenting as a science experiment. For more than two years we needed to record every ounce of liquid that went into Ezra's body. I am not good at math. I cheated my way from the multiplication tables through algebra. I didn't fill in most of the math portion of the SATs. Jeff, on the other hand, tried to do his math SATs, and somehow managed to score even worse than I did. Between the two of us we managed a subpar level of competence that was good enough to feed our baby, but poor enough to rightly suspect that each of us was doing it wrong and was off by precious ounces. We fought most viciously during the middle of the night. If our house had been wiretapped, you might have thought that we were running a meth lab: Male voice: "How many ounces of liquid did you pour in this morning? I can't read your handwriting." Female: "I can't remember!" Male: "What were you thinking?" Female: "At least I write down what we're doing!" Male: "But you have no idea what you're doing!" Female: "Right, but I'm writing it down anyway, you idiot! You don't keep track of anything! We can't do this together. Get the fuck out of my way, I need to mix up a batch!"

Jeff says he still loved me. He just hated everything I did and every decision I made, and he made it clear he didn't agree with me on a single course of action that had to do with Ezra's care.

Jeff says we stepped through a portal into an alternate reality. I was certain we had fallen through the looking glass into a world that was always there, we just didn't know it existed. While other families are celebrating holidays with their newborns, families of kids with chronic illnesses are camped out in hospitals. Somehow, during the first two years of his life, Ezra's emergencies always took place on holidays. Thanksgiving, Christmas, Fourth of July? But Big Mac never failed to materialize. We lost faith in each other, but Columbus was convinced Ezra was strong and resilient and sometimes that was the only thing that kept me going.

During the time that Jeff was fantasizing about a life of seducing women with his tale of our child's rectal woes, I fantasized about becoming the Martha Stewart of the parents-of-chronically-ill-children set. I was sure I could beat this thing and become the best mother of them all—if only I could wrestle control of the situation and didn't have to deal with Jeff's bothersome opinions. As I fell asleep at night, I pictured myself on the *Today* show exhibiting the new and improved colostomy bags that I had whipped up in my spare time. Why not a bag for every season? Blue- and pink-shaded Easter bags, a fall bag in the shape of a pumpkin. Immaculately dressed and coiffed, I'd hold my kid in one hand, feed him through a tube with the other, sort medical bills with my teeth, all the while describing how I had adapted to my unexpected role as parent of a chronically ill child. "I've had to make concessions," I'd confess. "Sure, it wasn't my dream that my kid would make the cover of the anorectal malformation magazine, but hey, a cover is a cover!"

In my real life, every day saw new examples of my failure to be anything like Martha. Once I was outside a department store when a poop rolled out of my son's pants and I kicked it under a decorative shrub. A woman who witnessed this act hissed, "I saw what you did!" Yeah, well, so what, that's a woman who's never changed a colostomy bag in an airplane bathroom! But I knew that Martha would never have done that. Meanwhile, I developed a twitch in my eye, I started taking Xanax and SSRIs,* my clothes were stained with bodily fluids and X-ray contrast dyes, and my coworkers' patience was tested by my need to constantly reschedule shooting days to accommodate Ezra's frequent surgeries. In fact, on our anniversary, during that first year of Ezra's life, Jeff valiantly tried to instill some romance into our lives, but my work ran late and Jeff spent most of the romantic meal he had planned for us being pissed off at me and drinking alone. With every area of my life in disarray, I gave up on perfectionism and went on a campaign to pass as a normal mom.

I tried attending a neighborhood Mommy & Me group. The other moms would go around the room and share: "My husband just doesn't understand—he dressed our daughter in a chartreuse onesie after I told him I wanted her in mauve." My turns usually sounded like this: "You know, those onesies are just impossible to get over a colostomy bag. Especially when the bag fills with gas, which it does a lot. If I don't empty out the gas every hour or so, it looks like he has a basketball growing out of his side! Anyhoo . . ." Silence. Looks of anxiety and suspicion. I know what they were thinking. Thank God I'm not her, and I wonder if she did something to cause those birth defects so I can avoid it when I have my next child. I know this because they'd grill me on how my pregnancy had gone, my diet and genetic history. The moms were

*They're not just mothers' little helpers anymore. In 2005, Americans made 169.9 million antidepressant purchases, according to health care researchers.

really trying to be nice, but for the next few years when I'd see one of these moms around town, they'd look at me with pitiful glances and slink away.

So, yes, I found a different kind of parenting group. But Jeff is completely wrong that this was a symptom of becoming unhinged. It was how I stayed hinged. The leader of the next group was a very kind older woman, a therapist, whose grandchild tragically was born with a very vital organ located outside his body. One mom had a daughter who was facing heart replacement. Another couple had an adult daughter with limited mental capacity, yet these amazingly resilient and devoted parents spoke enthusiastically about trips they took in an RV specially outfitted for her needs. It would be accurate to say that each family faced harrowing obstacles, but I found them inspirational. They helped me put our problems into perspective, and besides, Jeff exaggerates; there was not one family with a crustacean for a child.

It's also true that I found great comfort in the support group for kids born with no anuses and we did have a party at our house for the Southern California members of the Pull-thru Network. They were an easy group to please; while other kid parties focus on themes and entertainment, these moms just wanted to know how many bathrooms I had at the house! This loose-knit group of families offered me comfort and useful little tips on things I never dreamed I'd need to know, like skin salves for stomach acid irritation caused by a leaky gastrostomy tube. They also saved our lives. One night when Ezra was about four years old, I called a VACTERL mom whose number was listed as the coordinator of our "medical supply closet." I was hoping to donate some leftover gastrostomy feeding tubes to another family. This mother, Kathy, alerted me to a condition called tethered cord. I had no idea what she was talking about. She explained that the spinal cord is something like a rubber band; it is supposed to taper to a thin filament as it reaches the sacrum (the triangular bone at the base of the spine that joins to the hip bone on either side and forms a part of the pelvis), affording the remaining vertebrae at the base of the spine a wide range of movement. Children born with the condition referred to as tethered cord can have a thick cord, or "fatty filum," wrapped around the sacrum that eventually, due to the growth of the child and the stretching of the spine, can cause the cord to snap, resulting in paralysis and incontinence, and unfortunately, once the cord has been damaged, it can't be repaired. It's a horrible condition associated with the better known and also terrible spina bifida. Remediation requires a neurosurgeon to carve into the vertebrae and untether the cord while employing enough dexterity to avoid accidentally impairing brain function or causing motor function damage—it's a hoot! As I hung up the phone with Kathy, I remembered that our son had, on one single occasion, complained of back pain. When I alerted Jeff to this, he couldn't recall that incident. Both Jeff and Dr. McAlpin felt sure Ezra didn't have a tethered cord, but I insisted that he have an MRI. I certainly didn't want the results to be positive; however, it pains me to admit that part of me was aware that a positive result would represent a vindication: it would prove that I hadn't been responsible for ordering an unnecessary procedure that at Ezra's age required sedation and always carries some risk. We found out the results immediately. The solemn looks on the technicians' faces as they wheeled Ezra out of the MRI told us my hunch had been correct. That was *V* for vertebral. Ezra now had an almost clean sweep of VACTERL anomalies. It was devastating news, and it was a hollow victory for me. We were advised we could wait to see if symptoms worsened, but Columbus called and said if it was his kid, he would schedule surgery immediately. In fact, he had a neurosurgeon standing by on call.

In yet another example of how we experienced events differently, while Jeff was exhausted by the surgeries, I was oddly energized by them. I found them comforting, even relaxing. Each reconstruction procedure, even the spinal cord untethering, as harrowing and exhausting as it was, served to channel my anxiety into specific, defined, and immediate goals. It felt proactive. We weren't just waiting out yet another prognosis. As long as I was busy, it gave me the semblance of control over our destiny. And at least we weren't home alone; at the hospital I could sleep because there was round-the-clock help!*

I liken those first few years to training for a triathlon. Just when you finish the bike ride, you have to jump in the water and swim, and then, oh yeah, you have to run. I'm not really cut out for endurance of any kind. My sister should have been the one with the kid with problems; she once did an Ironman. The closest I have ever come to any sort of athletic competition was the time I tried to see a full twenty-four hours' worth of plays at the Edinburgh Theatre Festival. That was in 1989 and I've been exhausted ever since.

In some ways, Jeff and I became more isolated as Ezra's reconstruction process went along. Once Ezra was appliance free and had a normal appearance, at least in clothes, friends would inquire, "He's OK now, right?" Following his birth, I spent a lot of time reassuring pregnant friends that just knowing us would make it impossible, statistically speaking, for their kids to be born with Ezra's birth defect. I made that up. It's not true but it sounds true. Even members

---

*If you need any evidence of the lunacy of the American health care system, our insurance company initially declined payment for Ezra's surgery, determining it was an elective procedure. I guess if you consider consigning our kid to a progressive wasting of muscle tissue, chronic severe leg pain, loss of motor function, and incontinence as small inconveniences—then, yes, it was an elective procedure.

of our family grew inured to our drama and they wanted closure. My own husband didn't seem to want to know that our kid had a chronic condition that required daily attention, most likely for the rest of his life.*

And then just when we thought we knew what we were facing, we heard more bad news. We were completely blindsided by the new diagnosis about our son's kidney when he was seven. The kidney's longevity was put into question due to its official characterization as "poorly organized" (which I assume is a trait inherited from me). Our nephrologist told me in our annual consultation that Ezra had a 95 percent chance of outgrowing his kidney in his adolescence. She predicted he would need a new one and was very upbeat about renal compatibility and the new transplantation drugs that are far less toxic than the old ones. The day I got the news, I lay down right there on the floor of the pediatric nephrology clinic and cried. After I told Jeff, he was so Zen in his acceptance that he refused to believe I had heard correctly and insisted we call our doctor so he could hear the news for himself. After we hung up the phone, Mr. Positive Thinking said, "A five percent chance of lasting—not bad."

This is emblematic of the general position Jeff has adopted. An attitude that, I suspect, reveals a vestigial magical thinking superstition. Though both of us enjoy a shared mistrust of religions, Jeff takes it to an extreme. He claims to be something of a Sam Harris acolyte, espousing a desire to see an end to all organized religion, far surpassing my own atheistic, secular humanist tolerance for all faiths. However, Jeff postulates that if he just continues to

---

*VACTERL occurs in approximately 16 out of 100,000 births. That's around 640 in the United States. Tethered cord has a rate of maybe .25 per 1,000 births, so it's much rarer. As of the writing of this book, children born with VACTERL get screened routinely for TC.

think positively and hope for miracles, Ezra's medical conditions will simply disappear as he gets older. This is being optimistic, he insists. Said point of view places Jeff squarely alongside Learning Annex seminar junkies and the famously superstitious, like Sharon Stone, who announced that bad karma had caused the 2008 earthquake in China. Who knows where this will lead? Will he advocate a return to sacrificing virgins in volcanoes, learn to bend spoons with his mind, or master the art of manifesting abundance in a one-hour seminar? My Zen husband also forgets that for at least three years after Ezra was born, he would turn to me, out of the blue, and ask me to list everything I had consumed during my pregnancy. He suspected that my having eaten sushi, which I did maybe twice while pregnant, was behind Ezra's birth defect, even though there is no known cause of VACTERL.* Meanwhile, Jeff characterizes me as a pessimist, but I predict that he'll be right there next to me, sucking down tuna juice from a knife hole in one of the sixty-five cans of tuna fish I've warehoused in case of an earthquake, fire, or flood. Should this come to pass, he'll never let me forget that I've forgotten to store a can opener, but I say tuna juice will be better than nothing!

In fact, our family was required to evacuate in 2007 during the fire season. I managed to grab the cat, a pair of Dolce & Gabbana shoes, my grandmother's silver, our important legal papers, and our kid. True, I forgot to pack panties, but I had the best footwear of the evacuees in our neighborhood.

Jeff and I never agree about the direction to follow for our son's health. This polarization plays out in a general way in most households, as every parent who has ever uttered the words "go ask

---

*Eventually, after meeting other VACTERL moms who'd never so much as tried sushi in their lives, he gave up on that postulation.

your father/mother!" can attest to, but when your child's health is on the line, the stakes are raised. That's why the percentage of unions that fail when a child has a chronic illness ranges at upward of 70 percent. I know of at least one fellow VACTERL mom whose long-term boyfriend checked out the very day their daughter was born. He had been a little wary of fatherhood to begin with, and when he learned about his daughter's condition, well, it was beyond his ability to cope.* So with all of our madness, we're bucking the odds.

This might just be the twenty milligrams of Cymbalta speaking, but I am willing to entertain the thought that just maybe, by never agreeing we work harder to evaluate and more thoroughly weigh our options, and this pushes us to make better decisions. This ersatz strategy is our own mini checks and balances system. We're what the founding fathers envisioned and the Bush administration successfully chipped away at! What is it they say in the military—no man gets left behind? None of us—Jeff, Ezra, or I— would last one minute in the military, but we live by that saying and we mean it. Especially the *behind* part.

---

*This mom, Michelle, is now a full-time caregiver as her daughter, Emily, has struggled with health issues far more complicated than Ezra's. Just to blow the *Lorenzo's Oil* devoted-parent stereotype, when I asked her recently if she wanted me to come over and babysit, she said, "Thanks, but what I really need is to get laid!"

"*The first half* of our lives is ruined by our parents and the second half by our children." —Clarence Darrow

why do we do it?

"Whether they [parents] believe in pushing their children to succeed or leaving them to find their own way in life, whether the home is filled with books or sports equipment, whether it is orderly or messy, the research shows, counterintuitively, that none of these things makes much difference; outside influences such as popular culture, friends or street gangs have a much greater influence on children than family life or even genetic makeup."

—Psychologist Judith Rich Harris, writing in the *Telegraph,* UK, 2008

top five things couples argue about in order of frequency

1. money.   2. sex.   3. work.   4. children.   5. housework.

A University of Michigan study showed that once parents stop making time for each other, recovering the relationship that made them want to have children to begin with most often proves impossible.

Only 38 percent of mothers of infants report having high marital satisfaction compared to 62 percent of childless women.   —Pew Study

A growing number of Americans are choosing to have children but not marry. This group, commonly referred to as "committed unmarrieds," numbers approximately 5 million. These co-habitating parents represent a number five times the amount as in the 1970s. In Europe, unmarrieds stay together longer than married parents.   —*Time* magazine, 2009

• • • • • • • • • • • • • • • •

7

. . . .

The Eighteen-Year Plan

"The surest way to be alone is to get married."
—GLORIA STEINEM

Since the dawn of time you could probably sum up the universal parental aspiration as "wanting my kid to have a better life than mine." Each generation hopes that the next generation will have it easier. The shoes found on the 5,300-year-old "Iceman" in the Tyrolean Alps were made of skins and braided-bark netting and stuffed with straw and moss. Very homemade. His parents probably made them for him. No doubt they argued about the ratio of straw to moss, the proper fit, and if the shoe needed goatskin insoles because their son had flat feet. We would have. The Iceman died crossing the Alps and scientists have long been stumped as to what prompted him to leave on a journey with no water or food to speak of in an attempt to cross the mountains at a time of year when several feet of snow made his trek perilous. We bet if his parents were even remotely like us, he was probably trying to get away from them.

She Says

In the first few years of Ezra's life, we spent much of our time shuttling in and out of doctors' offices and surgeries. In spite of all of his reconstructive surgery, our child was busy with his own agenda: being a baby who was going through all the normal developmental stages. That left us with the question of how we were going to be that postmodern, cool new family. We could barely go a few blocks from home without having some kind of emergency. Neither of us ever figured out exactly what the hell this concept was supposed to mean anyway.

The only thing I could come up with was to try to distinguish our family from my own upbringing. In terms of parental supervision, my 1970s childhood was something like growing up at the intersection of Laissez-faire and Benign Neglect. This has worked out just fine for my sister, who has always had the work habits of a highly efficient attorney, which is what she became. I've always had messy closets, I crammed for tests, and I dropped out of the college I was lucky to be accepted to in the first place. Only the right combination of pharmaceuticals and the pressing and constant need to earn a living have allowed me to manage a modicum of order (barely) and a smattering of accomplishments (dubious). So to ensure that our son has every advantage, despite our own admittedly ad hoc lifestyle, I've been striving to provide him with a solid foundation on which to build an orderly life. There's only one thing standing in my way: my husband.

Jeff didn't support the idea of a family philosophy or a single one of my plans when we got pregnant and so it's not surprising that when I suggested, "We should really get educated about what we're doing here," Jeff balked. It's ironic, because Jeff was a history major. Every major undertaking in history has a plan, right? There was the five-year plan, the seven-year plan, the Marshall Plan—damn it, I thought if it was good enough for the rebuilding of Western Europe, it's good enough for us! Sadly, if it's not a plan that involves de-panting me, Jeff doesn't want to hear about it. However, if I even casually mention that I might be able to squeeze in some sex at, say, 8:30 p.m., at 8:29 p.m. and fifty-nine seconds, Jeff will be in the bedroom with his cock out, but should I mention that we have a nursery school orientation at some Academy of Entitled Offspring, this type of appointment simply doesn't stick in his brain.

The problem with trying to construct the Gurkahn Eighteen-Year Plan was that as hard as it was to absorb anything from *What to Expect* when I was pregnant, it was even harder to concentrate now. I had spent my valuable scant reading time on the subject of pregnancy, when what I really needed to read about was what happens once the baby comes out, and now it was too late. If I actually had the time and mental acuity to read more than one sentence after our kid was born, did I really want to spend it reading books about parenting, which was now my life? I did manage to read a paragraph or two about childhood development before my eyes glazed over. In case you never get the chance to read them, here are my one-sentence summaries: Piaget: *Children develop in stages, not all at once. Your kid will never paint like Picasso and play like Bach at the same time.* Sears: *When baby cries, pick it up. Often. You'll never sleep alone ever again.* * Steiner: *If you're raising children who will have to work for a living, you can't afford to follow my kooky bohemian theories. Never read this book.* So I took what I thought was a reasonable course of action. I enrolled in an infant development course.

---

*Brazelton: More of the same as Sears, but T. Berry Brazelton is just so much fun to say.

Classes at the Resources for Infant Educarers (RIE) institute teach a philosophy that emphasizes allowing infants to develop at their own pace. Simple toys that encourage exploration as opposed to providing passive entertainment were recommended. The rules include no TV, no mechanized toys, no bouncers, and no putting babies into positions they couldn't get into themselves. (This way they'd build confidence in their eventual independent mastery of walking, instead of being dependent on you to "walk" them around.)

Best of all, the classes were exquisitely quiet—no moms swapping stories—and the policy was strictly to observe without interference. I could see how their nonintervention rule could work to my advantage. The black string that was being used for Ezra's esophageal dilations attracted a lot of attention. Well-meaning people would not only inquire about it, one day a complete stranger in an elevator reached into his mouth and tried to pull it out. Because that string went through his mouth down into his stomach portal and up his esophagus (an endless loop through his internal organs), this appeared to cause Ezra enormous pain. "I thought your baby had a cherry stem in his mouth!" the lady shrieked as Ezra howled. By the time I started RIE classes, I had attached a notice onto his stroller: "Yes, I know my baby has a string in his mouth." I knew he'd be left alone at the institute.

Jeff likes to say the *R* in RIE stands for "ridiculous." I know that RIE sounds a little extreme (OK, it *was* a little intense), but in practice it was basically infants rolling around on blankets in a circle, ringed in by moms. Some of the ideas just made sense. For example, every parent knows that no matter how much money you spend on a toy, your kid will end up spending more time playing with the box it came in. The class I attended had a warm and easy-going teacher, Janet, whose sense of humor made some of the more severe rules more palatable. As luck would have it, Janet got pregnant with twins, and she was replaced by Lucinda. Where Janet had been warm, approachable, and bubbly, Lucinda was sullen, distant, and sported a short choppy haircut that suggested she had styled it herself with a dull blade. Both her personality and voice had the affect of a recent lobotomy patient. Her placidness was tempered only by her strict adherence to the rules of RIE. But how much damage could she do? We were basically sitting on our asses observing our children, who were barely more than soybeans, right?

When the babies reached twelve months, Lucinda announced that she was ready to facilitate the first official snack time. She placed wooden cable spools in the play area, but before she could put the orange slices and cups of water on top of these makeshift snack tables, one oversized child clad only in a diaper (sort of a baby Spartacus) started knocking the spools over and rolling them toward the other children, some of whom were still crawling and not terribly swift at that. It seemed about to escalate into a slaughter of the innocents, but no one said a word. "Shouldn't we do something?" I volunteered. Lucinda wouldn't budge. "Nobody move. The rules are no intervention of any kind. The children are scheduled to have snack time today and snacks they will have! We need to let them adapt to their environment!" Adapt to their environment? Was this an infant playgroup or a demonstration of survival of the fittest? I hadn't just spent a quarter of a million dollars and the better part of the last twelve months nursing our child to health to have his head cracked open by a baby gladiator! I picked up my child and dragged the spools out of the play area. Some of the mothers looked aghast while others followed my actions, but the chain of command had been breached. Lucinda excused herself, went into an adjoining office, and softly shut the door. We could hear her phoning someone to come in for "backup." Backup for an instructional course on human development? We knocked and waited for maybe forty-five minutes. She never came out. That was the last any of us ever saw of Lucinda. She phoned me a few weeks later and left me a long rambling message, at the end of which she demanded that I apologize to her. A replacement was brought in, but I was persona non grata at the RIE center and was never invited back to the class. I still maintain that it was worthwhile. While other toddlers were flinging themselves down stairs and were covered in bruises, Ezra was far less accident-prone, but Jeff maintains that the best thing to come out of RIE is that he gets to tell people that I was kicked out of an infant observation workshop.

If Jeff deemed RIE ridiculous, he characterized my television-viewing guidelines as patently idiotic. This despite the fact that the American Pediatrics Association has been saying for years that children under the age of two shouldn't watch TV.* You don't need a Ph.D. to observe that a kid in front of a television turns into an inert receptacle and you might as well remove his brain and sell it on eBay to the highest bidder, who will no doubt be a parent in Asia, where they recognize that a child's brain is the key to greater earning power in life.† That's right, I'm just the kind of hypocritical person who makes a living on TV but doesn't want people to watch it. At least not shows that I'm not in.

---

*The APA: Although certain television programs may be promoted to this age group, research on early brain development shows that babies and toddlers have a critical need for direct interactions with parents and other significant caregivers for healthy brain growth and the development of appropriate social, emotional, and cognitive skills. A full 80 percent of the studies done conclude that higher amounts of television and other media exposure are associated with negative health effects in children and adolescents.

†One recent study found that if American students did as well as those in several Asian countries in math and science, our economy would grow 20 percent faster. (Nicholas Kristof wrote about it in the *New York Times* in 2008.)

YOU SAY TOMATO, I SAY SHUT UP

Sadly, I discovered early on what everyone who can't afford child care finds out really fast: babies don't need TV; parents do. Sure, it was all well and good when you're paying people to watch your child, but once you're on your own, the minutes stretch into aeons, especially when your kid is sick. One such night Jeff was working late and little Ezra had something as ordinary as a cold and was screaming his head off. I couldn't listen to my supposedly relaxing *Liszt for Light Sleepers* or *Mendelssohn for Munchkins* CDs one more time. So I plopped him in a swing (non–RIE approved; I cheated on that too) and turned on the tube. It was one a.m. and we watched the only thing that held Ezra's attention long enough to get him to stop crying: Chucky III. That's right, *Child's Play 3*, a movie about a sociopathic doll that kills people. Ezra calmed down and fell asleep just as Chucky decapitated his last victim. The next day Jeff danced a little victory jig when I told him I would rethink the no-TV policy.

I am still fighting the TV battle to this day because although we've found consensus on one area of parenting—our kid's attendance at a school with rigorous academic standards—when it comes to actually fulfilling these expectations, such as doing the homework they assign, Jeff complains more than Ezra. Despite our numerous discussions about imposing the no-TV-on-weekdays policy, I'll come home and find them settled in front of the screen on a school night because, according to Jeff, "sports is not TV." Nor is *House*. "It's a *medical* drama." Nor is *The Simpsons*. "It's the Halloween episode." Nor is *Family Guy*. Why? "Because . . . Because . . . it's so funny!"

There's a lot of TV on TV. With eight hundred channels there's always something on that fits Jeff's exceptions. Put the Internet and YouTube into the mix, and it only makes more sense to me that we need some kind of scheduled media-viewing timetable or at least a reliable reward system. Unfortunately, I'm too disorganized to ever remember and Jeff is too uninterested to recall what kind of plan I come up with during any given week. Did we agree that if the kid does the homework, he gets a half hour of TV? Or was it if he does his homework *before* we have to ask him five times, he gets that privilege? Does that include thirty minutes of reading, or did we decide we don't want to *make* him read because that might turn him off reading? We can't keep it straight and no matter how many times we've imposed a "you're losing your allowance, TV, Internet, or iPod" punishment, it never holds for more than thirty minutes before one of us caves in. Well, Jeff caves in. That's why I've advocated for the simple, one-stop-shopping, no-TV-during-the-week rule.

Not that I haven't tried some sort of visual aid to remind my family. I can't begin to quantify the amount of time and money I've spent on crafting reward charts, posting schedules, not to mention placing in- and out-boxes around our house to collect the reams of homework and school announcements that threaten to turn our home into utter chaos. I've tried everything from magnetic boards to my own homemade calendars to map out lists of chores. Not a single one of my programs has ever been followed. Within one day of being posted, a chart will be covered with Jeff's doodles (satirical caricatures of me); by the end of two days, you can barely read the thing because he's added silly nonsense words beside entries for tasks that must be completed. A column that previously read "Make bed" might now read, "Professor Q. Quakerman declares, we won the game: 44 to 44!" I'm not making this up. I haven't a clue what it means, but I do know that by the third day Jeff pays it no more attention than if it were written in Cyrillic and, of course, our son follows Jeff's lead. And so by the fourth day, if the chart/board/list hasn't already fallen behind some piece of furniture at the close of day three, it's crumpled in a corner gathering dust. Our in- and out-boxes are filled to the brim with Jeff's receipts and stray scraps with telephone numbers. It's a wonder any of us gets dressed and makes it out of the house each day in matching shoes and isn't wandering the streets aimlessly.

I have no more succeeded in crafting a daily routine than I have in declaring our home a demilitarized zone. "Isn't it enough that there are wars around the world and gang violence in our neighborhood middle school; do we really need our kid to be wielding a toy gun?" I pleaded with my spouse when Ezra was a toddler. "Good luck with that!" was the only support Jeff was willing to offer in my war against warfare.

"Trust but verify." If it was good enough for Ronald Reagan, surely the Gurkahns could carry out this policy? When Ez was little, I requested that friends and family forgo giving Ezra toys that came with guns, guns that turned into toys, or toy guns. As it turns out, the only thing harder than getting on the same page with your partner is trying to tell your extended community that you are following a style of parenting that's unfamiliar. Yes, that appeal worked so well that I'd find myself sitting up all night, discarding gifts and disarming toy soldiers who packed the most miniature of weaponry imaginable before Ezra could get a gander at them. I was a one-mother UN monitoring agency working to stop the arms proliferation in one toddler's toy chest. Up until the time that Ezra was four, I managed to reach a kind of détente on the issue with Jeff, right up to the day I had the temerity to take our kid to the Autry Museum of Western Heritage. Going to a museum fit my educational mandate for an ideal outing. What I didn't know was that the Autry museum is basically an institution dedicated to the history and celebration of the firearms of the Old West. For two hours we walked past row after row of display cases crammed with rifles, muskets, derringers, revolvers, and ammunition. I might as well have arranged a tour of the Smith & Wesson factory. By the time we made it to the gift store, Ezra was hanging on my leg, begging me for a toy pistol. Other parents were staring at me as our child threw himself on the floor and wept until I agreed on a compromise purchase. I begrudgingly bought him a real leather holster and a matching cowboy outfit. Ezra loved that outfit so much he wore it every day for three months. He slept in the thing. You can even see him wearing it in the adorable pictures from Jeff's sister's wedding. And what's in the holster? Why, it's a gun Ezra made himself out of LEGOs. That was the day I waved the white flag, surrendered, and Jeff went out and bought him a Nerf gun. The sole concession I've managed to negotiate is a prohibition against shooting me in the face.

All of my plans, schemes, and agendas fuel Jeff's characterization of me as overly strident and have earned me the nickname Sergeant Gurwitch in our family, but it's just not true. Maybe it's a little true. But I can only hope that somehow, despite Jeff's insistence that our child grow up in that hilarious land of imagination known as Jeff's id, it doesn't result in Ezra's running off to join the circus or get us a visit from social services. You see, in his role as Carnival Cruise director of fun, Jeff has taken to providing voices and personalities for all of our little one's stuffed animals and takes pleasure in entertaining Ez's friends with their antics. Besides the overwhelming amount of exchanges I have personally been subjected to from a trash-talking turtle, as Ez has gotten older, his stuffed animals have taken on a tone that is decidedly PG-13 heading in R-rated territory. There's a moose named Melvin . . . who's gay. This moose isn't just a little gay, he's so swish, he's practically having a sexual identity crisis. Moose also has a partner in crime, a bear who addresses our son's classmates with inappropriate salutations. Every time the phone rings, I imagine it's a social worker who wants to know why children are being greeted at our house by a stuffed animal saying, "Hey, bitches!"

All of which is to say that I'm not giving up my rank as Sergeant Gurwitch anytime soon, because in spite of Jeff's best efforts, our son is a well-adjusted kid who's enthusiastic about school. He's confident (RIE) and independent (Sears) and artsy (Steiner) and he's never actually shot me in the face, so mission accomplished. And we all know what happens when you utter those words. We're so fucked.

He Says

Who knew that fun was so bad? To Annabelle all manner of fun is equivalent to a sugar-coated junky kid's cereal: it might be tasty but it'll rot your teeth and give you type 2 diabetes. Bad, fun, bad! Fun, you and your buddies silly, goofy, and laugh riot are not welcome in Ms. Gurwitch's House of Superstructured Seriousness. So, fuck you, fun, and the funny little horse you rode in on!

There must be some kind of balance between structure and spontaneity in the face of the complexities of child rearing in the early twenty-first century. You would hope that we might find some middle-ground flexibility. Alas, Annabelle sees flexibility as a threat to her parenting agenda. I'm less coparent and more, mortal parenting enemy.

I'm not completely as averse to rules and structure as Annabelle alleges I am; it's just that I have some experience with it and I'm not the biggest fan. My family wasn't so much *Father Knows Best* as *Father Knows All and Don't You Dare Cross Him*. He was a sort of benevolent, generous, and sometimes even silly dictator. My dad was equal parts Groucho Marx, Santa Claus, and Saddam Hussein. A dictator is still a dictator and let's not forget how "weird" I was to him as a kid. To say I was the black sheep of the family really doesn't paint me black enough. My mom was super overprotective of both my sister and me. I was the only person I knew growing up who had babysitters younger than I was because "a girl, even a younger one, is more mature and responsible than you are to take care of your sister." Gee, thanks, Mom. I wonder if she ever knew how humiliating it was for me, a high school junior trying to get a freshman babysitter to tuck me into bed.

As was every Jewish boy I ever knew growing up, I was expected to get good grades. Unlike most of them, I didn't. This must have been a big disappointment to my parents. In eleventh grade, on my New York State–mandated Regents geometry exam, I got a 56 out of 100. I only got a 56 because the geometry genius I had cheated off of all year finished the test so quickly that I could copy only about half the answers. My father was furious with me and insisted on making me take the test over. I told him that he should be satisfied with a 56 because I was never going to do better. He wouldn't listen to reason, forced me to study all summer, work with a tutor, and take the Regents exam again. Months later I asked my dad if the test score ever came back. It did. I asked what I got. A 19. I couldn't help but laugh at my sheer ineptitude. It was so bad, I was almost proud of myself, but my dad couldn't even look at me when he told me. It must have been humiliating for him. I can't say I blame him—my father put himself through college and law school playing the saxophone in his own orchestra and his reward is a son with the mathematical aptitude of an early hominid.

I wasn't allowed to watch TV during the week (had to sneak it). I was expected to keep my room clean at all times (it never was), have good manners in public (couldn't quite get the hang of that knife and fork thing), and never to talk back or question my parents' decisions (something I did on a regular basis). Furthermore, from third to ninth grades I went to military school. The establishment in question was a private day school in Albany, New York, and I wasn't sent there because I liked killing cats or burning down houses, but because my parents thought I would get a better education at a private school. The local Christian Brothers Academy was too Christian and the Hebrew Academy was far too Jewish, so this left just one establishment: the Albany Academy for Boys, founded in 1813, a bastion of white Anglo-Saxon old money elitism and virulently anti-Semitic—perfect! We wore West Point uniforms to class and learned how to drill with toy rifles. I entered the Academy's battalion a buck private and after years of practicing, taking part in the school's competitive and ceremonial drills, and marching in Veterans and Memorial Day parades, I left the Academy a buck private. I sucked at being a boy-soldier and hated that given just the slightest rank, even the nicest of classmates immediately turned into sadistic, power-mad assholes. So, yes, I was slightly skeptical about all the rules and guidelines Annabelle was so hell-bent on giving to our son, Ezra.

Annabelle thinks it's ironic that because of my history degree I wasn't prepared to help her implement her Eighteen-Year Plan. But talk about "magical thinking," anyone who has ever studied even a shred of twentieth-century history can tell you that these five or seven or however many year plans were hollow and doomed-to-fail policies of totalitarian communist governments. Ladies and Gents, I give you the Soviet Union. Oh, I'm sorry, it doesn't exist anymore. I have always felt that both parents and superpowers should avoid enforcing idealistic dogma, because it will inevitably fly right in the face of a little something I like to call *reality*. But reality never stopped Annabelle. Not when she could make a plan, follow a philosophy, attend a class, or put her trust in anyone or anything that claims to be an authority. This was how we landed at RIE.

RIE was insane! Don't take my word for it; just go back and reread Annabelle's description. Essentially, RIE is baby-raising Marxism, founded by the late Magda Gerber. She started developing her ideas during the 1950s while managing an iron curtain Hungarian orphanage. (I rest my case.) It's a quaint technique that professes to give the baby the space to learn on his own from his environment without parental intrusion. I wager Magda thought that an RIE-trained infant would naturally choose communism over capitalism. Inevitably, the whole thing's fated for disaster as soon as the babies are big enough to begin to exercise that inconvenient little thing called free will. I love it that Annabelle initiated the RIE Rebellion of 1998 that made her persona non grata at the place she had defended so rigorously. Like a pretentious university student who sees herself as part of the working classes, Annabelle would be the type of revolutionary idealist who fights to see the cause succeed, but soon finds fault with it, voices her dissent, and is subsequently executed. The road from dogmatic idealism to hypocrisy is a short one. I remember how when we first started living together and I was making a cappuccino and farted in front of her, Annabelle admonished me, "I hope we're not going to be a couple who farts and burps in front of each other all the time." And just as she said it, Annabelle sneezed with such force that she pushed out a fart so loud it startled her; she gasped and then burped loudly. "I don't know about *us*," I shot back, "but *you* will be."

And let me set the record straight on another Annabelle misconception about RIE: Ezra did not fall or have accidents as a baby because of RIE, but because he just naturally had good balance. Contrary to Annabelle's assertion, I did go a couple times to RIE class and witnessed what was going on there. Let's just say that compared to the other bumbling, stumbling RIE infants, Ezra was a baby Baryshnikov.

I'm astonished that Annabelle failed to mention the other massive attempt to have some structure in our lives when Ezra was an infant. Bedtime: from six to nine p.m. every night, baby Ez had severe colic and couldn't fall asleep. This was in part because Annabelle and I were sent home from the hospital with only a modicum of instruction and even less practice on how to work his feeding tube. Bringing home Ezra reminded me of getting my first computer in the late 1980s. I had never used anything vaguely computerized before; I didn't even know how to type, but the cocky salesman guaranteed that I'd get the hang of it in no time. If that computer had been a baby, I would have killed it several times over. Obviously, we didn't kill Ezra, but we were unknowingly and improperly letting too much air from the feeding tube enter his stomach and giving him really bad gas.

The only thing that got him to fall asleep was to strap him in the car and drive and drive and drive. When he finally conked out, I'd drive back to the house and as delicately as defusing a bomb begin to unstrap him from his car seat. As I gently lifted him out, he'd inevitably wake up and start screaming his head off, and then it was back into the car and drive, drive, drive! By the time Ezra stopped crying and fell asleep I didn't just want a glass of wine, I wanted to smash the bottle over my head.

Even as Ezra got older, there were nights where he refused to sleep and would work himself into such a feral crazed state—thrashing, bucking, and barking—that I was tempted to go all Mutual of Omaha and shoot him with a tranquilizer gun. So when Annabelle brought up Ferberization, I was actually open to it if it meant just one more minute of sleep.

Dr. Ferber's method depicts the ritual of your baby's learning to go to sleep by himself as the child's natural progress toward nocturnal self-reliance. What to the untrained ear sounds like a baby wailing in desperate protest of abandonment is, for Ferber, a child learning how to self-soothe himself. Like many theories, Ferberizing seems reasonable until you put it into practice and have to wait outside your newborn's room while he "cries it out" for a half hour, or in the infant/parental-crying continuum, *a light-year*. Hearing someone else's baby crying is annoying; hearing your own baby wailing is what I imagine it feels like to endure electric shock torture. The current of Ezra's cry would surge through my head, skin, and every nerve fiber. An infant has a brain the size of a chipmunk's, for chrissakes. They're not "crying it out" because it's fun. They're desperate for comfort, love, and warmth. How can denying a helpless baby natural parental compassion help in its further emotional development?

As the wailing and gasping for air that emanated from Ezra's bedroom continued unabated, I imagined what he might be like years later as a young man: "Why are you shooting heroin, Ezra?" "Oh, it's no big deal. I'm self-soothing. You know, I don't want to bother my parents—they're trying to sleep." Nocturnal self-reliance . . . Ferber . . . Schmuck. So we never made it through Ferberizing and in the end one or both of us would go in and soothe Ezra. I hoped this experience would help Annabelle see the wisdom of flexibility or, at the minimum, teach her not to attempt to live by didactic proclamations, particularly when Dr. Ferber himself began recanting his method soon after we abandoned it. But it fell on deaf ears (perhaps because she was shell-shocked from all the Ferber baby crying), and by then Annabelle had found a new cause célèbre: *no toy guns*!

From third through sixth grade I shot Kenny Lashin. It was a comic-book gun game we made up featuring my very lifelike sound effects. I'd shoot Kenny with machine guns, silencers, shotguns, grenades, and poison-tipped darts and he would die. Kenny was a grand master at dying. He'd twitch and shudder with each bullet, dart, or flesh-impaling shrapnel. Kenny was my own one-man Sam Peckinpah movie.

It wasn't that I was a giant gun nut, but, as a general rule, little boys love guns. Being a girl and growing up with a sister sibling, Annabelle missed the whole boy-gun love affair. By the time Annabelle began to experience boys, they had pretty much put away their toy guns for a ticket into her pants. True, there are some boys who never outgrow their fascination with guns. They become skeet shooters and hunters, gun aficionados and collectors, gangsters and Republicans, NRA members and Texans.

Because there is no stopping little tykes from playing with toy guns, I wasn't against Ezra's having one. It's not as if I wanted him to go around town with a toy Glock or Luger in his tiny hand. Nerf makes nifty Nerf guns and there's always the amusing but annoying squirt guns, but Annabelle was against them, too, until he started making them on the sly out of LEGOs.

After Annabelle saw the folly of her ways about guns, I thought maybe she'd loosen up a bit, but she was just getting started. Annabelle's next crusade against fun was the evil of video games. I was flabbergasted. I had no idea I'd married an Amish. She lectured me about the dangers of video games, sent me e-mails, cut out articles, gave sermons to all our friends who had gaming systems about how they were raising a generation of warlike kids desensitized to violence, addicted to immediate gratification, and incapable of sustained focus. Her diatribes generally had the effect of sucking all the joy out of the air wherever she went. She'd sternly harangue any parent within earshot about how a gaming system hooked up to the TV tethers kids to some vile mind-control umbilical cord. In time, and after every single one of Ezra's friends were given Xboxes, Sony PlayStations, and Nintendo Wiis, Annabelle relaxed her no-videos edict and allowed him a portable video game player. The result: Ezra played video games everywhere—in the car, in restaurants, on five-hour plane rides, at friends' houses, on the toilet, and under the covers of his bed so we wouldn't hear him when he should be sleeping. Once again for Annabelle, it was game, set, and match. Reality!

My wife's need to regulate and structure doesn't just have jurisdiction over Ezra's life; I, too, have been subjected to her edicts. One I especially disliked was attending a Friday-night playgroup. This wasn't as much a playgroup for kids as it was an excuse for their parents to get together and drink. The venue revolved—each week it was held at a different house. The couples brought their babies, toddlers, or small children along with gallons of cheap wine and tasteless food—mainly varieties of cheeses so bland they were not even worth downing a Lactaid for. Kids were stuffed with gobs of delivery pizza and then left to their own devices while their parents got smashed. Why did Annabelle find this weekly occurrence so crucial? None of these people were my friends. Just because they were all parents of similarly aged kids didn't make me want to hang out with them. And to be honest, all the couples seemed odd to me. Several group members were divorced; they came each week weary, sad, lonely, and overwhelmed. One frantic single mom seemed always to be on the verge of tears or was already crying her eyes out. She had a little boy who ate food only if it was white. There was a married couple whose giantism was only half as interesting as the fact that they were both named Fred. And then there was Tim Sands, who wore a mullet haircut, and his son with the same mullet haircut whom he called Son. No one knew the kid's actual name. Maybe Son *was* his name. Tim was divorced and in the music business, but like everyone else who lives within a fifty-mile radius of Los Angeles, his dream was to write a television show. When he tried to give me the script he eventually wrote, I flatly refused to read it for two reasons: one, I'm in the TV-pilot-writing business, so reading it could result in a conflict, and two, I didn't much care for Tim, his mullet, or his son named Son, and I didn't want to read anything he wrote. But did that stop Annabelle? No, she had to read it. She didn't dare alienate anyone from her sacred Friday night, drunken-ass parents' group.

CUT TO: Several Tim Sands–less years later, I was having dinner with friends at a local bar when none other than ole mullet-head arrived and came right up to my table as if we had been in touch on a daily basis. After the "how's it been going?" was over, Tim launched into a monologue about his TV pilot—the one he had given to Annabelle that I refused to read. Apparently, it was called *Hollyweird* and was about a bunch of actors who are hoping to get their big break by working children's birthday parties dressed as cartoon characters or superheroes. By chance, Tim had recently seen me on an episode of *Entourage* in which I had a very minor role. The director, my friend Larry, had asked me to come in and play the part of an unemployed actor working as a clown at Ari Gold's kid's birthday party. The script called for me, at an inopportune moment, to hand Ari my pathetic headshot and DVD résumé, which he used as a drink coaster and then told me to fuck off. It's maybe all of two minutes of airtime. Everyone in LA has hired wannabe actors at one time or another to work children's birthday parties. It is one of the most common jokes in town. Nevertheless, Tim Sands had the audacity to accuse me of contacting the Emmy Award–winning writers and producers of *Entourage*, *slipping* them his unproduced pilot script so they could steal his "idea" for a two-minute scene that had nothing to do with the rest of the episode. I informed Mullet Man that what he was accusing me of was wrong in so many ways and on so many levels that I didn't even know where to begin. But Tim wouldn't let it go. He actually said that if he wasn't committed to being nonviolent, he'd beat the crap out of me. I had to laugh, eager to please. Annabelle and her structured Friday night playgroup almost got me into a bar brawl with a guy sporting a mullet.

I'm still not quite sure what Annabelle expected to happen with all her parental bylaws and stipulations. Did she really think that Ezra could somehow escape being part of the supercharged modern world of distractions, gadgets, and media manipulation and remain some kind of pure and pristine being? As for me, maybe I'm lazy, too rebellious, or just a huge pain in the ass, but I don't see the harm in letting Ezra goof off, act silly, eat a little Cap'n Crunch, or even watch TV and play video games during school nights once in a while, and if I'm wrong . . . we are so fucked.

"Men don't like to cuddle. We only like it if it leads to ... you know ... lower cuddling." —Ray Romano

"no sex, please, we're married" read the cover of Newsweek in 2002

The magazine reported that many of the 113 million married Americans are too exhausted or grumpy to have sex. Psychologists estimate that 15 to 20 percent of couples have sex no more than 10 times a year; 3 times a week is the number reported by newlyweds, tapering off with time. The average is 68.5 times a year; still, estimates indicate that marrieds have 6.9 more sexual encounters per year than the unwed who are the same age.

the trajectory of passion?

Elle magazine (2006) says that passion fades for 70 percent after the first year together, for 58 percent after two years, 45 percent after three to five years, and 34 percent after six years or more.

Percentage of women over seventy-five years of age who would be happy to never have sex again: 36.
Percentage of men over seventy-five who are OK with that: 5.

Percentage of marrieds who cheat: 22.
Percentage of women who cheat: 15.
Percentage of men who would cheat if they felt they wouldn't get caught: 40.

"We don't know whether people who are happy in marriages have sex more, or whether people who have sex more become happy in their marriages or a combination of the two." —Tom W. Smith, University of Chicago

8

. . . .

Back to the Pussy

"Suffering, emptiness, darkness are nothing more than interruptions of a cosmic orgasm that grows forever in intensity."

—I.B. SINGER

In the beginning, there was sex and it was good. In the middle, it became something to schedule, like a tennis lesson or flu shot. In the end, it has to be done with the help of creams and gels, prescription pills, and perhaps even a pulley or two. Our advice: Take full advantage of the beginning. Try to enjoy the middle as much as you possibly can. And for the end, be sure to stock up on plenty of KY jelly.

He Says

If it wasn't for the fact that I love pussy so much, I'd have given up on the whole marriage thing a long time ago. Ever since the birth of our son eleven years ago, I've been on a never-ending quest to get back to the pussy. My wife's. But getting there is nearly a Herculean task demanding the patience of Mahatma Gandhi, the perseverance of a Chicago Cubs fan, the focus of Tiger Woods, and a mind so warped, so perverted, so single-minded in its pursuit, that it can withstand almost anything. Because what having a child does to your sex life is not unlike what happens when a majestic eagle is hit with a surface-to-air heat-seeking missile. No longer is there spontaneous, stepping-out-of-the-shower-I-have-to-have-you-on-the-bathroom-floor. "What if he walks in and sees us?" No more do-it-with-the-sunrise-I-have-to-piss-hard-on-warm-and-cozy-from-spooning sex, because our kid is right there in bed with us every morning—sleeping in the middle, sweeter than honey on a Hershey bar, cuter than anyone has a right to be, and more demanding of attention than Madonna at a Madonna concert.

But eleven years after our son's birth, one would think that maybe, just maybe, my wife and I could resume our mutual desire to get her off. I mean, how long could she keep using that "I just had a baby" excuse anyway? The truth is, Annabelle's high tide of horniness began to recede innocently enough just after Ezra was born when she began to take antidepressants. The SSRIs dovetailed nicely with all the recently acquired anxieties caused by Ezra's health complications and created a perfect storm of lack of libido. The antidepressants had beneficial results for Annabelle, and sure, she might have been able to function better in her career, but was it really worth it? I saw the drugs as working for her the way the Hoover Dam operates. They stop up the flow of lust and then carefully funnel it to generate more stability for her to use effectively in her workplace, in better ways of dealing with her parents, in coping with the garden varieties of daily stress, and generally in not succumbing to bouts of low self-esteem that were once so fantastically channeled into sexual energy. Annabelle readily admits that she often used sex in very self-destructive ways, as did all my favorite girlfriends. I immediately picked up that scent of self-destructive sexuality and wanted it in the worst way. It goes without saying that sex is always hotter with crazier women. How did I miss Annabelle's slutty years! She'll counter that if I'd got them, we never would have lasted and is that something I could live with? (I won't answer that—*dead giveaway.*)

When it comes to sex, we definitely do not see eye to eye, crotch to crotch, or even eye to crotch. I want to have sex every day; Annabelle wants to do it only once a week. So we compromised: we have sex once a week. (If I'm lucky.) However, once in a great while this can actually work to my advantage. Because our lives are too complicated and chaotic to pick a set date to have sex, every day brings with it the possibility that today could be the day it happens. And because I'm the one who always initiates the sex process, I try every chance I can. Sometimes Annabelle forgets we've already done it once that week and we actually do it twice. (That's the way I stick it to the man, or in this case, the woman.)

By this point in Annabelle's life, many things have changed both inside and outside her pants. No longer is she just horny for horny's sake; she's a mother and homeowner, a talented, hardworking, ambitious career woman who is very, very—and I can't stress this enough—very tired. Yet this fatigue is just the beginning of obstacles I have to wade through if I am to get back to the pussy.

The only time we have for sex is at night, after Ezra has gone to bed. However, our son doesn't like going to bed. It is as if, in some brilliant Oedipal tactic, he delays his sleep to worsen my chances of getting into the body from whence he sprang. Each step of his bedtime process is met with a determined resistance the likes of which haven't been seen since the Battle of Britain. Moving through his homework, bath, brush, snack, pee, and good-night reading, he has to be begged, badgered, bribed, and cajoled every inch of the way. Getting him to bed is an act that utterly drains our life force. And by "life force" I mean my wife's desire to have sex. After the epic bedtime melee she inevitably asks what time it is, and when I offhandedly tell her it's almost ten p.m., she moans, "Already? That's like one a.m. for me." Let me explain: ten at night is one in the morning for her because she spent a day or so in New York earlier in the month and now she's permanently on East Coast time. It's not really possible to be jet-lagged two and half weeks after spending less than forty-eight hours in New York, but she is.

Because of our regional time difference, if any sex is to be had, there's precious little time to get it on before she literally passes out. At first I casually hint, "Oh, c'mon, please, I'm begging you. Lord God, have mercy; I need some!" Then I hunker down for the *rehash*. The rehash is a retelling of the day's events, which I've already heard; future scheduling details we've already discussed; and a laundry list of what's going on in her life I already know about. "The new tiles have come in for the upstairs bathroom." "Yes, I know." "I have an audition tomorrow, so you're going to have to pick him up from school." "OK." "Did I tell you I read that Bonnie Hunt still claims to be thirty-six years old?" "Yeah, twice." "Oh, and we have to get Ezra into a summer camp as soon as possible." "Sure." "I'm not kidding." "All right." "I mean, seriously, like *right now*." It's the "right now" that bugs me. Right now? Like it can't wait until, say, tomorrow morning so we can take this precious brief time to please, please get back to the pussy!

OK, so I completely blow the rehash. It's already two o'clock in the morning her time so I have to regroup fast. Time for . . . the *massage*. The *massage* is a foolproof way to relax and put Annabelle in the mood. I start with the feet, work up to the calf. Then I rub the neck and shoulders and finally the head. At this point in her life, my wife prefers a head massage to getting head, claiming it "gets her out of her brain and into her body." The massage works; Annabelle closes her eyes and says, "Do you mind if I'm a lie-backer?" The lie-backer is when she's too tired to do anything else but lie back and let me do everything. I don't mind the lie-backer. It makes me feel like a conductor on a sex train: "Station stops at French Kiss, Nipple-Suck, Clit-lick, Anal Stimulation, Vibrator City, and Orgasm. Last stop, Orgasm, all aboard!"

All that remains between me and the lie-backer is . . . the *minefield*. The minefield is a series of questions and/or statements my wife lays in front of me like land mines. If I answer them in the correct manner, sex will follow. "I feel bloated." "You don't look bloated." You get the game. But if I respond improperly: "Is my butt looking bigger? "No bigger than usual." "So, you're saying my ass is fat!" "No, I—" Click. I just stepped on a land mine and *boom!* "Great, you think I have a huge ass! Well, maybe I'm just too busy working and helping Ezra with his homework, and paying our mortgage, and doing our taxes, and sorting out our medical bills, to focus on getting my ass in shape every second of the day? Sorry it's not good enough for you. Thanks a lot!" By this point, I'm just a defeated, dejected, despondent shell. I surrender: "I love your ass, but you're tired so why don't you go to sleep and I'll go downstairs to watch *SportsCenter* and down Pinot Noir until I pass out." But now she's all "I still want some action." And then she surprises me by assuming the lie-backer position. This is it, now or never. I dive into bed anticipating all the exciting station stops ahead on the lie-backer express, just as things are picking up speed between the nipple-suck and clit-lick, she pulls the emergency brakes. "I have a right to be tired, right?" Shit, a last land mine. "I shouldn't feel bad about being tired, right?" "Say nothing," I tell myself. "Say *nothing*!" But she keeps at it. "I work hard, Jeff. I do a lot for this family. I'm entitled to feel tired." "Say nothing, say nothing." "Don't act as if I'm the only wife in the world who gets tired. A Pew research survey recently polled working mothers and found out . . ." Christ, it's no use. I can't control myself any longer. "Hey, do you want to do this or not! It's like four o'clock in the morning your time and I can't take it anymore. Be tired, be more in your brain than you are in your body, be any way you want. Just please, for the love of all that's holy and sacred and good, can we please, please, get back to the pussy!" And then she'll say, "You know, I can't have sex when you're so angry at me." And it's *SportsCenter,* bottle of Pinot, here I come.

She Says

My husband says that "he can't get back to the pussy often enough," but like many men and women, I suspect that we have a very different idea of what having sex often actually means. In the first few years after our son was born, it's hard to remember if we had any sex at all. Ever since Bill Clinton tried to redefine what sex with "that woman" meant, there have been lots of definitions of what constitutes sex. In addition, in some parts of the world, mere skin-to-skin contact is considered illicit, so if you count collapsing on top of each other in exhaustion as sexual contact, then, yes, we had lots of it. But once we hit eight years of marriage, once a week, as a fail-safe number, seemed like an acceptable amount to me; however, Jeff feels it would be perfectly reasonable to have sex at least twice a day, a scenario that would leave me bedridden with cystitis. Admittedly, I've always thought of sex as a great way to get to know someone and have struggled with seeing sex with the same person as a compelling activity. I am willing to give it the old college try, although that may not be a terribly appropriate phrase to describe this effort, because in college no one had to try very hard to get me into bed. So perhaps the most significant part of this equation is the amount of time and energy I can devote to the pursuit of an orgasm at this point in my life.

I am going to give an example of my average day at the time when Jeff and I commenced our relationship.

Wake up at eight a.m., check clock—too early—get back in bed. Get up at nine-thirty, pet cat for an hour—she's the cutest thing in the whole world! Go to yoga class, meditate, drop by Farmers Market for a coffee, browse around—I love patchouli. Go to an audition where I read to play the artsy English teacher of a young actor named Ryan Phillippe in a failed pilot that I get offered on the spot. What a great day! Drive home, stopping to look at antiques in a quaint little boutique, but I don't buy anything because I'm a free spirit and I don't want to own too many things. Arrive at apartment, spend close to an hour looking at my hair color in mirror—should I go more red or not? Not sure. Go to acting class, work on relaxation exercises and imagining a really icky smell. Come home, take a leisurely bath, and then try on five different outfits for date with Jeff—I want to look great for him. Spend half an hour placing candles strategically around bedroom, pick out perfect music to have sex to—hey, what about some Portishead? Dance around the house for a half an hour, throw extra clothes in a heap into closet, and voilà, I'm ready. Answer door to Jeff; we see *The Sheltering Sky*, the most moody, weirdly erotic, and slowest-paced film ever made by Bertolucci and that's saying a lot. A perfect date film—we debate its meaning for an hour, which gets us so turned on we have to rush home and have sex, still talking about how we love Paul Bowles and how maybe we'll go to Morocco one day. We're going to roam the world and never lead boring middle-class lives—we're unencumbered by traditional roles and values and we might just go and live in Morocco, only with bank accounts and better plumbing. We fall asleep wrapped tightly in each other's arms. We wake up, go out for coffee, and afterward have sex again; we both pet the cat for an hour and make plans to have more sex later that night. Hot!

The following is a brief summary of my ordinary day after

thirteen years of marriage. Get up at six-thirty a.m., which is really nine-thirty a.m. my time because I was in New York last month, so I'm already running three hours behind. Down a double espresso so I can appear sentient and not frighten our child as I attempt to drag him out of bed. I lovingly make him pancakes, but "Mom, these pancakes taste too eggy" is my reward, and because I feel guilty that I am traveling so much, I remake pancakes from scratch all the while reminding kid that children are starving down the street in East Los Angeles. Then I drive the carpool, depositing the children at school, and then head across town to have night guard adjusted. Doctor tells me my jaw clenching at night is causing my neck pain, and I should "relax more." I pencil in "relax more" in my "pending" list and note that I'd better get another job soon or I won't even be able to afford a new night guard to grind through as I hit the road for two auditions while applying makeup and shoving food in my mouth at the same time.

At the first interview, the director mistakenly thinks I am Annabeth Gish, a perfectly lovely actress who is just not me. He insists on talking about "we"—she and he worked together—and he simply will not accept that I'm not Annabeth Gish and becomes irate when I decline to discuss it. I leave feeling vaguely confused— am I her? I might be. At the second audition I see every actress who has ever, and I mean *ever*, starred in a sitcom, including people as varied as Bonnie Franklin, from *One Day at a Time;* Katey Sagal, from *Married with Children;* and Mel Harris, from *Thirtysomething,* a show about a kind of ennui that at the time it was on I didn't recognize as my life. Because forty is the new thirty, I suppose it makes sense that at fortysomething I would now understand *Thirtysomething.* Of course, actress years are like dog years, only shorter, so at fortysomething in show business I'm like eightysomething and virtually unemployable. I wait for an hour to read, miss my yoga class, add "do yoga" to my "pending" list for next week, then swing over to get a Brazilian, because it's date night and I want to make an effort for Jeff.

As I undress at Faces, which is an ironic name for a salon that mostly attends to crotches, my Eastern European waxer, Mischa, is admonishing me for missing appointments, and I'm too embarrassed to explain that since my original waxer, Sasha, died of breast cancer last year, it's been too depressing to come in for a wax. But I know they need the business so I buy a series of treatments that I'm sure I'll never have time to come in for, and while she's buried in my now hairless nether region, I'm on the phone with other moms coordinating summer camp schedules when a call comes in. It's Jeff, wondering if he was supposed to pick up Ezra or if I was on my way? I remind him that I have my legs over my head right now, and he tells me not to worry, he'll be happy to pick up the kid because he's so looking forward to going down on me tonight. But that call is interrupted by a message from the contractor confirming that the tiles have come in for the upstairs bathroom renovation. I feel strangely turned on by the idea of new shower tiles. Meanwhile, a text message appears on my BlackBerry from the babysitter, whose car has broken down and she can't make it tonight. I call and cancel plans with Jeff, who's so mad I promise him we'll grab some time later tonight. While I drive home, our stockbroker calls to explain that although our pension plans are worth less than when we initially invested with him, they were actually worth more for a two-year period six years ago and we've only lost money that was profit anyway and so even though I am a moron at all things financial, even I can deduce that by the time Jeff and I will be cashing in these accounts, we'll be lucky to have enough to afford our membership dues in AARP with the proceeds. The fact that I thought of myself and AARP together sends me into an instant spiral of anxiety. How did I get so fucking old! There must be some mistake! The years 1985–88 were such a waste—I want those years back! I want back all the hours I got sucked into watching *Rock of Love*! The time I've spent deleting e-mailed invitations to join Plaxo, LinkedIn, and Twitter? I want that back too! I want every minute I've spent on hold with customer service centers returned to me. I'm so old I need every available minute to make money for when I'm even older! By now I have a big fat TMJ headache as I inch my way home through the Los Angeles traffic.

Get home, feed kid, struggle through fifth-grade math, beg him to commence bedtime routine. We read, he wants Dad, he wants me, Dad, me, Dad, then says he wants some Mom time; and I know that he knows that I know that the Mom years will soon be coming to an end, so I can't refuse and I stay with him until he falls asleep, grab a quick shower, and then head to my office to pay our medical bills. Call downstairs to tell Jeff to turn off ESPN and meet me upstairs soon because I'll be ready for some "action" right after I figure out our health plan's newly required co-payment policy. I'm halfway through the pile when Jeff races upstairs to check on my progress and gives me the once-over. "Aren't you going to put a cute outfit on?" Jeff says with a groan. "I'm sorry. I meant to," is all I can manage to say, and the truth is I really did intend to wear thigh-high stockings, heels, and a skirt for Jeff, but after I showered I didn't have the energy to get dressed up for him. So I end up right back in my ratty sweat pants and T-shirt just like every other night since our kid was born. He sees me covered in insurance claim statements and hisses, "Aren't you ready yet?" By now it's almost eleven p.m., which is really two a.m. my time, so I can barely hold my head up as I reply that we had better start to make more money or one day we'll be forced to figure out the new Medicare drug benefit and then we'll really be screwed! He takes this as an opportunity to remind me that talking about money before sex is a turnoff. I remind him that talking about money is only a *turnoff* if you're talking about not having money; talking about money before sex when you have money is actually a *turn-on*.

By now my neck really hurts, so when we finally make it into the bedroom, Jeff starts to massage the place that most directly connects to my vagina, which these days, is my head. It's so relaxing that I start to fall asleep so I ask Jeff if a hand job is OK, but no, he wants it all. To liven things up, Jeff suggests I talk to him. I begin a rapturous description of how nice the new bathroom cabinets are going to be, but he says that's not the kind of talk he meant. I know it's not, and I can't believe I'm the kind of person who wants to talk about a bathroom renovation—when did I become so bourgeois? It's just that I'm so tired . . . So I ask, "Do you mind if lie down while we do it?" Yes, here comes the lie-backer: as I lie there it occurs to me that this will be the only time we'll have a chance to talk about the camp Ezra should attend this summer because the forms are due tomorrow. Jeff would like to switch the topic and get back to the pussy, but when did it become "the pussy"? I say, "I know California is a community property state, but it's still my pussy!" But Jeff has made the lie-backer, for its horrible nomenclature, a veritable orgasmatron. He has special talents—it works every time, and I achieve orgasm as we are in the middle of discussing the registration process. I've got just enough energy to fit in forty-five seconds of snuggling before we each assume our sleeping positions on our designated sides of the bed and then hear the pitter-patter of little footsteps: Ezra slides in bed between us, Stinky jumps on top of me, and we all fall asleep. Hot!

Psychologists predict gay spouses will experience happier unions. Gay and lesbian couples tend to assign household labor more fairly and resolve conflict more constructively.

less is more

People spend more time with their kids now than they used to. Even though both are working more hours, moms spent 20 percent more time in 2000 than they did in 1965; for married dads the number has doubled. Parents are more kidcentric now. But is that a good thing? The Family and Work Institute, which studies problems in contemporary working families, has found that most children don't want to spend as much time with their parents as parents assume; they just want their parents to be more relaxed during the time they spend together.

family values, washington style

Gingrich, who frequently campaigned on the sanctity of marriage and family values, then divorced his second wife after acknowledging his relationship with his current wife, a former congressional aide more than twenty years younger than he is and with whom he was having a clandestine relationship during the Monica Lewinsky hearings. Newt "Family Values" Gingrich announced his plans to divorce his first wife while she was recuperating in the hospital from cancer surgery.

the worst is yet to come

Participants in a University of Michigan study were asked how strongly they responded to questions such as "My spouse gets on my nerves." In every age group, people were more annoyed with spouses than with friends and family and the annoyance only increased the longer they were married.

9

. . . .

Slouching Toward Cooperstown

*"Even his griefs are a joy long after to one who
remembers all that he wrought and endured."*
—HOMER, *THE ODYSSEY*

There is a pervasive cliché that men are gonzo over sports and the women they are married to can't understand it.

But clichés are often true for a lot of people a lot of the time. That's how they became clichés in the first place. For instance, the apple doesn't fall far from the tree, or between a rock and a hard place. When it comes to sports, our son is the apple, and Jeff's fanaticism for sports continually puts our marriage between the rock and the hard place.

She Says

I hate to make it sound like our house resembles those ubiquitous commercials where a husband and his pals are camped out in the living room and the pastel-hued twinsetted wife is doing one of two things: shaking her head with a mixture of irritation and love as she places bowls of starchy foodstuff in front of their large bellies or shaking her head with a mixture of irritation and love as she's shoving her coat on so she can make her escape to the mall. It doesn't. Except for the Super Bowl or the World Series, rarely do my husband's buddies come over to sit through ESPN News, ESPN Highlights, ESPN Lowlights, ESPN Minutiae, or the myriad other ways the all-sports network has contrived to fill air space twenty-four hours a day. No, most days, it's just Jeff camped out with his hummus and avocado wrap, yelling at our television while I walk by seething in genuine disgust at what appears to be a huge time suck and is setting a bad example for our kid, when I would prefer to see him sitting in front of his computer Googling old girlfriends so at least he'd have the appearance of doing something productive. I thought I was marrying a comedy writer; I had no idea that Jeff had ever harbored hoop dreams, Heisman delusions, or boys-of-summer fantasies. While we were dating, I had observed him watching games on TV, but somehow the extent of his devotion just didn't register. When I offhandedly mentioned it to him, he allowed that he tried not to miss the play-offs. I had no idea he meant the play-offs of every single sport. I had no idea that every single sport even had a play-off. If the javelin throw had play-offs, he'd watch them. I suspect that from the moment our son was conceived, Jeff was hatching a plan. Like the husband in *Rosemary's Baby* who just couldn't wait to deliver their child to the neighboring Satanists, my spouse, unbeknownst to me, was plotting to pimp our kid to the neighborhood athletic associations.

It's not like I'm anti-sports; everyone in Miami Beach played tennis when I was growing up. I've watched my share of Super Bowls and I've got a fairly reliable outside shot in H-O-R-S-E, but I didn't grow up playing team sports so I was entirely unprepared for Jeff's machinations. It started innocently enough: I had been genuinely enjoying myself, having a great if not exhausting time indulging our munchkin in his desire to toss or kick a ball from sunrise to sunset, which had the added bonus of serving as my personal fitness regimen. In a town where people regularly throw fistfuls of cash at strangers to nag them into shape, I had my own trainer, who employed one of the most sophisticated motivational techniques known to our species: working-mother guilt.* So imagine my surprise when Ezra and I were playing in the backyard and Jeff barked out this pronouncement: "If our son wants to be a professional baseball player, you're not stopping him." Huh? The kid was two years old. But that was the moment my spouse chose to inform me, in an excited, almost anguished tone of voice, that he himself might have had a career in professional sports had his family been more encouraging, and now I might be denying his son the same opportunity and he was not going to stand for it. I was stunned.

Some kind of early childhood imprinting has left my husband with the impression that nothing could be better than a career in sports. Jeff has formed this opinion despite the fact that aside from a few brief encounters at parties with that human phenomenon known as Lance Armstrong, we don't actually know any professional athletes who could give us a realistic depiction of the profession. That's like having an audience with the pope and concluding that joining the clergy affords one a glamorous lifestyle. Try telling that to Coach Kahn.

There's my husband, Jeff, and then there's his alter ego, Coach Kahn. Jeff has a self-deprecating sense of humor and can experience

---

*Between Ezra's athletic prowess and two weeks of delivered Zone meals, I was able to lose most of my pregnancy weight pretty quickly. The Zone works. If you're frugal, you will feel compelled to follow the program and not cheat, because it's expensive. You will also be hungry. Very hungry. Around noon on the first day of my delivered meals, I called the company to make sure I understood the system properly. "So you guys deliver one meal at a time?" Apparently, I had eaten the entire first day's meals for breakfast. Lunch and dinner were so small, I assumed they were garnishes.

complete (if fleeting) happiness in the enjoyment of a delicious meal. Coach Kahn, on the other hand, takes things superseriously and the only thing that will satisfy him will be to see the fruit of his loins take his place among the pantheon of greats in Cooperstown. They are exact opposites. Okay, I might be exaggerating a little— Coach Kahn would probably like to get into my pants too.

Mighty Mite Rebels, Orangemen, the Giants, the Orioles, the Yankees, the Rangers, the Red Sox, the White Sox, the Orioles again, the Yankees again, the Titans, the White Sox again, the Purple Yankees, and the Toluca Lake All Stars. In chronological order, those are the teams our child has played on.* The kid is eleven. You don't join teams until you're four. You do the math.

I can't remember the justifications for all the moves; all I know is that like our Russian ancestors who trudged from shtetl to shtetl, Coach Kahn schleps our kid from league to league as if they are escaping a pogrom.

To this day it's a complete mystery to me how he finds these teams and how many leagues there are in each and every neighborhood. I am loath to make the distinction, but it does seem to be the dads who pass this information around. Do they actually speak of it, or is there something in the male DNA code by which this information is shared? Each organization has its own code of conduct and commissioners, and you have to know the secret handshake or someone who has an *in* in order to penetrate the labyrinthine system. It's no secret to anyone with athletically inclined kids that each and every one of these youth teams is something of a personal fiefdom ruled over by a coach whose child, coincidentally, happens to be the star player of the team. Each team has its own hierarchical structure that must never be challenged or your kid will find

---

*I had to ask Jeff the names; there's no way I could ever remember them all.

himself warming the bench all season. Think feudalism meets the Moose Lodge. Coach Kahn quickly adapted to the system and began ingratiating himself with the coaches, offering to run practices and doling out batting tips, because he just loves to pass on his passion for sports to children, and more important, he was determined to secure a good spot for our future Hall of Famer.

The thing was, Ez really seemed to love the game and exhibited remarkable hand-eye coordination, so my husband decided he needed to become the coach of a team too. It was adorable to see the kids on Jeff's team all suited up at this young age. The only problem was that at seven years old, not all of them had developed the long attention span required for baseball. *I* don't always have the attention span required for the game. As an employee of Ted Turner's, I was once given the honor of being the captain of the Atlanta Braves for a day. After I jokingly suggested that the team play only five innings because I found nine to be a tad repetitive, I think I escaped bodily harm only because earlier that week the Braves' pitcher John Rocker had made racist remarks* and manager Bobby Cox didn't want to draw any more negative attention to the team.

Meanwhile, on our field of delusions for men who are living out their childhood dreams through their sons, one kid was drawing circles in the dirt, another was counting the clouds overhead, and another was in tears. Often the crying child was our very own offspring. Why? The way Coach K singled him out, you might imagine our tyke was being scouted for the majors right then and

---

*"New York City is the most hectic, nerve-racking city. Imagine having to take the 7 Train to the ballpark, [it's] like you're riding through Beirut next to some kid with purple hair, next to some queer with AIDS, right next to some dude who just got out of jail for the fourth time and some twenty-year-old mom with four kids. It's depressing. Asians, Koreans, Vietnamese, Indians, Russians, Spanish people, and everything up there. How the hell did they get in this country?"

there. "Ezra, ready position," "Ezra, don't look down," "Ezra, don't look up!" "Run hard, Kahn, run hard," "*Head in the game*," "*Head in the game!*" Head in the game? The kids were hitting a ball off a tee, for God's sake. It was not an uncommon occurrence for me to show up and inquire how the game was going only to be told, "I don't know about the team, but your husband's on fire!" Coach Kahn's reputation for toughness was sealed when he threatened to bench a player because said cutie had forgotten his team cap. When did "Thou shall not forget your hat" become a commandment! It's kind of funny when you realize my husband is as passionate about baseball as he is about seeing the end of all organized religion, and yet his adherence to following the rules of the sport has exactly the same kind of rigidity that you see in only one other group in the world: religious fanatics. Fearing that we would have to relocate to a new community and live under assumed names in some sort of Little League protection program, I gently suggested that perhaps he should retire from coaching temporarily as the kids headed to coach pitch.* He agreed to hang up his official coaching hat, but felt they needed to change leagues—again.

Out of the frying pan into the fire, as the saying goes.

Jeff sussed out a new league, where, as fate would have it, Ezra was placed on the one team in this league headed by a coach who didn't believe in keeping score in games with young children. Each week Jeff was increasingly agitated by this coach, who, by a coincidence, was an old friend of mine.

I wasn't present when "the incident" occurred, but as I later heard from numerous sources, Jeff got into a screaming match with my friend in full view of the seven-year-old players. The fallout

---

*I might actually have said, "If you insist upon coaching ever again, I'm going to divorce you and you're going to scar your child for life, asshole!"

from this incident became extremely uncomfortable for me as word spread through the community. I'd find myself at my friend's house agreeing that my husband had been over the top, but it felt icky, as if I were betraying him. Something had to give. Is there nothing more painful than watching women like Hillary Clinton, Silda Spitzer, or Elizabeth Edwards publicly stand by their men? I've always thought I'd never do that. Certainly, Jeff's behavior wasn't reaching a level of public humiliation—it was more on the scale of neighborhood disaffection—but a choice had to be made. I stood by him . . . in public. I cut back my time with my friend, but that didn't stop me from reading him the riot act in the privacy of our home and everywhere we went together for the next month: "Did you go off of your medication? You are fucking out of control, and you have got to get hold of yourself!!"

From the fire into the flames? There's just no idiom that truly conveys going from bad to worse. The next league Jeff shuffled Ezra to practiced in a local park named for the Elysian Fields, the area of the Greek underworld that was the final resting place of the souls of the heroic and the virtuous. But in modern-day Los Angeles, the Elysian Fields is the home of a cliquey group of coaches and families, who, as it turned out, didn't much like our kid's emotionally expressive artistic temperament. I thought it might be a good life lesson for our child to experience this kind of thing—after all, not everyone is going to appreciate your uniqueness—but Jeff insisted on making it known that he wasn't happy and things were spiraling down again as Coach K started to make regular appearances at Elysian Fields. During the time our issue played on that team, a day didn't go by that Jeff and I didn't argue about how hard he was riding our child on the field and how much he was rushing him through his homework so he could not only arrive at practice early but also attend supplementary practices for practice!

Coach K became fixated on the idea that our son should be working toward winning a college baseball scholarship,* even though his entire body could fit inside the pant leg of any one of his teammates. The tension escalated to the point where our son turned around on the plate one day and, seething, said, "Shut up, Dad!" The next week Ezra insisted that Coach K cease all talking during games and he was eventually exiled to the outfield, where the team could see him yelling from a distance but, fortunately, couldn't hear his admonishments.

It was only a short time later that Coach K announced that he'd found the über league of all Little Leagues that was definitely going to be the launching pad for Ezra Kahn's career. This new league is widely known as a competitive hotbed of Little League intrigue brimming with power struggles between dads vying for status and position for their progeny.

Jeff loves it! More important, Ezra really enjoys playing in this league; he's made good friends and seems eager to put in the time, even though joining up means he has to play on two teams at once in order to keep a position on the travel team. Honestly, I don't see how these kids can be expected to keep it all straight. In the last league, you could steal but you couldn't lead off the base, but in the new one, you can take a lead, but if it's a close play at home, you have to slide or you're out. I have no idea what this means and if I saw it in the field, I'd be just as confused as I am writing about it. I can only hope that this kind of thing will serve as some kind of sequential-thinking exercise so our kid will do better in math than either of us.

Maybe it's a form of Stockholm syndrome, but I get it. I have no idea whether Ezra will stick with the sport, and the health of his

---

*On average, the best-paying sports scholarship is men's ice hockey ($21,755). Baseball is the second-lowest men's sport ($5,806).

kidney may well dictate his career trajectory. But with all of the reconstructive surgeries he's weathered, it's amazing that he's so athletic.* It has also been a real opportunity for me to work on that Zen acceptance of life that Jeff says he's adopted in relation to Ezra's health. For instance, we were on a tour of a school recently and were trying to make a good impression with the admissions director when a child stood up, pointed at Jeff, and announced to the classroom, "That's the dad that yells in the stands!" Oh, that was so funny.

He Says

Annabelle is not the first person to assume that I'm not into sports (because of my smallish stature) at first meeting me, but I assure you that sports and being a really good athlete were the most crucial and important aspects of my life right up until the second a girl touched my penis.

OK, perhaps if you grow up a member of the Taliban, it's how fast you can saw off an infidel's head that ingratiates you to your fellow men, but in most places in the world it's sports. Over the years sports have given me many advantages. It's like having an invisible passport that can get you past all the boundaries of men regardless of geography, politics, and racial, religious, or socioeconomic backgrounds. It's our one common male language, and I feel that it is my paternal duty to pass on the love of sports to my own son, who,

---

*High-contact sports like soccer, football, and hockey are considered verboten by most pediatric nephrologists, but both baseball and basketball fall into the medium-contact range. Some of our nephrologist's patients even have special protective padding made to allow them and their parents peace of mind when participating in those activities. If Ezra really does continue, he'll face pitches going upward of 60 miles per hour, so I keep the phone number of an orthotics specialist on my desk.

I might add, is not unlike his father in the lack of largeness department and could really benefit from the world of sports.

Annabelle would like everyone to believe that I hatched some
sinister, predestined *Rosemary's Baby* conspiracy to embroil our little
Ezra into the *dark* world of athletic competition, but that's not what
happened at all. Here's the real story about Ezra and our family's
journey into the world of kid sports:

At around the age of two and a half, Ezra was watching Tiger
Woods on TV when he suddenly, as if hypnotized, walked out of
the house into the backyard and began hitting plastic golf balls
with his plastic clubs. That little boy could swing. The golf club became a baseball bat and a year and a half later Ez was playing on his
first Little League team, the tiny T-Ball Giants. At his very first
game, the gung-ho coach took notice and soon Ezra was his star
rookie, playing at the pitcher position and smacking homers off
the T-stand.

Ezra didn't just like baseball, he loved it. My heart fluttered
and danced. My son loves baseball! He couldn't get enough of it.
We played after school every day. He wanted me to continue to
play even after the team practices ended. Every night, in our backyard, he had me throw him pop-ups until the sun set and my arm
turned to Silly Putty. And it still wasn't enough for him. "One
more pop-up, Dad. Just one." One more really meant a hundred
more, in the dark, with Annabelle yelling at us to come in for dinner, until my arm and shoulder finally gave out. Every night I
slathered my achy limbs with Tiger Balm. All my T-shirts smelled
as if they'd been washed in menthol. For my little future Hall of
Famer, it was nothing but baseball twenty-four hours a day. That's
why I simply suggested to Annabelle that if Ezra wanted to play
professional baseball, she wasn't going to stop him.

For Ezra's second season of T-ball, I volunteered to coach his team. I became "Coach Kahn" only because I was trying to be a good, involved parent and not some kind of sports Svengali, as Annabelle would have you believe. There is also a long and storied history of fathers and sons in sports: Tiger Woods and his dad, Earl; Michael Jordan and father, James; Archie Manning and his sons Peyton and Eli. Maybe if Hitler's daddy had played some sports with him, things would have turned out a lot better. Admittedly, my coaching style could be polarizing. Some parents adored me and loved my zeal, while others gawked at me with bewildered irritation as if I just cut them off on the freeway and then shot their tires out. After hearing some of the disgruntled parents gripe about me, Annabelle appointed herself our family's official anti–baseball commissioner, whose first order of business was to conclude that playing baseball would interfere with the rigorous academic expectations of first grade. And so Anti-Commish Gurwitch and Coach Kahn would go at each other over our son's baseball passion as if it were the Little League version of the Scopes trial.

Ezra's skills were improving so rapidly that it was only logical for him to graduate from hitting the ball off a tee and move to a league where the coaches pitched to the players to hit. For the new coach-pitch league, I hooked up to manage the team with another neighborhood sports dad, Tom. I thought we'd make a good team because where I have a hyper, nearly hysterical sideline demeanor, Tom's coaching is elegantly understated. As luck would have it, the new league had no umpires to officiate, leaving it up to the coaches to determine who was out or safe. So it should come as no surprise how quickly things deteriorated when a couple of opposing coaches bitterly questioned one of Tom's on-field calls. There were angry accusations, name-calling escalations, and then the macho challenge of "Okay, let's go, you and me, right here, right now" was brazenly hurled at Tom by an undersized yet rabid opposing coach who was clearly in dire need of a Xanax. Soon parents from both sides started weighing in and kids began to cry and wander off the field looking for someone to hug. A coach on-field rumble was just the kind of damning evidence anti-Commissioner Gurwitch was looking for to slow down Ezra's baseball career as well as the perfect thing she could demonstrate to all our friends, family, neighbors, and even strangers on the street as proof that she was right about my being way too intense. (Being right is Annabelle's national pastime.) Fortunately, cooler heads prevailed, but I decided to switch leagues after the season. The anti-commish declared I was dragging Ezra from league to league as if we were some kind of roving panhandling baseball gypsies, but there was rhyme to my reason. If one league didn't have umps, shouldn't I find one that did?

The new league I found for Ezra's fourth season had not only volunteer umpires, but also this really cool eighteen-year-old high school senior who was the coach of Ezra's team. I was ecstatic to learn from Coach Teenager that he intended to lead the team to victory right up to the championship game at the end of the season. He seemed so perfect I barely gave it a second thought that he had a co-coach. She was a team mom who was usually very, very busy with work, but would be there in case he couldn't make it, which would "hardly ever" happen.

Before the first game, Coach Teenager's assistant coach strutted onto the field wearing a Ramones T-shirt and a bat slung over her shoulder like an Israeli soldier's Uzi and brazenly announced with a George W. first-term swagger that she *did not* believe in competitive sports for kids, that winning and losing were *irrelevant* to her and *completely contrary* to the way she ran *"my team."* Although

Coach Teenager had said he was in charge, it was clear she was the boss. It wasn't long before he alleged that he had become unexpectedly busy preparing for college and faded away, paving the way for Cruella De Coach to assume full control. The tension between Coach Snow Queen of Narnia and me escalated to an nearly Shia versus Sunni level as she proudly came unprepared to the games without such trivial details as batting orders and which positions the kids were to play. Still, I had no idea what kind of car bomb was waiting for me until one sunny Saturday before our weekly game when Coach Nurse Ratched caught sight of me setting up the kids for warm-ups. It must have been the last straw for her and the moment she had been waiting for to let me have it. She lambasted me loudly in front of all the kids, parents, and my own son. She rhetorically barked, "Are you the coach?" This was followed by "You don't touch *my* players." (I later learned that one of the team's overtly PC moms was incensed that while coaching first base I had adjusted a player's feet to help him learn the correct way to stand on a base.) The tirade continued with "If you want to coach your own team, *go get fingerprinted*!" (As in most leagues, coaches must be fingerprinted to prove that they aren't sex offenders.) She kept howling "Go get fingerprinted," as if instead of being at a Little League game, I was now the object of scorn at a NAMBLA protest rally. I could only presume that in Coach Lady Macbeth's eyes, moving a kid's feet was tantamount to reaching into his little pants and adjusting his tiny baseballs.

To make matters even worse, the Lizzie Borden of Little League, was an old friend of Annabelle's as well as a member in good standing of Hollywood's powerful lesbian elite. Besides the loss of friendship, Annabelle feared that she and I would find ourselves pariahs in the gay showbiz community on the order of the Reverend James Dobson and the post-Ellen Anne Heche. This made my situation at home particularly precarious. Although Annabelle professes to have sided with me, it came at a cost. Let's just say that it's hard to take your wife seriously when she's telling you that *you* need anger management while she's screaming her lungs out at you.

And so we switched leagues again. This one had well-kept fields, a great snack bar, genuine uniforms and caps, an electronic scoreboard, and the players, not the coaches, pitched to the batters, but three practices a week had the anti-commissioner and me at each other's throats about Ezra's eroding homework time. I was trapped. If Ezra didn't show up for practice, he would never have a chance to prove his worth to his new coaches. So I overrode Annabelle and made sure Ezra attended each and every practice. We were rewarded for all our time and effort with a pathetically coached team that lost most games, sometimes by twenty-five runs or more, and with Ezra spending half the time on the bench. I don't want to say that his coaches were lazy, narrow-minded, biased, and had no clue how to coach baseball—OK, yes, I do want to say it. Providentially, around the end of the horrific season Tom called to tell me he was very happy with a new league he'd found and suggested we try it.

I was flabbergasted by how well Commissioner Gurwitch took the news. "You've gotta be kidding me! God, Jeff, when will it end? Did you ever think the coaches, umpires, and parents might not be problem, but you are?" I made my case for relocating: Ezra loved baseball and deserved to be at a place that appreciated his talent, hard work, and dedication. Finding the right Little League was like dating: you had to go through a few losers before you married the right one. "Like I did with you, right, honey?" Annabelle rolled her eyes, let out a sarcastic chortle and said, "We'll see how long this one lasts."

At the new league, Ezra's ability and work ethic were immediately recognized during the league tryouts, and many of the coaches wanted him on their teams. These coaches were all dads of players and they also reminded me a lot of, well, me: basically nice guys, slightly neurotic, good senses of humor, sometimes temperamental and irrational, but loving fathers and intense advocates of their sons, such as the ex-army helicopter pilot named Buzz—that's right, Buzz, a pitch-perfect name—who actually shouted this during his son's at bat: "C'mon, Seth! Placate my adult insecurities and faded dreams!" Yes, I have finally found my people. Even Anti-Commissioner Gurwitch agrees that it's a good fit. So you see I'm not this crazy, out-of-control Coach Kahn caricature that Annabelle cooked up. I'm just a sane, loving activist of my son's baseball talents. Right? Sure, along the way there have been coaches, parents, players, lesbians, umpires, little siblings of players, the people who ran the concession stand, the ice-cream-truck driver who played that insidious repeating ice-cream-truck music, and even strangers walking their dogs who utterly detested me. Sure, it almost destroyed my relationship with my son and my marriage to Annabelle, but it's all been worth it because after the long and precarious journey, we've finally made it to the right Little League.

OK, I admit the new league's not perfect. It has its share of politics, rumors, gossipmongering, social cliques, and a player caste system as rigid as anything you can find in India. And it's also true that if I put as much time and energy into my writing career as I continue to put into Ezra's baseball, by this point I could have written at least three *War and Peace*–sized novels, a dozen screenplays, a half dozen plays, two books of short stories, and a collection of poetry, not to mention having a regular magazine column, my own comedy show on the Web, and still have time left over to resculpt my body at a gym and invent my own language. But it's been totally worth it because nothing is better than seeing your son smash a hit into the outfield, round third, and score or make a great catch. And last year, after he made the last out and his travel team won a big tournament, he leaped into my arms like Yogi Berra did to Don Larsen after he pitched a perfect game in the 1956 World Series. I know, no matter what happens after Ezra's travel team, the Titans, goes to play in Cooperstown in 2010 for the Field of Dreams Tournament, he'll always remember that day he jumped in my arms to celebrate the victory. And if he does ever forget, I'll be sure to remind him.

what's love got to do with it?

Researchers from Australian National University tracking 2,500 couples, married or living together, from 2001 to 2007, have identified what it takes to keep a couple together: Couples in which one partner and not the other smokes are more likely to have a relationship that ends in failure. A husband who is nine or more years older than his wife is twice as likely to get divorced as are husbands who get married before they turn twenty-five. Sixteen percent of men and women whose parents ever separated or divorced experienced marital separation themselves compared with ten percent for those whose parents did not separate.

varieties of marriage

Polygamy: The Practice or condition of having more than one spouse at one time. *Bigamy:* Marrying one person while still legally married to another. *Polygyny:* The condition or practice of having more than one wife at one time. *Endogamy:* Marriage within one's own tribe. *Monogamy:* Marriage with only one person at a time. *Arranged:* The selection of a marriage partner may involve the couple going through a selection process of courtship, or the marriage may be arranged by the couple's parents or an outside party, a matchmaker.

study confirms in-laws are the chief cause of divorces

Data in the 2004 National Population and Family Development Board study in Malaysia revealed that "meddlesome in-laws" are the number one reason why Indian couples get divorced. Ironically, most of these marriages were arranged by the same in-laws who later cause conflict with the spouses they once chose.

10

. . . .

They're Not Our Fathers' Fathers-in-Law

"Serpentine, Sheldon, serpentine!"

—PETER FALK'S SAGE ADVICE TO ALAN ARKIN,

THE IN-LAWS

*M*eet the *Parents:* for some it's a hilarious movie, but for others it's a much more serious proposition. In Kyrgyzstan one-third of marriages are initiated by the kidnapping of a bride from her parents' home. The night of the abduction she is spirited away to the home of her new family. Her would-be in-laws are charged with persuading the intended bride to stay overnight. If they succeed, the deal is pretty much sealed. Apparently their cajoling goes something like this: "Everyone thinks you're a big fat whore now, so why put up a fight?" It may not be elegant, but it's damn persuasive. In Botswana, the entire family, led by the groom's parents, assembles to petition a bride's family in a lengthy dowry-negotiating process. "Hey, you want her, put up or shut up." She's like an NBA free agent.

For people like us who live two thousand seven hundred and fifty-one miles away from one set of in-laws and one thousand four hundred and thirty and a half miles from the other (not that we've done the math), we're coming up with new ways to screw it up.

He Says

Last December, I was on my way to LAX, which, depending on traffic, is about two or three light-years from where we live in Hollywood, to pick up my mother-in-law—that's right, I said I was picking up my mother-in-law from the airport, all by myself. Before I got married I was always of the mind that two parents were plenty and shuddered at the thought of having to deal with another set. Parents were the enriched fluffy white bread to my artesian whole-wheat, flaxseed, gluten-free, Kalamata olive loaf. What could possibly be less romantic than interacting with your in-laws? Having tea with the Taliban? Catching the swine flu? Watching *I'm a Celebrity . . . Get Me out of Here*? In-laws are a relationship of obligation and that was what I was always trying to get away from my whole life. But, and this is the bottom line, if you're going to get married, then having in-laws is inevitable, like jury duty, rain after you've just gotten your car washed, and acid reflux the millisecond you turn forty.

Meeting Annabelle's folks did not bode well for me because historically I don't make the best first impression. Let's not forget that for half a decade Annabelle wasn't sure whether she should date me or have me arrested for stalking her. On the other hand, it's true that once people get to know me a little more, they really warm up to me, except, of course, my own parents. Unfortunately, because my in-laws live so far away, it would be next to impossible for us to spend enough time together for them to get over the horrible first impression and grow to like me, so I figured the whole thing was doomed from the get-go.

The first time we met was in San Francisco. They were in town for Passover to pay homage to Judaism's own Lisa Gurwitch and her family. Meeting my in-laws-to-be at a seder had all the makings of a disaster of a biblical proportion. Besides family and religion, the only thing missing from the trifecta of things that turn me into a cynical, sarcastic, belligerent asshole is musical theater. That piece of the puzzle was solved when Lisa instructed us to begin the Passover meal by singing "There's No Seder Like Our Seder" to the tune of "There's No Business Like Show Business." I also noticed that Annabelle's mother, Shirley, asks a lot of questions. I'm talking peppering anyone within earshot with inquiries the way antiaircraft guns fire thousands of rounds of artillery into the sky to shoot down an enemy bomber. Did I write for TV or film? Did I usually work during the day or night? Did I work at home or in an office? Did I drive to work? How far was my drive from my house? Did the building have parking? Were the bathrooms nice? Where did I go for lunch? Was I a vegetarian? Is chicken still considered meat? Are your friends writers too? Where do they work? Do you ever work with them? Are most writers vegetarians? Do they eat chicken? How far do your friends have to drive to get to work and what are their names and addresses? I could barely answer one query before the next was fired off. Finally, I gave up and without saying a word I got up from the table and walked away in the middle of dipping the bitter herbs.

Annabelle's dad was another story altogether. At six feet four, Harry Gurwitch is a mammoth of a man, born and raised in Mobile, Alabama, and with his gruff southern baritone drawl, he comes off like a Jewish Foghorn Leghorn: "I say, I say, Jeff, do you like to smoke them Cuban cee-gars?" "I bet y'all play lots of golf out there in sunny Californ-i-a." "I say, Jeff, you ever attend one of those legendary Los Angeles airport-adjacent gentlemen's clubs?" I hate cigars, never golf, and was not about to swap any strip club shop talk with my future father-in-law, so I did my best to keep changing the subject to Miami sports teams: Dolphins, Heat, Marlins, Panthers, even jai alai. I also couldn't help observing that more than golf, cigars, and even strip clubs, Harry's greatest love is food, and he seemed to be on an almost spiritual quest to keep eating it every chance he got. There was breakfast, postbreakfast snack, prelunch treat, lunch, late lunch nibble, predinner appetizer, dinner, dessert, and the before-bedtime nosh.

The next day Harry and I went off to spend some bonding mealtimes together, starting with the after-breakfast snack. Alone at last, the big guy overshared with me his proclivity for a couple of the famous body parts of Halle Berry. During our predinner appetizer, we began to disagree about politics (Harry's an anti–gun control, antitax, probusiness Republican), so Harry switched gears and pitched me his idea for a TV show. It was about a bookish lawyer lady. By day she's a boring banker, but at night she sheds her Brooks Brothers business suit, pantyhose, and briefcase for latex heels, whips, and chains and makes a killing as the city's most notorious dominatrix. With Harry's southern pronunciation, *dominatrix* sounds more like "domin-a-tricks." I knew I was sounding snarky when I told him that it could be called *Law & Order, S&M.* Harry missed my ironic tone and, thinking I was being sincere, offered me the job of head writer when he and I sold *Law & Order, S&M* to a network for millions of dollars.

I never expected my in-laws to like me. We have practically nothing in common except that we all love, adore, and are annoyed by Annabelle. Thirteen years into our marriage and objectively speaking, I'm not a good son-in-law at all. I see them only once or twice a year; I don't call them very much and never send them cards on their birthdays or anniversaries, but for some reason they seem to really love me. A lot! The only explanation I can think of is that I had inadvertently set the bar so low with my in-laws when I first met them that it takes only the smallest gesture of goodwill to endear myself to them. In fact, if I do anything, if I throw Harry and Shirley any kind of bone, such as sending them some photographs of Ezra, they are so eternally grateful for them that it actually makes me feel completely guilty for not doing more in the first place, which makes me want to do more for them and that's exactly why I was going to pick up my mother-in-law at the airport. I volunteered. I'm so guilt ridden I actually want to do it. Also, because Harry and Shirley live so far away from us, there is no way they can just drop by every Sunday afternoon the way my grandparents, Katie and Pat, did for my entire childhood. Without the geographic proximity and weekly visitations, familial provocations and tensions are vastly reduced and in their place there is something I call distance empathy. By the time I finally see them, I have accumulated almost a grain silo full of compassion for my in-laws. And to top it off, there is their grandchild to add to the mix. This is what I refer to as the "Ferrari factor." That is, if you're lucky enough to own a Ferrari and get to drive it every day, eventually it becomes just the car you drive even though to everyone else on the road "you're driving a fucking-a Ferrari, bro!" For me, that Ferrari is Ezra. I get to see and be with him every day, but his grandparents get to drive the King of Cute so rarely that I don't think it's much of an exaggeration to say that it's something they live for. Consequently, when either of them comes to LA, I really want them to be able to take a turn behind the wheel of that truly amazing entity Ezra.

So last December, when I finally arrived at LAX to get Shirley, she was nearly jumping out of her skin with excitement. Annabelle had signed up our son to attend a cotillion, as if there's nothing a ten-and-half-year-old boy wants to do more than put on a suit and tie and dance the fox trot and the waltz with an equally formal, white-gloved ten-year-old girl. My wife had a theory—she always has a theory—that a cotillion, although as obsolete as pay phones and GM, could instill in Ezra the importance of social courtesy and allow him to slowly ease his way toward being with girls. As with most theories, this one didn't stand a chance in reality. The cotillion is basically a preteen Best of Show—fine for the parents of the young pups to come ogle their offspring and take numerous embarrassing photos, but unnatural and torturous for the little ones. For the up-coming Cotillion Christmas Dance, boys were to dance with their mothers and girls with their dads. Unfortunately—or conveniently, depending on how you see these things—Annabelle was leaving for a job in New York on the same afternoon, so she suggested that her mom, Shirley, come to town and be her Cotillion Christmas Dance replacement. By her reaction, it was as if Shirley had just been nominated for the Nobel Peace Prize. And now, as she and I headed from LAX to our house in the hills of Los Feliz, she had, depending on traffic, a two- to three-light-year car ride home to ask me questions about the cotillion, and I was helpless to escape. "When does it start? How long does it take to get there from your house? What will Ezra wear? Does he know all the dances? When do I get my turn to dance with Ezra? How many boys and girls take part in the cotillion and what are their names and addresses?"

The next day it was up to me to get my mother-in-law and Ezra ready and over to the dance and document the whole thing with photographs. The pictures tell the story, Shirley all smiles and joy towering over Ezra as they danced. He looks embarrassed, in-credulous, and silly with laughter and pain as he tried to keep his balance with his grandmother accidentally stepping on his feet half the time. Shirley, conversely, appears to be tripping on ecstasy. Ezra's cotillion was her Woodstock.

I knew that Ezra hated the cotillion from the depths of his soul, and after that Christmas dance, he never stepped foot, let alone danced, in that hall again. Shirley, on the other hand, had no idea how much he loathed going. To make his grandmother happy, Ezra put up an excellent façade, making sure that he played the part of the good and loving grandson. I know exactly where he gets this talent. I witnessed it the first time Annabelle met my parents before we were married. She transformed herself: she was spunky Cameron Diaz in *There's Something About Mary* meets lovable Julia Roberts in *Notting Hill.* She was parental catnip, completely irresistible.

My parents have been separated since the early 1980s, and although amicable, they live very distinct lives. The first one to meet her was my mother, who views all interpersonal relationships through the prism of a Hallmark card that's been soaked in maple syrup and dusted with sugar. My mom treats Valentine's Day with the same sense of tribute as the Fourth of July and with even more reverence than the highest of the High Holy Days, Yom Kippur. She flew out to LA, and my tough-minded, unsentimental, all-business Annabelle took my mom on long *meaningful* hikes and *intimate* lunches, basically hitting all the right notes that ensured she would live up to my mother's idealized, saccharine picture of mother-daughter-in-lawdom.

And again, when Annabelle went to Albany to meet my dad, she was nothing short of brilliant. I was extremely anxious about her meeting him because although my dad can be delightful, warm, and very funny, he can also be harshly judgmental, fundamentally suspicious, and so highly prize his own opinions that he can make Nancy Grace seem as tolerant as Wolf Blitzer. Yet there was Annabelle, fearlessly engaging him on his home turf.

Conversely, I reverted to my twelve-year-old self when I thought that I had lost my expensive new sunglasses. They were Oliver Peoples sunglasses and I cherished them. My father pushed a pair of his sunglasses at me, claiming they were as fashionable and provided just as much UV protection, meaning they were ugly as sin and were purchased at a local Albany drugstore around the time of the Iranian hostage crisis. Then he took me aside and sternly reprimanded me for making way too big a deal about it, which had the effect of making me act even more like a preteen.

Living distinct lives doesn't stop my parents from presenting a united front when it comes to chastising me, and pushing all of my emotional and psychological buttons. After my dad called my mom to tell her about "the sunglass incident," she called me in a state of sheer panic. Fearing that my appalling conduct would cause Annabelle to call off the wedding, she advised me to run out and buy her a dozen roses, a Hallmark card, and a cute, cuddly stuffed teddy bear wearing a T-shirt that had "I Wub U" written on it and beg her forgiveness. I was in the absurd, incredibly awkward position of defending myself to my parents by claiming that Annabelle, whom they practically worshipped, had her faults just as I did. So not only was I a jerk about the lost sunglasses, but I was also being a dick about my parents' fondness for Annabelle. It was John Mahoney all over again! He was the boy my parents were constantly comparing me to when I was growing up. John Mahoney gets all A's. John does all his homework right away when he gets home from school. John always gets the lead in the school play. John's the class president and quarterback of the football team. He makes his bed every day after he's finished all his morning chores. John Mahoney doesn't get detention, play with firecrackers, talk back to his parents, or fight with his sister. I never could figure out how my parents knew so much about John Mahoney. And now Annabelle could do no wrong, according to them. Was she going to be my marital John Mahoney?

During the more than fourteen years since meeting my parents, she's proved that John Mahoney she is not. Annabelle, with her heartfelt and captivating original encounter with my parents, had set the bar *way* too high. After her pitch-perfect first impression, everything she's done since seems to pale in comparison. Expectations set that loftily can only be met with disappointment, like Gretchen Mol's career after the 1998 *Vanity Fair* cover. There was no way Annabelle would be able to keep up with my mother's virtually religious devotion to schmaltziness. Annabelle is solidly indifferent to all noneating holidays and hasn't bought a Hallmark card in . . . ever. As for Annabelle and my dad, I'm sure that every time we have all gotten together since she first met him, my dad is thinking "What the hell happened to that gal who came over to my house and dazzled me with her impeccable material and timing?" With expectations that elevated, there was no place for Annabelle to go but down.

As for me, all in all, I consider myself pretty damn lucky that Shirley and Harry hold me in such unearned high esteem. And knowing Annabelle as I do after thirteen years of marriage, those first eighteen years of her childhood could not have been a picnic for her parents. So that makes me feel for them as well.

She Says

I hate to burst Jeff's bubble, but he needn't have worried. As a son-in-law, he had my parents at "Hello."

With those thousands of miles between us, my parents met very few of the men I dated, although I did bring home one boyfriend from my freshman year in college. Jacob was the son of a famous French socialist philosopher, but all my parents knew was that he had a shaved head, owned only one set of clothing, and his bathing habits were decidedly European. He wore a black leather motorcycle jacket with skin-tight jeans tucked into knee-high, shit-kicker, steel-toed lace-up work boots; his one T-shirt had an engorged penis hand-painted on it. He wore that to the beach. He spoke no English. We also spent most of our time in Miami doing coke. That went over so well, they didn't meet another person I dated for ten years.* My folks never met my first husband until after we'd eloped, so by the time I got engaged to Jeff, the fact that I had chosen to marry someone with whom they had even a slight chance of having something in common was so astonishing that I might as well have informed them that I had grown a second head. Really, all Jeff had to do was conjugate a few verbs correctly, dress seasonally, and he was in.

By now, they simply cannot believe anyone has agreed to stay married to me for this long. My mom loves to characterize living with me as a hostage situation. A few years ago, when she was purging her house of all evidence of my youth, she returned a ransom note I sent to them from summer camp when I was the same age our son is now. It reads: *Send me candy & comics or I won't write you again, love, Anne.*

If Jeff has been a gift sent from heaven for my parents, I've been the Trojan horse of daughters-in-law. As most actresses will admit, we want you to "like us—really, really like us!" Even though I have been cured to some extent of "Actressy," I can still come down with an acute case when under pressure, and that's what happened when we headed east the first time I was to meet Jeff's dad. I rallied to give a stellar performance for my new role as future daughter-in-law to Bob Kahn, the man who had sent us a note both congratulating us on our engagement and reminding us that half of marriages don't last (all in the same sentence).

*Jacob lives in Europe and is an award-winning director and a dad now. He owns numerous articles of clothing at this point.

Bob graciously gave me a driving tour of Albany, but it wasn't to point out the historic sites of New York's capital city; instead he drove us past the homes of people Jeff had grown up with and gave me the rundown on their parents' divorces. Bob did them all. Bob divides the world into two categories, people whose divorces he's done and people whose divorces he hopes to do in the future. Maybe it was because Bob saw me as a future client, but we got off to a great start.

Jeff's boyhood home, my father-in-law's lair, is something out of the space-time continuum. With its gold-veined mirrored walls, chrome fixtures, and love beads in the doorway leading to the basement, the interior has remained exactly the same since Jeff and his sister were toddlers, as Bob mainly resides at the home of his longtime girlfriend, whose divorce he did. Jeff had regaled me with descriptions of his parents' home, and it lived up to the advance word.

Walking in the house requires navigating through piles of books, legal papers, stacks of case documents—it's like strolling around inside a filing cabinet. Bob had a cat, named Cat, who was consigned to only one room in the house, the kitchen. She seemed resigned to her role as lone full-time inhabitant of Bob's home and contentedly lazed on top of one of the taller stacks. I imagine that when she expired, some five years ago, she simply crawled into one of Bob's expandable cardboard folders and filed herself under Case Closed.

That night Bob magnanimously offered to let us sleep in his private sanctuary. On his *water bed*. I had no idea anyone still owned those things. It was the technological equivalent of sleeping on a pager. The next morning Bob made an entrance into the chamber, clad only in his Jockey underwear and an undershirt. He slapped his chest and declared, "Maybe you're marrying the wrong Kahn." Jeff says he doesn't remember this happening, but he can't be sure, as he believes he might have suffered some sort of "humiliation embolism" at that very moment.

If visiting Bob's house was a trip backward through time, visiting Ilene's home was an expedition to another planet. I had managed to make a great first impression in Los Angeles, but her home was alien territory for me. As Jeff has explained, Ilene once had her own gift shop and boutique that specialized in Mylar balloons, knickknacks, and novelties. Some of these items migrated from the store to her home, along with coffee mugs that remind you of things you might have forgotten, like "A smile is just a frown upside down." Every surface is a vehicle for a message: "Be the best *you* you can be." "Find your inner princess." "I ♥ Love." It's all very upbeat, which is something many people find comforting. I'm just not an upbeat person. Manic, sure. Upbeat, not so much. It was also intimidatingly clean. Ilene is an admitted germaphobe who has her laundry going day and night, and you could perform open-heart surgery on her "I'd rather be golfing" welcome mat. I might have had a frozen expression on my face throughout our stay, but any discomfort on my part was completely overshadowed by the Sturm und Drang of Jeff Kahn's hometown visit.

From the moment we drove by the WELCOME TO ALBANY, CAPITAL OF NEW YORK sign, Jeff transformed into a petulant teenage Alexis de Tocqueville, treating us to long-winded tirades about the preponderance of big-box stores and the oppressiveness of the cookie-cutter bedroom communities that surround Albany proper with their artificial lakes and confounding nomenclature. "Turning Leaf Manor—is that a housing development or a rehab community or both?" Because he's a major food snob and a picky eater, getting him to agree to a meal at one of the local eateries—Ruby Tuesday, T.G.I. Friday's, or across the street at Applebee's, which is down the block from the area Olive Garden—was tantamount to inquiring if he'd prefer to be drawn and quartered or tarred and feathered. Then he lost his sunglasses. The Sunglasses Incident lives in infamy in the Kahn family lore. Bob's teasing Jeff was perhaps a little excessive, but it was Jeff who was being a total pain in the ass. I found myself in agreement with Jeff's parents that he was simply unbearable to be around. By the end of the trip we were all mad at Jeff, and I left thinking, "Well, that went pretty well."

Jeff's right, though, I was a hard act for me to follow. Sometimes, when I'm drinking a cup of tea in our "I'm a ten-year-old trapped in a thirty-year-old body" mug, courtesy of Ilene's store, I feel guilty that I've cheated Ilene out of the daughter-in-law experience she deserves. I don't play golf; I don't get manicures; and romantic comedies with Matthew McConaughey (especially ones where he takes his shirt off, which is all of them) make me want to run through the streets and stab people in their eyes. I'm sure Ilene is still stumped as to what kind of person doesn't find a lithograph of two anonymous cherubic children holding hands while running on a beach with balloons adorable. Sadly, for Ilene, I'm just the kind of cynical person Jeff would go for, so since that first meeting I've never managed to deliver on the initial promise of more meaningful encounters. As for Bob, I haven't been able to schedule enough time or summon the intense energy that I lavished upon him at our first summit. I had set the bar too high.

Our annual pilgrimages to Albany did provide me with some of the most wounding ammunition I can deploy when trying to escalate a fight with my spouse. Just uttering the phrase "You're exactly like your dad" cuts right to the quick. On the other hand, saying "You're nothing like your dad" produces the same devastating effect. I use one when Jeff loses his temper and the other when comparing him to how successful his dad has been in his chosen profession. It works like a charm every time! But it was practically a conjugal vow to view our parents through each other's eyes, so five years ago I started letting Jeff and Ezra take the trip upstate without me. Instead, I see them at a restaurant of my husband's choosing, in neutral territory, like Manhattan. Not being present to witness Jeff's crabbiness on these family visits spares me from taking a polarizing position. I'm making this sacrifice for the good of my marriage, damn it!*

Getting to choose the kind of relationship you want with your in-laws is a luxury that would have been unthinkable for my parents, whose early life together, not unlike Bob and Ilene's, was conducted near their in-laws. My parents shared meals, child care, and business interests with both sets. We've had friends who've had their in-laws move in with them for either health or financial reasons, or both. Jeff and I haven't faced that kind of challenge yet. Not that my in-laws would ever want to live with us. I think Ilene would prefer that we cast her onto a slab of sea ice in the Arctic Ocean before subjecting herself to my ridiculously poor housekeeping habits. Jeff has promised that should my parents ever need to live with us, we'd find a way to accommodate them. That he would even offer makes me love him more than ever, and I'd be sure to call home often from ports around the world because I'm more likely to sign up with the merchant marines than live with my folks again.

As employment opportunities shift to different parts of the country, many more people will likely find themselves in the same position as Jeff and me, living apart from their parents and thus spared that daily or even monthly in-law squabbling. Is this good or bad? Have we fetishized traditional cultures where multigenerations live in close contact? A 2008 Harvard study showed that

---

*I just thought of this excuse, and I've kinda convinced myself of its logic.

Japanese women who live with their in-laws are more than three times more likely to have heart attacks than those who don't.* That study didn't factor in the financial benefits of having in-house babysitting or the kind of familial bond your kids get to enjoy when they grow up near their grandparents, but with the age of marriages and childbearing creeping upward, who knows what the future will look like? It's notable that when Big and Carrie got married on the big screen, neither set of in-laws was in attendance.†

What kind of future does this portend for Jeff and me? Just the other night, Ezra held my hand and asked me to stay with him for a few minutes before he fell asleep. I lay down next to him. I was silently congratulating myself for raising a kid who wants my company when he whispered softly, "Mom, I want to spend as much time with you now, before I start to hate you." Parenthood is so humbling. I'm just someone's future mother-in-law whose visits will be carefully measured out or made fun of. If I'm lucky.

*Oddly enough, living with in-laws seems to have no negative health benefits for men. Go figure.
†Jeff just thinks that Robert DeNiro and Diane Keaton were unavailable.

GURKAHN RELATIONSHIP QUIZ

Not sure how your relationship is stacking up compared to ours? Add your scores together and you'll see whether you should be saving up for retirement together or packing your bags right now. Good luck!

1. How good are you at influencing your partner?
   a. I'm Alan Dershowitz!
   b. Only when there are copious amounts of alcohol.
   c. Almost as good as I am at predicting earthquakes.
   d. I'd have better luck getting Rush Limbaugh to admit he's been wrong about anything he's ever said.

2. Are you competitive with each other?
   a. We're cocaptain cheerleaders on our Team Marriage—*Go us!*
   b. It's hard to say, but I think I'm winning.
   c. Yankees versus the Red Sox, but worse and without the multimillion-dollar merchandising revenue.
   d. Have you heard about that little feud between God and Satan? Yeah, it's like that.

3. When things don't go your way, do you sulk or withdraw?
   a. Never. I'm a happy, well-adjusted person raised by happy, well-adjusted, and loving parents.
   b. There are times when I sulk and my spouse withdraws and when my spouse pouts, I withdraw, but never at the same time or for more than a month or two.
   c. I sulk and withdraw only when I'm awake.
   d. Like a kid whose parents have confiscated all of his video games and given them away to less-fortunate children.

4. Do you have fun?

   a. Always—being with my spouse is like renting our very own fun house in the middle of the funnest street in Funtown, USA!

   b. It's possible if enough antidepressants are mixed with several other, less-legal drugs.

   c. If you call Guantánamo Bay fun, then yes, we have fun.

   d. What's this strange word *fun*? Nope, never heard of it.

5. How much anger and irritability do you feel?

   a. Our relationship is like a Buddhist temple on the Buddha's birthday.

   b. We get pissed at each other, but we're not Baldwin and Basinger.

   c. Let's just say it's a very good thing we believe in gun control. A very, very good thing.

   d. I'm Mount Vesuvius and he/she is Mount St. Helens, and it's go time, baby!

6. Do you feel included in each other's lives?

   a. There is never a moment when we are not together in body, mind, and spirit. We're not two beings; we are one joined in holy matrimony.

   b. Kind of, but I feel that the cover charge is way too steep, and the drinks at Club Spouse Inclusion are really watered down.

   c. I remember once being asked about something while we were planning the wedding. That was the last time—ever.

   d. I have a better chance of being invited to take over North Korea.

RESULTS:

7–9: You're in amazing, glorious, perfectly blissful union and we fucking hate you—a lot. Stop gloating.

10–18: OK, you have some problems and it's probably going to get worse, so get some therapy quick and buy a really good vibrator.

19–26: It's bad; very bad; very, very bad—we can't help you. Sorry.

27–28: You have entered Jeff and Annabelle territory, from which there is no escape. Call your lawyer immediately.

69 percent of disagreements that arise in a marriage are never resolved.

—*How to Survive Your Marriage*, 2004

how do you split this marital asset?

Dr. Richard Batista of Long Island, New York, donated his kidney while married to wife Downell. In their 2009 divorce petition, he is asking either to have the kidney returned or to receive a million dollars in compensation.

my chemical romance

Love produces chemical reactions in the brain, but what if you aren't in love anymore? How can you produce the same results?

Serotonin (falling in love): sunlight, SSRIs, warm milk, chocolate

Oxytocin (trust and bonding): have baby and bond with it, eat more chocolate

Endorphins (security of long-term love): go for a run or a swim, chocolate again

Phenylethylamine (adrenaline rush of affair): climb Mount Kilimanjaro, meditation, caffeine, just give up and buy the chocolate already

70 percent of couples argue about money at least once a week.

—*Smart Money* magazine

O brave new world that has such people in it! Could Shakespeare have envisioned this tempest?

A British couple, Amy and David Pollard, split up after she caught him cheating in Second Life. The two spent many hours of their marriage in the online world as their vastly more attractive avatar characters Dave Barmy and Laura Skye. They married in 2005 in both worlds. In 2008, with the help of an online detective, Amy caught David's avatar having sex with a pixel prostitute. Pollard is now engaged to the woman whose avatar he was caught cheating with.

11

. . . .

I'm OK, You're the Problem

"In the early years, you fight because you don't understand each other. In the later years, you fight because you do."

—JOAN DIDION

Socrates is quoted as saying, "The unexamined life is not worth living." Records of that time suggest he also fought with his wife on a regular basis. Big surprise.

She Says

Every few months for the first maybe nine years of our marriage, I'd get fed up with how much we argue and try to persuade Jeff to attend couples therapy sessions with me by citing the role of a referee in sports. "Players need someone from the outside to judge," I've offered. But Jeff has countered with "Unless there's a guy in a striped shirt with a whistle who can follow our marriage around and call us on our shit when and where it happens, I'm not interested."

However, I've managed to wear him down and we've seen a few counselors. We'd meet up at one of these offices and, inevitably, one of us would be running late and we'd argue about being late, and then proceed to tear each other to pieces. I assumed that the point of going to couples therapy was for me to convey my perspective to the therapist, who would naturally agree with my point of view, that once Jeff was reprimanded by an objective third party, he would have to follow my directives to the letter. I have heard that is a misinterpretation of the goal of therapy, although I suspect I am not at all alone in my reasoning. There is a saying often bandied about: would you rather be happy or would you rather be right? Right, of course! Being right is what makes me happy. Emotions come and go, but the certainty that you're right never fails to comfort you as you stalk off angrily to your separate corners and obsess over the details of your disagreements.

He Says

I don't dislike therapy. How else could I have found out that everything I've ever done wrong was really my parents' fault? Couples therapy, on the other hand, is the worst. It's like a fifty-minute argument in some stranger's living room.

So, why did I allow myself to be dragged into these couples therapists' offices? Easy. After each session I felt shitty, but Annabelle felt great, and if that's not good enough, she felt guilty that I felt so bad. The combination of her feeling both good and guilty made it much easier to get into her pants. Yes, I might be superficial and have a one-track mind, but at least I'm consistent.

She Says

We tested the therapeutic waters together with a matronly and taciturn therapist named Diane. These were expensive exercises in futility during which Diane would nod, I would vent, and Jeff would stew. I would feel much better following Diane's sessions, but Jeff wanted to throw himself from a window. So we broke up with Diane and rebounded with Glen, who may or may not have been wearing an ill-fitting wig. Jeff and I argued so vehemently about the status of his piece that we couldn't focus on ourselves, so we dumped Glen. Next, we hooked up with New Age Donna; traditional Charlene; Bonnie, the very Waspy lady whom Jeff scared every time he raised his voice (which was often); a cadre of intensely serious middle-aged men with receding hairlines and soothing voices; my rabbi and spiritual adviser Mel, whom Jeff respects but had vetoed for our wedding and in whose company he could never resist ranting against organized religion even when the subject was division of household chores.

In one of our sessions—I believe it was with Diane, but it could have been Charlene or the very Waspy lady Jeff scared—we were asked to do a marital therapy exercise. I was eager to try it. Jeff considered it a waste of time but agreed because leaving the session early would have meant getting stuck in rush hour traffic. The assignment was titled "The Fondness and Admiration Catalog." We were told to list the things about our partner that bother and annoy us. Then we were to explain why we justify putting up with them. I believe the object is perspective, assuming that each participant will examine their list and realize how small and petty their concerns are in the face of the deep love and respect they have for their partner, and thus build on the fondness and admiration.

Here is the actual transcript from that session:

JEFF

You're asking me what bothers me about Annabelle. Seriously? Christ, where do I even start? [He takes a moment to think about it.] OK, it never ceases to boggle my mind how Annabelle opens up boxes of cereal, cookies, bottles of medicine, packages of smoked salmon, and containers of cheese as if she were a feral, starving animal with large claws, huge fangs, no sense of reason, and lacking the ability to use logic or opposable thumbs. I'm pretty positive that most chimps, a majority of orangutans, and even bottle-nosed dolphins would do a much better job of opening things than Annabelle. I am forever having to find new ways of salvaging these shredded boxes and containers with Scotch tape, safety pins, or just abandoning the destroyed packages altogether and emptying the contents into plastic bags, which, by this time, I have to buy in bulk. And then she has the nerve to yell at me because plastic bags are bad for the environment. If they are so bad, maybe she should learn how to open up cardboard!

I am also constantly amazed at Annabelle's bed-making technique. Annabelle leaves the blankets in the same crumpled jumbled mess from the night before and then casually drapes the bedcover over them. The pillows are then pushed and squeezed under the lumpy covers. It's not so much making a bed as it is stuffing it like a cannoli.

And how is it okay for her to take all the cups and glasses from the kitchen and leave them in her upstairs office? I'll be at a loss about where they've all disappeared to when I remember how she hoards them, and then I have to go upstairs to retrieve all the coffee- and wine-encrusted cups and glasses.

Even more aggravating is that although she's completely addicted to coffee and uses the espresso machine sometimes up to five times a day, Annabelle refuses to clean, add water to, or care for it in any way. She treats the machine as if it were her personal little coffee bitch, exploiting and mistreating it until it dies an ugly, dirty, dehydrated death from neglect and abuse. I spend almost half of my morning cleaning the espresso maker of excess grimy coffee grounds, removing the caked-on soy milk, and adding the life-sustaining water until the next time Annabelle tries to kill it. And you should see how she keeps the inside of her car! It's as if everyone in the city of Los Angeles opened her car doors and emptied everything out of their pockets and threw it in. Riding shotgun in Annabelle's car is equivalent to sitting in the back of a garbage truck on pickup day. I'm no clean freak by any means, but after driving with Annabelle, I not only need a shower, I also need to be deloused. It's really very nasty.

ANNABELLE

Jeff doesn't like my housekeeping habits very much, which is interesting considering that Jeff engages in a mortal struggle with kitchen appliances on a daily basis. Recently, Jeff squared off with our toaster. Ezra and I were happily reading *Harry Potter and the Order of the Phoenix* when the tirade began. Was the battle between Lord Voldemort and Harry raging in our very own house? No, it was just Jeff. "Ugh, ow! Shit, fuck! Annabelle, why did you buy this piece-of-crap toaster?" Scuffling and metal-on-metal clanging sounds ensued. In the morning, I inquired, "Who won?" but I needn't have. When I went downstairs, all traces of that toaster were, as they say, toast. Jeff's ire is not limited to appliances; it also stretches to answering machines, shoelaces, traffic lights, phone solicitations, and (especially) organized religion.

True, no one will ever bounce a quarter off a bed I've made, but Jeff leaves traces of his presence everywhere.

Every morning the same sight greets me. Wadded-up damp towels gather in a wet heap that looks as though an old man has curled up by the side of the tub and expired there. In addition, Jeff refuses to adhere to the new regulations of our recycling program. He's a one-man superfund site. He reacts to my reminders as if I have personally set out to regulate him, not that these are instructions from the City of Los Angeles. Consequently, I spend a great deal of time keeping our reusable resources from sitting in a landfill for the next millennium.

My spouse also doesn't take into account that I spend much of my day in the car, making it, in effect, my secondary residence, but Jeff has turned our house into the equivalent of my car's interior. Either Jeff is turning into his dad or his history major's interest in ancient civilizations seems to have degenerated into a compulsion to create piles. These mounds of detritus act as a Rosetta stone to the life of Jeff Kahn. Receipts, phone numbers, tax-filing information, price tags from new clothes, movie theater stubs can be found in interesting configurations scattered onto every flat surface in the house. This makes living with Jeff both a fire hazard and fantastically entertaining for someone whose hobby is scrapbooking. Sadly, not being crafty in any way at all, I have been reduced to placing smoke detectors all over the house in case any of Jeff's structures should ignite and reduce our home to a pile of ashes.

JEFF

First of all, 98.9 percent of the time I throw the right trash into the right recycle bin, so why does my accidentally putting one recyclable item into the wrong wastebasket make me, according to Annabelle, the captain of the Exxon *Valdez*? Let's talk about how well all of her initiatives have worked out. One year she insisted on fruit-sweetened whole wheat cupcakes for Ezra's birthday party. Some of the boys threw them on the ground in disgust while others used them as baseballs and batted them against the side of our house. They were so dense, they're still decomposing in the backyard three years later.

ANNABELLE

I'm glad Jeff mentioned that birthday because Jeff always makes fun of my attempts at organizing structured activities. That particular year, for Ezra's birthday celebration sleepover, I hired a cousin and her friends to come and set up play stations where they supervised cookie baking, arts and crafts, and soccer. Jeff made fun of this and said that I had overscheduled the boys. So the next year I let Jeff have his way, and we made no plans at all for the annual event. The boys all went outside to play in the backyard. In less than ten minutes, these parochial school boys had transformed into a marauding gang. One boy was tied to a tree, with two or three others taunting him with a big stick, while another band was in the center of the yard jousting with chairs. The only way we were able to reestablish order was to get pizzas and permit the entire bunch of hooligans to throw slices at one another until they exhausted themselves. It was a nightmare. I'm still tired.

JEFF

Please, you're always tired and when you're not, you're on the phone. Who is she talking to all the time? Not me, that's for sure. She positively refuses to be accessible to me during business hours, which consist of the moment she wakes up to the second she goes to sleep. You'd think she was on staff at the State Department. Ezra and I have even come up with a nickname for her: Phonabelle. Interestingly, when she's on the phone, she becomes this completely different personality. She's . : . nice. Phonabelle has a hi-how-are-you, over-the-top, artificially upbeat can-this-person-really-be-my-wife voice. The voice is very different from the one who answers the phone when I call. That phone personality answers with something like this: "What is it, Jeff?! What? Make it quick because I'm on the other line on a very important phone call." Between all her calls and the countless time spent checking her e-mails on her "Crackberry," Annabelle has a communication device plastered to her face for three-fourths of the day. For the other fourth, she's sleeping. All of this leaves precious little time to, say, go see a movie or have oral sex.

ANNABELLE

It amuses me that Jeff takes my occupational hazard of talking on the phone as a personal indictment against him, when it sometimes appears as though our entire family schedule revolves around Jeff's obsession with a particular bodily function. Basically, his day is a continuum of bathroom runs, which makes it impossible to calculate the timing of everyone else's use of that room. Inevitably, I might amble into said room at the same time that Jeff has headed in armed with the entire newspaper, the new Philip Roth novel, and the *Mahabharata.* Jeff is convinced that somehow I am conspiring to keep him out just because I also use the bathroom to shower and put on my makeup; however, it would be impossible to plan my visits because he seems to need to go all day long, after which we stage a daily reenactment of the scene from *Marathon Man:* "Is it safe?"

JEFF

Here's another thing that drives me nuts: she cannot master any technology invented after 1989. Now, admittedly, I am no techno-wizard at any level, but compared to Annabelle, I'm Steve Fucking Jobs. Annabelle has never figured out how to work the DirecTV, the DVD player, or, of course, the TiVo, all of which our son had mastered by the age of three. This means that after I've finished saving the espresso machine from certain death, I segue into my other identity as Annabelle's techno-slave. I'm up and down the stairs all day long trying to solve the many technical mysteries that never cease to bewilder Annabelle and grind her life to a complete halt. She'll call me to her office to see what's wrong with her computer or printer, and a majority of the time I'll take one look and tell her that because the printer and computer run on electricity, it might work better if she remembered to plug them in. Later at night I have to turn on the TV set for her, remind her how to use the DirecTV remote, and also work the TiVo, a task that Annabelle finds as perplexing and unimaginably complicated as the string theory. If it was left up to her and I didn't push to upgrade our technology into the twenty-first century, Annabelle would be listening to cassettes on a Sony Walkman, watching VHS tapes, and working on her nine-inch black-and-white laptop with a rolling trackball by gaslight.

ANNABELLE

Jeff is right. I can't figure out the remotes. They annoy me and I can't help it; I just don't feel like learning how to do it because, let's face it, all of this type of information becomes obsolete the minute you learn it. The small space I have left in my brain is currently occupied by user names, passwords, membership numbers, credit card expiration dates, and e-mail addresses, all of which will have to be updated constantly, leaving no more room for any new information and instructions. I know that once I conquer the TiVo, the new downloadable chip will be ready, and by the time I can figure out how to add music to my iPod, I'll be downloading songs straight into my all-in-one phone, and if I ever bother to learn how to do that, you can bet that the very next week Apple will invent a way to upload tunes right into my brain.

JEFF

Annabelle will not let me listen to music in my car when I'm driving if it's any louder than a Jennifer Lopez movie dialogue whisper. I love to listen to music when I drive, but straining to hear lyrics by the Strokes at a volume only a dog can discern is absolutely maddening. This prohibition doesn't just apply to music loudness, it also goes for controlling car temperature, speed, and when I can or can't honk the horn. Annabelle is not just my navigationally challenged copilot, she's my passenger-side Mussolini.

ANNABELLE

I might be his passenger-side Mussolini, but he's a veritable Stalin behind the wheel. He acts as if he's the dictator of the road with his stream-of-consciousness narration of everyone's mistakes. Other cars, trucks, motorbikes, bicycles, pedestrians, squirrels, potholes, a stop sign—you name it and Jeff honks at it. The only things that enrage Jeff more than other drivers' habits are his own errors when he's playing sports. That's right, Jeff himself is a bad sport. I signed us up for a weekly family tennis lesson, but every time Jeff missed a shot, he'd curse at himself and throw his racket down in disgust. Both of these expressions of bad sportsmanship were accompanied by loud growling through clenched teeth, which was sometimes sprinkled with expletives. When he played, it sounded like he was on the receiving end of a Civil War–era amputation. His claim that "lessons were ruining his game" was a novel one; meanwhile, our child was privy to all of this behavior. What kind of role model was he being by being such a bad sport?

JEFF

Speaking of bad sports, it really irks me that Annabelle refuses to wear lingerie. Not on Valentine's Day, my birthday, or even our anniversary. She claims to be just antilingerie. She finds garter belts and thigh-high stockings silly, needlessly provocative, and objectifying, three things I hold very dear to my heart. Yet I doth think the lady protests too much because there is plenty of evidence to the contrary. I have personally seen dozens of photos of Annabelle wearing very sexy lingerie all through the 1980s and early 1990s. She insists she never wore it to be sexy for a guy, but as a sort of neo-postmodern-feminist, mini-Madonna fashion statement. "Just for herself." Well, I am sorry, but I don't buy it. I mean, even Annabelle will freely admit that the period from the 1980s to the early 1990s was the prime of her sluttiest years. Those fortunate boyfriends and suitors got the emotionally desperate, nearly nympho lingerie-adorned gamine that I somehow completely managed to miss by marrying her.

ANNABELLE

Jeff would like me to wear sexy lingerie. I get it! Let me state for the record that I have never been a lingerie girl. Jeff thinks I am making up the fact that I was wearing these items in public as a political statement. He forgets that I am not of the current generation of postfeminists who feel perfectly comfortable popping out babies in their twenties while simultaneously piercing their labias for a QuickTime video to be posted on YouTube. No, I am age wise, an annoying postfeminist feminist who wore lingerie outside the bedroom to break down stereotypes, but inside, I always preferred to wear the pants and not the panties. OK, sometimes I wore neither, but never did I don a garter belt or push-up bra. Meanwhile, the only thing Jeff says more often than "Would you please put on a pair of thigh-high stockings" is "How's my hair?" If Jeff were a Hindu, that could be his mantra. Ironically, his hair always looks the same to me.

JEFF

The fact that Annabelle thinks my hair looks the same all the time speaks volumes as to how little she actually looks at me. My hair's been every which way since we first met. Back then it was big and puffy like a cloud. Then I cut it mid-length, then went short, then very short, then I grew it out long and curly, and then cut it short again and now it's between looks. I don't know what it is. I mean, how is it? How's my hair?

That's when Susan or Donna, or maybe it was Bonnie or Glen said, "Great work." They appreciated our honesty and were very much impressed by our attention to detail.

JEFF (INTERRUPTING)

We have more. I can't stand the way she uses the phrase "Don't micromanage me" every time I disagree with the way she's doing something, for instance, loading the dishwasher without first rinsing out the meat-stained dishes.

ANNABELLE

Jeff has this whole list of words and phrases I can't say. Jeff thinks the word *property* is an erection killer. What am I supposed to say, "Jeff, the land our house is sitting on's tax bill arrived in the mail today"?

At this juncture, the therapist says, "That's all we have time for today, but you two should definitely come back." In fact, she/he suggested we come back twice a week for the next six months if not for the rest of our natural lives. Annabelle assured her/him that we'll consider that, and so we dutifully made our next appointment and slunk out of the office.

As we drove home, the Strokes playing at a barely audible level in the car, we talked about the session. We both acknowledged that we really did need to pick our battles. One of us, noting that the timbre of our exchanges can be a little too heated, suggested that perhaps we should ratchet down the tone. One of us said that *ratchet* was about to become as overused as *micromanage*. One of us agreed that we would try not to use the word *ratchet* quite as much, and the other agreed that although SSRIs had eroded the partner's once full-throttled libido, it probably was important to function in the world as long as the music could be turned up just a little. Agreed. Then we calculated how much the next six months of counseling would cost. Though mathematically challenged, even we could figure out this one. Once a week at $175 for six months came out to $4,200. We weighed our options. That was enough for three nights plus tax at the surreally luxurious Post Ranch Inn in Big Sur (ocean views, five-zillion-thread-count sheets, Lindt chocolates on the pillow) or four and a half months at a youth hostel in Flagstaff, Arizona (towels and linens included, shared bath). Come to think of it, in total we've spent enough money on therapy over the years to make a monthlong barge trip down the Seine ($25,000) or a week's worth of dinners at one of Napa Valley's most celebrated restaurants, The French Laundry, without wine, of course.

It's our belief that it's ultimately more cost-effective to complete the fondness and admiration exercise over tiramisu with candlelight instead of sitting on a sofa in front of a stranger trying not to make eye contact. The latest data tells us that there are more than fifty thousand couples therapists practicing in the United States today, so clearly, many other couples are spending as much as, if not more than, us on counseling and the latest innovation:

conjugal boot camps. Statistically speaking, after four years, upward of 38 percent of couples who seek out help end up divorced anyway, so we have a suggestion for couples who are thinking of sinking all of their hard-earned money on therapy: Go to Paris instead. Get drunk and eat great food. You might eventually get divorced, but at least you'll have the memory of harping at each other in front of Notre Dame instead of in some cramped, windowless therapist's office.

field guide to the vacation trajectory of a married couple

prewedding weekender: the fuck fest

Two sex-filled days and nights at a picturesque Santa Barbara hilltop hotel

year one: napa valley bacchanalian bliss

Drinking wine, eating great food, more wine, more food, wine, food, wine, food, sex, sleep, food, wine, a little biking and tennis, food, wine, sex, sleep, sex, spoon the rest of the night

year two: romantically rustic

A cozy cabin in the woods of Big Sur. We soak in a hot tub, make a wood-burning fire, screw. Jeff is so happy he's inspired to gobble at a flock of wild turkeys that live on a farm next door to the cabin. Turkeys mistake Jeff for female bird in heat and attempt to ravish him. Turkeys chase him back into cabin, perch overhead, and peer through skylight while we try to have sex. Nothing can deter us; we're passionately aflame! Gobble gobble!

year three: we always had paris

This was the high point of our marital vacations. We drop off kid at Grandma's in Albany. We saunter guiltily but very happily down the Avenue des Champs-Élysées eating seven meals a day. Luckily, we had no idea that this was our last gasp of vacation grandeur or we might not ever have left France. As it was, it took several garçons to pry Jeff's hands from that last bowl of steamed mussels or we would have missed our flight home. Au revoir, joie de vivre.

year four: intervention convention

Four years into our union, it was a hostage-style, no-one-gets-out-of-here-alive journey to the center of our relationship. Annabelle spent the entire weekend weeping and wondering if we should have a second child. Somehow, in the middle of this emotional meltdown, Jeff discovers there's an all-girl anal porno in the room's DVD player. Imagine that—all-girl, all-anal, conveniently left in our room. He spends two days trying to convince Annabelle that he didn't put the movie in there and proceeds to memorize each scene for later reenactment. Meanwhile, Annabelle breaks her indoor crying record.

year five: reality bites

We stop in at the relatively inexpensive Harris Cattle Ranch for a one-night vacation en route to the annual Gurwitch family Thanksgiving dinner in San Francisco. Ezra takes a few bites of Annabelle's tri tip, a delicious yet sinewy cut of cow, when that old persnickety esophageal stricture makes an untimely appearance. It forms a net across his esophagus. We spend most of the night trying to coax it down, and a large part of the next day debating whether to take him to a hospital in LA or to a hospital in SF. Just as we decide to head back to LA, Ezra raises his fists in the air and announces, "It's down!" We drag ourselves to San Francisco, but when we arrive back home, we are greeted by an overflowing toilet. Spend much of the night and next few days washing down floors with bleach. All in all, an utterly unrelaxing holiday.

year six: the frugal family freebie

A lovely two-plane jaunt with hours of layovers to picturesque Albany, New York. It may sound like a good idea to take up Jeff's parents on their annual offer to babysit while we take it easy in our hotel. Can any couple manufacture romance at the Capital District's Viewcrest Suites, which has neither a view nor a location on a crest, but occupies an uninspired spot on an industrial stretch of highway where each prefab room smells more like spoiled fish and old socks than a youth hostel on a fisherman's wharf? Come on, we dare you!

year seven: asian con-fusion

Jeff surprises Annabelle by making reservations at a hotel near home, cleverly eliminating costly travel expenses. We eat a delicious Asian-fusion dinner and arrangements have been made for Annabelle to have an hour-and-a-half shiatsu massage. Jeff neglected to factor in that Annabelle had just returned from New York and is still on East Coast time. The effect of the three-hour difference and the relaxing massage is to put her in a state of deep sleep that she awakens from only a half hour before checkout time. Number of times we had sex: zilch. Number of cold showers for Jeff: four.

year eight: the florida bathroom keys

Annabelle takes a road trip with her parents and Ezra down the Florida coast to the Keys. Ever taken a road trip with two people in their seventies? The foursome toured exhaustively every bathroom from Miami Beach to Key West. It takes almost nine hours to make the five-hour drive.

year nine: eat and run

Jeff surprises Annabelle on their anniversary by taking her to a special dinner one hundred miles up the coast at the Hitching Post Restaurant, made famous in the movie *Sideways*. Annabelle packs away half a cow, while Jeff downs an entire family of roasted quails. We skip dessert and rush back to Los Angeles. Lots of indigestion and gas, but the food was delicious and we saved a good seventy-five bucks in sitter sleepover charges.

year ten: anniversary spa somnambulist splurge

Jeff surprises Annabelle on their anniversary with a weekend getaway to a spa in the Santa Ynez Valley. Kid is farmed out to friends so more cash could be funneled into a bank-breaking (but desperately needed) getaway. Spa splurge saw Annabelle sleeping through the first day and most of the second as Jeff retreated deep into some local Pinot Noirs for some trying-to-forget-I'm-married time. Total amount of time spent together: an hour! But oh, what an hour it was!

year eleven: evacuation vacation

No cash for a vacation due to Writers Guild strike, but luckily the national park that borders our neighborhood catches on fire. Our mandatory evacuation order gives us a chance for a spur-of-the-moment getaway to a friend's guesthouse, recently vacated by the teenage son. Teenage son never actually cleaned said guesthouse nor changed sheets or bath towels. Ever spend the night inside a high school boys' locker room? With ants?

year twelve: our $22,065 staycation

This year we go for broke with an overnight visit to Beverly Hills's most expensive chalet: Cedars-Sinai Hospital. Ezra develops intestinal blockage due to scar tissue from earlier surgeries, causing him excruciating discomfort and requiring emergency care. Our little trouper dodges a surgical bullet when his intestines right themselves without the aid of anything more than one night of a hydrating IV drip. Throw in an extra $65 for Annabelle to get an emergency Thai massage the next day. Anything is worth it for the health of our son, but with that bill of $22,000, we'll be vacationing in the backyard in a makeshift tent for the foreseeable future! Take our advice: if you want to treat yourself to something special, they charge only $8,725 for one of those super-duper new high-resolution MRIs. Food and parking not included.

year thirteen: the $14.98 fakation

As the economy completely collapses, we can't afford to leave our bedroom, much less travel anywhere overnight. We let kid have free rein over downstairs TV for the night while we retreat to our bedroom. We sip twelve-dollar California wine and watch a marathon of our favorite HBO shows on our nineteen-inch flat-screen TV. Laugh about how improbable it is that all those supernatural freaks have ended up in one backwater Louisiana town until we fall asleep in our clothes. Loved every moment of it.

12

. . . .

Anything Goes

"Marriage brings one into fatal connection with custom and tradition, and traditions and customs are like the wind and weather, altogether incalculable."

—KIERKEGÀARD

What do those red-string Kabbalah bracelets, books such as *The Five People You Meet in Heaven,* and the countless mass e-mails about miraculous stories of healing and personal salvation that you absolutely must forward to another ten friends or you won't have good luck for the next decade have in common? They confirm a recently published study by the Pew Research Center that large numbers of Americans are desperately looking for forms of "transcendence from everyday life" without any cumbersome dogma and irksome hard-to-follow doctrine. But what does this mean in practice? If you're not actively fearing retribution from one vengeful God or another, it can be difficult to get motivated enough to keep up any kind of observances. Complicating matters is our hectic schedule, which means that our family's daily rituals include the sacred search for the misplaced house keys, crossing our fingers that we still have enough coffee and soy milk left to make our morning lattes, and the mystical hope that our son will remember to bring home that night's homework assignment. Over the years we've cobbled together a set of old-fashioned, new-fangled, and just plain absurd customs into our set of Gurkahn traditions. Here are some of our favorites:

He Says

The Three Nights of Hanukkah

Here's a holiday that commemorates a short and victorious war that Israel won over the Syrians more than two thousand years ago. Wow, have times changed! Can you imagine Israel and Syria fighting a war now? True, the kids like Hanukkah because they love any festival that celebrates military victories and miraculous oil that burned for eight days more than it had any realistic right to burn, God be praised. Yeah, right. Kids like presents and that's exactly what Hanukkah, in its calendar proximity to Christmas, is all about. You all remember Christmas, the celebration that honors the baby Jesus' first shopping spree at an indoor mall?

Every year Annabelle and I are resolute in trying to give Ezra a sprinkling of his religious heritage by lighting the Hanukkah lights and saying the prayers. We also appreciate how the glowing lights seem all the more cheerful set against the early darkness of that time of year. The first day of Hanukkah, I've set out the menorah and loaded it with the two candles. It's rarin' to go! We all gather around, light the candles, say the prayers, and then give Ezra a present from one of the grandparents or aunts or uncles. The second day of Hanukkah is much like the first, but Ezra is late coming downstairs, while Annabelle forgets she's got dinner on the stove and when the smoke fills the house, she runs off to turn on the ceiling fan and open all the windows. Before the second candle is lit, Ezra asks for his present. I dig out another grandparent/relative gift.

This one is never quite as good as the one from the first night and Ezra cynically returns to his homework far less enthused. Night three, Annabelle is not at home. Ezra is in the middle of homework and doesn't want to come down unless he gets the present first. The candles don't seem to stay in the menorah very well and I have to keep putting them back after they fall off. We manage to light the candles, but don't bother to say the prayer. Night four, Annabelle and Ezra are both not home and I'm off in my office at the computer writing or looking at free Internet porn. Night five, none of us are at home. Night six, Annabelle is thinking Hanukkah is over because she can't remember when it started and has put the menorah away and none of us bother to do anything about it. Night seven, I feel guilty and look for the menorah, but I have no idea where Annabelle put it. Desperate, I put the candles in a loaf of bread and instead of the traditional blessing, Ezra thinks it's hysterical to sing "Happy Birthday to Jews." We laugh, the candles fall over, and I blow them out. The last night of Hanukkah finds all three of us at a good friend's Christmas party eating a decidedly un-kosher holiday meal of ham and imported cheeses, the three of us downing Lactaid tablets because Ezra is, like us, lactose intolerant. Next year I'm sure we'll try to do all eight nights, but predictably, we'll get to night three and that will be that. Who really knows for sure whether that oil lasted for eight days; maybe it lasted for only three and they thought, Hey, that's not long enough for a winter holiday that will someday have to compete against Christmas; let's make it eight. So maybe we Gurkahns are not just lazy and religiously apathetic but more historically accurate.

She Says
Groundhog Day the movie meets Halloween 2005

Honestly, three days of any holiday is enough, right? I like things that can get done in a twenty-four-hour time frame. That's why Halloween seems manageable. Unfortunately, we're still celebrating Halloween 2005. In 2005, I went all out. I bought pounds of candy to hand out to the neighborhood kids, and I even managed to buy and put up the decorations a week in advance. It was the first time in my life I had gotten the seasonal decor right, so it seemed a shame to take down the ghost faces I had attached to our trees right away. I intended to leave the decorations up for only an extra week, but that week turned into a month and by 2007 the bark had started to grow around the edges of the masks. Now ghoulish foliage is just part of our direction lexicon, "Oh, you can't miss it; it's the third house on the left, the one with the perpetual Halloween decorations."

That year was also when Fraidy Cat wandered out of our house and took up residence inside a hedge outside our front door. We couldn't see her, but we could hear her horrible garbled meowing from deep inside the bush. We all felt awful about Fraidy, except for Jeff, who took to calling her Freaky. I was so desperate I consulted a pet psychic. It took her all of about two minutes and seventy-five dollars to come to the psychic revelation that our pet didn't like being called Freaky/Fraidy Cat and we needed to start calling her Esme again. If we did that, pet psychic lady predicted, she'd come back inside the house. Even though Jeff positively loathed this cat, out of love for me or because I yelled at him, or both, he joined me in a daily ritual of begging Esme to rejoin our family. Neither the name change nor the whole cans of tuna with which we tried to entice her lured her back indoors.

Late one night, about three weeks after receiving the useless pet psychic's advice, Jeff and I heard some scuffling in the bushes, accompanied by loud hissing and a short high-pitched meep. Jeff opened the front door of the house and saw

Esme/Freaky/Fraidy Cat's limp, matted fur ball of a corpse in the mouth of a coyote. Acting on instinct and perhaps too much Pinot Noir, Jeff grabbed one of Ezra's dinky Star Wars light sabers—really nothing more than a flashlight outfitted with a flimsy plastic cone—and gave chase. The coyote sauntered brazenly up the street, leaving Jeff out of breath as he brandished his plastic weaponry. Esme/Fraidy/Freaky was gone forever.

So for Halloween 2005, Jeff marked the spot where Fraidy Cat was taken from us by scrawling "RIP Fraidy" on a stone leading up to our house. Each year we turn over the marker, while other folks decorate their yards with faux gravestones. Since that year, our *descansos* is the real deal.

And 2005 also marked Ezra's refusal to wear a one-stop-shopping costume. It had been so easy when he couldn't speak, just stuffing him into a little soft suit and voilà, instant cow or pumpkin. Once he could voice his own opinions, he was Spider-Man each Halloween (and many other days of the year) until 2005, when he announced that he wanted us to make a costume together. Clever and crafty parents turn their kids into pieces of sushi, iPhones, or wind turbines, but due to our combined negative organizational skills, by 5:30 p.m. we were tearing through our closets to hunt down old clothes and applying makeup for beard stubble to achieve that costume favored by harried parents everywhere: the hobo. I've tried to help him keep his hobo au courant by making timely signs that vary from BROTHER CAN YOU SPARE A MILLION to WILL WORK FOR HEALTH CARE BENEFITS (which would be both a trick and a treat). Last year, deep in the grip of the Twilight book series, Ezra added fangs and became the first hobo vampire in our neighborhood.

Because we don't really get a lot of trick-or-treaters, since 2005 we've been sheepishly doling out that same Halloween candy. We've barely made a dent in the stash, so we'll be hauling it out every year for the foreseeable future. Maybe that's the one trick we're actually pulling off. We've made time stop and it's always 2005 at our house, at least for one night every year.

He Says

Father's Day, Fight Club

Another great nouveau Gurkahn tradition is to take Father's Day and drain every last drop of joy out of it. Perhaps this stems from Annabelle's habitual indifference and perpetual disregard for sentimentality, or from my inheriting from my mother more of a weakness for contrived holiday sappiness than I had originally thought. It's true; I actually don't mind these minor manufactured celebrations. It's one day on which you can grant the other person appreciation and acknowledgment, however brief or even artificial. I know it's not like winning an Academy Award or Pulitzer Prize, but sometimes it just feels good to be recognized.

A few years ago Annabelle was in a showcase of short plays written by teenagers. Why she chose to be in those plays, I don't know. For my Father's Day present she got tickets for Ezra and me to see her in the teenagers' plays. I don't think she did this with any malice, but if there is one thing worse than going to see mediocre theater in Los Angeles, it's going to see mediocre theater in LA that's written by teenagers. I don't know who liked it less, Ezra or me.

Afterward, there was a supremely vague plan to go out to a Father's Day lunch and an even vaguer idea as to where we were to go. As we headed out to find a restaurant, I was about to turn off the narrow side street near the theater when a megalodon-sized Hummer limo came out of nowhere and turned into the street at the same time. He saw that I was turning and could easily have stopped to let me scoot by, but instead he proceeded to barrel to-ward my car like a tank running over a bicycle. He rolled down the limo window and barked at me in broken English to back my car down the street and let him through. I rolled down my window and told him to let me through. He got angry, I got angry; he started to curse me, and I cursed him back. Annabelle hit the fan. What was I doing? What if he had a gun? The mention of a gun sent Ezra into hysterics, imagining I was about to be shot. The Father's Day standoff continued, the limo driver and I screaming and cursing each other, Annabelle reprimanding me in a shrill hate-filled voice, and Ezra bawling his eyes out. Finally, I gave up and let him pass. We didn't go to a restaurant and instead drove home in a bitter silence interrupted only by Ezra's postcrying snif-fles. I spent the rest of the day in Annabelle's doghouse—by myself and watching an NBA play-off game. She went to bed without even saying good night as the game segued into *SportsCenter* and a night spent sleeping on the couch.

After that, Annabelle was conspicuously out of state and not present for three years' worth of Father's Days. Then last year—surprise, surprise—she's in town and promises to take me to one of our favorite French restaurants for lunch. She's all sweetness and light, swearing we have to end our dismal Father's Day custom of absence and loathing. On the way to the restaurant, out of nowhere, Annabelle suddenly states she wants us to have a talk about our finances. She says we never talk about them. I say we always do, even, for some insane reason, on Father's Fucking Day. She pushes, I resist, she insists, I lose it, and soon we are at each other's throats about it. The restaurant plans are scrapped once again and it's back to the doghouse/couch/TV sports for me. Thus, another Father's Day bites the dust.

This year, I plan to let Father's Day come and go by treating it like any other Sunday. That might not make it a very special day, but it also might not suck ass.

She Says

Toothy Booty, or Bad Business in the Land of Fairies

The tooth fairy visitation and honorarium is one of those childhood conventions we have tried to observe with some reliability, but due to our incompetence, competitiveness, and inability to stick to a plan, our tenure in fairydom had an inauspicious beginning, inconsistent middle, and is heading toward a crash-and-burn finish line.

One of the unexpected side effects of having a kid with a chronic medical condition is that you are always primed to leap into crisis management mode at the smallest sign of trouble, so when Ezra was in kindergarten and he yelled from his bedroom, "Mom, my tooth fell out," I screamed, "Oh my God, Jeff, his tooth fell out; let's go to the hospital!" I was already herding a confused Ezra into the car before I remembered that young children's teeth are supposed to fall out. After he went to sleep, we were stoked—Ezra's first lost tooth! Jeff had what sounded like a plan. "Wouldn't it be fun if we could tell Ezra we saw the tooth fairy? Better yet, what if he could see her?" Jeff suggested that we should make a tooth fairy visitation video every time Ezra loses a tooth. Jeff would film it and I'd be the tooth fairy. Maybe it was because I was so excited to have gotten a part without having to audition that I instantly agreed, and we sprang into action.

See, it sounds like a good plan until you really start to think about it. "What should the tooth fairy wear, Jeff?" "A sheet." "Too scary, she's not the tooth ghost!" I settled on an elaborate beaded jacket that my mother wore in the 1960s. I looked like a tooth maître d'. Now we're standing outside his door debating about the story line. "What should I say?" "I don't know, something tooth fairyish." "What do I do if he wakes up?" "You're the actress, do what the tooth fairy would do!" After debating this for a solid thirty minutes, Jeff realized that there was no tape in the camera and we stalked off to our separate corners. That seemed to be that—our child seemed destined for a fairy-free childhood.

The following morning, Ezra woke up ecstatic; he received two separate envelopes with a total of forty dollars. Huh? That's a sum that's going to be hard to produce every time the kid loses a tooth! As it turns out, both of us had separately left twenty dollars under Ezra's pillow. In an attempt to cover up our mistake, I came up with the great idea that there's an East Coast fairy and a West Coast fairy, and because we are often visiting family back east, Ezra falls into both of their jurisdictions. The very next time Ezra loses a tooth, he goes to bed early for the first (and as it turns out the only) time in his entire life because he's anticipating his toothy booty, but Jeff and I both agree that forty bucks is too steep for one tooth and decide to cut the prize in half. To soften the disappointment the next morning, we contrive a new twist to the tooth fairy tale: because we live so far away, the East Coast fairy is often unable to come, depending on how many teeth have been lost along the longitudinal lines for which she is responsible on any given night. If you want to confound a six-year-old, use the word *longitudinal*.

Tooth after tooth had us doling out cash and coming up with more and more East Coast tooth fairy excuses: She must have gotten caught in the jet stream and high winds prevented her from coming on time. She got confused with the time change. She's on strike for a better benefit package. Due to tough economic times, cross-country fairy flights are almost nonexistent now.

Cut to this year: after a long dry spell of no lost teeth, Ezra announces a tooth has come out during the day and he and I enter into a debate about whether there really is a tooth fairy. He's eleven so it's a tough sell, but he's still in that prepubescent phase, perhaps best characterized by the tagline for the television series *The X Files:* "I want to believe." I'm Mulder and he's Scully and if I say it just right, I know I might just suck him in one more time. In an effort to make the fairy sound more plausible, I posit this line of reasoning: "I know you don't believe in Santa; I mean, how can one guy circle the globe in a single night, right? However, there are thousands of fairies of all different types; the tooth fairy is merely one category of fairies that operates out of regional chapters, one of which is located right in our hillside neighborhood." He looks at me incredulously. I elucidate, "Don't believe me? What about leprechauns, who are a close relation of fairies? The Irish are famous for their belief in little people." (I neglect to mention that the Irish are also famous for their drinking.) Ezra's still skeptical and announces that he doesn't think Los Angeles is magical enough to attract a legion of fairies. Uncertain, he goes downstairs to get Jeff's take on the tooth fairy. My husband is so over the Gurkahn tooth tradition that he informs our son that the real tooth fairy is a transgender pixie who eats the old tooth and pees it out of her penis as money. "If that's the cash you want, you got it." Ezra giggles and then turns deadly serious. "Is that really true?" Thank you, Jeff.

The next day Ezra is completely disappointed that the tooth fairy didn't come at all. Jeff and I were so tired from arguing about why we keep up this canard that we fell asleep thinking the other was going to make the deposit once again. When he's not looking, I slip a five-dollar bill in an envelope inside the pencil bag Ezra takes to school along with a note that reads: "To Ezra, Love, TF." When I pick him up later, Ezra excitedly announces that he found a love letter in his pencil case with money and wants to figure out which girl is TF. When I inform him that TF stands for *tooth fairy* and not a girl at his school, he curses me and kicks me out of his room. I guess paying for his braces one day will be the punishment for screwing up the tooth fairy for him. This ritual has been a complete dental disaster. Thank God, he has only one more tooth to go.

He Says
A Long Day's Journey into Date Night

We try to go out once a week to a movie or dinner or just have a glass of wine and talk. One night a week, just Annabelle and I together, sounds simple . . . And yet I do believe that it might be easier for Iraq to self-govern than it is for us to pull off date night. But every week, we try.

In order for date night to have even the slightest chance for success, we need to find a sitter for Ezra. This means calling, e-mailing, and texting all the sitters we have on tap at any given time, which varies from zero to three. If one can be procured, inevitably they cancel at the last minute. Most explanations have to do with cars: they won't start or have stalled; a tire has gone flat; a battery died; brakes don't work; a front window was smashed; a boyfriend needs it tonight to drive to Lincoln, Nebraska, to visit his sick mother. We've heard myriad excuses ranging from spontaneous sore throats to one sitter who announced on the day between agreeing to come over and the actual date night that she had a hit song in England and sitting was now conflicting with her band's UK tour.

When the sitter cancels at the last minute before date night, we shift into plan B: get Ezra a sleepover. As every parent discovers, sleepovers are the bartering exchange we use instead of money to help out on one another's date nights. We take their kid one week; they take ours the next. After driving him down the block or across town, depending on whom I've bartered with and how far they live from us, we're free at last for date night! Not so fast. We still have to pick a movie to see, but we've missed all the early showings due to driving Ez to the sleepover and Annabelle will be too tired for the later ones. I'm hungry, but she's already had dinner and doesn't want to eat too much late at night. We decide to just get a glass of wine at a local wine bar that also has food, perfect! She says that because we don't have to make a movie or be back in time for a babysitter, we can relax and take our time. So Annabelle goes to take a shower and get ready for date night.

This sounds reasonable, so we quickly kiss and I head downstairs to pour a glass of wine from what's left over from last night's bottle and wait for her to finish getting ready. That's when I notice that there's an unopened Netflix movie that's been sitting on the coffee table for the last seven months. I pop it into the DVD player, get another glass of wine, and start to watch. It's one of those French movies I had read was "sensual, provocative and emotionally insightful" in the *New York Times,* but we never got to see it when it was in the theaters because it's so difficult to go and see movies on date night. I gather from the subtitles that the film is about people who are unhappy, smoke a fuckload of cigarettes, have extramarital affairs, and talk incessantly. It's a lot slower paced and harder to follow than I thought it would be, but it's set in majestic Paris and the French actresses as always are incredibly sexy. I think what the hell, I'll just watch a little of it until Annabelle is ready to go. The next thing I know, the film is over and it's three in the morning. I must have fallen asleep, which means I missed the classic French cinematic climax when the couple confront each other for having affairs, scream, cry, then have sex and smoke cigarettes. I go upstairs and find Annabelle sleeping on top of the still-made bed in her cute date night outfit and holding the latest copy of the *New Yorker* open on her lap, the lights and the TV on. It takes me ten minutes to find the TV remote and turn the set off. Then I remove the *New Yorker* from her hands and go to take a bath. Yes, yet another date night success for Annabelle and Jeff.

She says
Home Alone

So true. But I would like to note that Jeff and I have substantially different expectations for date night. The part of date night I always hope for is a chance to go out with my spouse in the company of other people. As long as the topic isn't religion, he can be really funny, entertaining, and cute. Usually socializing gives me a jolt of the falling-in-love dopamine rush of "Jeff is adorable." Having other people with us on a date also ensures that we get a break from falling into the scheduling discussion that composes the majority of our exchanges on a daily basis. However, besides resolving all the things that can go wrong in our attempts to exit our home, it's tantamount to winning the lottery when friends we both like are available when we are and also have a babysitter on the same night. That is why that Friday night playgroup we had when our kid was an infant worked for me. It was a fail-safe way to ensure we'd have conversations with other adults. As of the writing of this book, however, every single one of the couples in that group is now divorced and unavailable for date night. Now that they are single, their date nights are literally date nights. So who's left to go out with? Like so many couples, we've lost track of many of the people we knew before entering the parenting years.

Here is a short summary of whom you can expect to socialize with when your children are young should you be lucky enough to find a way to leave your domicile on date night, or frankly, any other night:

People you will spend time with

Parents of children whose kids are the same age as yours. Parents of children whose kids are the same age and sex. Parents of children who are the same age, sex, and who make around the same amount of money as you. As much as it's fun to get together with others, if you don't have some parity, you can't vacation together and eventually you will fall off their list. Parents of children who are the same age, sex, have relatively similar financial resources, and also live within five miles of your home.

People you won't spend time with

Single people. Especially single people who don't have children. Single childless people who live outside a five-mile radius of your house. However, if you find single people who think your kid is almost as amazing and cute as you do, and are not put off by the suggestion that they come to your dwelling because you have no babysitter, you may get to enjoy their company. This has happened to us on several occasions, and we always provide dinner out of gratitude.

People you break every rule and make time to see

Friends you grew up with. Work buddies you call when either of you or both are out of work and need to commiserate. People who call and say they are getting divorced and need your support. People who've been diagnosed with cancer. Relatives who've traveled by plane to see you. Relatives who have traveled long distances by car, bus, or train (but not to see you) can be worked into preexisting plans if time permits. For example, "We're going to see our kid play a maple tree in the school Thanksgiving play, wanna come?" Otherwise, forget it. (I have a cousin whom we both adore, but she's single and even though she lives within two miles of our house, we haven't seen her in three years.)

All of which is to say, it really helps to like the person you're married to, because when you have young children, most of your date nights will be spent solely in their company.

She Says

God of the Interfaith Faithless

Kids raised in nonreligious homes, according to studies, tend to seek out religious organizations when they're older in higher numbers than children raised in households with some exposure to religion. Clueless as to how to process this info, we've pieced together a smorgasbord of Episcopal school, three nights of Hanukkah, soap bars in the shape of a meditating Buddha, watching *South Park* episodes together, and attending the occasional gospel sing. Confusion abounds.

Jeff insists he's an agnostic, but remains open to a Supreme Being, however unknowable or unlikely. I consider myself a secular humanist atheist. I can't conceive of any God who would create something that tastes so delicious, allow us to invent the tools to harvest it, and then not want us to enjoy something as fundamentally scrumptious as shellfish. It defies both gastronomic and evolutionary reasoning. Still, when Ezra recently asked me if it was OK to pray to God even if you're unsure there is one, I jumped upon this as an occasion to institute a tradition of nightly prayers because it's a much better way to end the day than playing with his iPod touch in bed.

Our bedtime prayers consist of a gratitude list we make every night. Sometimes it's being thankful for his home, friends, and favorite teachers. Other times it's being grateful for the Jimi

Hendrix version of "All Along the Watchtower," PlayStation's NBA '09 Live, and his own flattering leg-to-torso ratio.

Sometimes we discuss world events at the end of the day and these inevitably creep into our prayers. For an entire month both Ezra and I ended our prayers with "At least I didn't have to saw off my own leg after being buried by a building in an earthquake."* Jeff's only participation in this ritual comes in the form of mocking us by suggesting that his evening prayer is being thankful that he doesn't have to participate in the nightly prayers. Then he makes his surly white stuffed bear Snow Ball say to Ezra, "Now you lay you down to sleep, you pray the Lord your soul to keep; now shut the hell up and go to sleep, bitch!" Oh, well, perhaps the lack of any formal religious training will cause Ezra to revolt when he's older and become a Hasidic Jew, a Mormon, or a New Age Druid who believes that godlike extraterrestrials are coming to take him to the planet Poetic Irony, where his parents are being permanently held hostage.

---

*Gong Tianxiu of Beichuan, China, not only sawed her own leg off, she also drank her own blood to remain hydrated after her husband died in their collapsed house in the earthquake of 2008. Driven by what she said was a "mother's love" for her son, she was determined to stay alive so that her child would have at least one parent.

Here's a list of marital conventional wisdom and how we choose to follow it:

1. *Conventional Wisdom:* Talk through the tough times.
Annabelle and Jeff: Pass. We prefer to just yell.

2. *CW:* Learn how to listen.
A&J: Pass again. Listening takes valuable time away from arguing and yelling.

3. *CW:* Learn how to compromise.
A&J: Still passing. Compromise is for pussies. We prefer to play the marital version of chicken—first one to back off from a head-on argument that could lead to a divorce loses.

4. *CW:* Forgiveness is the most important value in a relationship.
A&J: More passing. What's the point of that? It's much more satisfying to stew about all the things our partner has done wrong. Building resentment is one activity we enjoy doing together.

5. *CW:* Never do anything without an enthusiastic agreement between you and your spouse.
A&J: Never do anything without enthusiastically disagreeing!

6. *CW:* Commit to be in it for the long haul.
A&J: We don't like the phrase *long haul.* We are looking for something between eternity and the beginning of the next school year.

7. *CW:* Make sure you have a shared vision of the future.
A&J: Future = Way Too Scary. We'd rather stick to what we know: arguing about the past.

13

· · · ·

Future Shock Spouse

"Ye who enter here leave all hope behind."

—DANTE'S *INFERNO*

The average life span for most people in the Western world has increased by thirty years over the last century. People are getting married later, but "till death do us part" still seems like an awfully long run. We find that phrase daunting. Will we wake up one day and realize we're just not that into us?

She Says

For more than a year, I had a gift box containing a small device sitting on my desk. It wasn't until our son asked, "Mom, how come you don't use your iPod Shuffle?" that I found out what it was. My Shuffle was so small, I thought it was a remote for an iPod, and because I didn't own one, I just left it there. A child correcting your knowledge of technology is one of the first signs that you are indeed getting older. (That and the use of the word *nowadays*.)

With each day bringing a reminder of how quickly time is passing, I decided that after thirteen years of winging it, Jeff and I should talk about where we see ourselves headed. There isn't a marriage book or counselor that doesn't stress the importance of having a shared vision of the future. The Marriage Builders, a popular advice Web site, puts it this way: "You wouldn't get in a car without directions to your destination, would you?" Clearly, they never drove to San Francisco with me. But this is a tough one for us. We don't even share a blanket anymore. We gave that up by the fourth year of our marriage. Too much squabbling over the temperature. I'm always cold, Jeff is always hot, and one of us might have sneaked a bite of cheese and need to be sealed into a Dutch oven.

When I told Jeff we should create a marital mission statement, Jeff flatly refused, calling this a symptom of my neurotic worrying about the future. Guilty. I'm guessing that it's not just me and that mainly women are pushing these kinds of discussions. We have to make plans because our physiology dictates time limits. Men also have a biological clock; it's just that theirs tells them things like buying overpriced sports cars is a neat way to blow a lot of cash or that having sexual trysts with hookers in midlevel hotel rooms or attempts at erotic encounters in bathroom stalls might be a terrific way to fritter away a career in politics.*

He suggested this discussion is merely my obsessing about aging. Guilty as charged. If sports is the universal language of men, as Jeff suggests, I'd venture to say that at a certain age, cataloging the psychological and physical effects of getting older is the glue that binds most women. Nora Ephron famously hates her neck, while Chrissie Hynde says she doesn't mind getting old, she just dislikes what she deems the humiliating process of getting uglier. Though Hynde's assessment seems like an extremely disturbing

---

*Add to that: having sex with your videographer or meeting up with your soul mate in South America on your constituents' dime.

sentiment, I'll be the first to admit that I've had things injected in my face I wouldn't clean my house with.

For all the new celebration of the *cougar*, no matter how smart and accomplished you are, you have to be taut and trim to get the same results as a guy. There's only one Demi and Ashton. It's a world of Michael Douglases trading up for the Catherine Zeta-Joneses. I would simply appreciate some advance notice should Jeff intend to exit our union, as it'll take a lot of work to get the ass ready if I want to go back on the market.

When I finally got Jeff to sit down with me, he admitted he hadn't ever thought that far ahead, because he was operating under the assumption that he would outlive me and take up with some very young, very attractive nymphet, whom he most certainly would *not* marry. That's it? That's his plan for our future? I was furious. Jeff has the audacity to think he's going to outlive me!! *That's totally ridiculous!!* As for his plan to seduce nubile young women, it's not that I object to a last-gasp sexathon, it's just that I'm a little dubious about his ability to attract sex-starved supermodels when his competition is going to be guys like billionaire businessman Ronald Perelman. I'm sure Ronny is a scintillating conversationalist, but one of his most attractive qualities is that he's packing an enormously large portfolio, while Jeff doesn't know the difference between a 401(k) and an ice-cream cone.

I naturally assumed, based on *every* available statistic, that I would outlive him, at which point, with Ezra safely launched into the world, I also have some plans. My list includes: traveling to Tuscany with my girlfriends who naturally will have outlived their spouses, walking across East Asia, digging wells in Africa, and election monitoring in South America or South Florida—the kind of do-gooder stuff I'm a sucker for.

Jeff tried to make his case for why he assumed he'd live longer than me. He threw out his low cholesterol number and that he goes to spinning classes twice a week. I retorted that I didn't know my cholesterol level offhand, but the mere fact that he has that number at his fingertips is not something he should advertise to his future dates. No woman under fifty wants to know that you know your cholesterol level. Add to that the fact that his spinning class makes him so tired, he takes naps afterward, something that is definitely not a turn-on to anyone over six years old, and then only after they've eaten milk and cookies and had story time.

We stalked off to our separate home offices and began pulling up Web sites that claim to predict your date of death. Big surprise: every one of them favored my sipping champagne on the Italian Riviera and strolling through Burmese rice paddies over my husband's fantasy fling with a coltish babe. I went to bed, happily tucked into my very warm comforter. It was maybe 1:00 a.m. when Jeff stormed into the bedroom, waking me from a life-extending good sleep, triumphantly waving a printed-out page from the sole death-clock site that had him outliving me. I had to explain that the result was suspect because he'd entered erroneous information to the effect that I have a negative attitude about my life. I'm not negative about *my* life; I'm negative about life in general. In fact, if there's anything positive about my psychology, it's my negativity. One of my favorite writers at the *New Yorker*, Dr. Atul Gawande of the Harvard School of Public Health, has written about the importance of critical thinking, which, he argues, leads toward improving systems. "In the running of schools, businesses, in planning war, in caring for the sick and injured, negative thinking may be exactly what we need." It isn't a stretch to see that these same skills are exactly what are needed to run a family.* In fact, numerous credible sources see a direct correlation between a reliance on positive thinking, which lulls people into optimistic complacency and overconfidence, and lack of oversight, fueling everything from the housing downturn, the stock market debacle, and the Bernie Madoff scandal. If anything puts me in an early grave, I predict it will be the stress of dealing with the health-insurance industry, whose own mission statement appears to be: "Band together to make it as difficult as possible for people to receive the health care benefits they pay for."

By 1:30 a.m., we'd come as close to a marital mission statement as we've ever come: "Our shared vision is to realize our dream of divergent futures."

At 2:00 a.m., the contest to outlive each other officially began.

The very next day, Jeff was a man on a mission. For all of Jeff's making fun of me, he's the faddist. Not a day has gone by since our contest began that we don't have blueberries in the fridge. Sure, sometimes we run out of eggs, butter, and coffee, but no matter what, we always have blueberries, whose antioxidant power Jeff believes will be the secret of his "win." One week he's gluten-free, the next he's cut out carbs altogether, but if new research announces that carbs are good, he's back shoveling brown rice into his mouth as fast as Joey Chestnut pounds Nathan's hot dogs. After learning that a restricted-calorie diet helps retard the aging process, he started eating less, mostly subsisting on hummus, flat breads, and vegetable tapenades. Upshot of that? Jeff does the majority of the food shopping and I hate hummus, so I've lost more weight than he has.

---

*One of the most surprising aspects of our marriage is how often I am called upon to give my "expert" medical advice. Annabelle, do you think my lymph glands seem swollen? I have a pain in my rib; do you think that's serious? Does my kidney area seem cold? "Yes, no, yes." "Really?" " I mean, no, no, yes." (If he asks again, I switch the order.)

From June through August of 2008, the faint smell of carp followed Jeff everywhere he went. As it turns out, Jeff had accidentally sat on one of the trendy fish oil gels he downs daily. This had the effect of pressure-sealing the omega-3 gel into the fabric of his favorite jeans, causing his butt to smell like old salmon. He tried washing these jeans to rid them of the odor, but all that did was spread the fish stink to the other clothes he was washing. The stuff was literally oozing from his pores; you could even catch the scent of herring now and then just walking through our house. Eventually, he cut down on the dosage and his entire wardrobe had to be fumigated.

His effort to keep fit and healthy was undone further after he began taking Advil to ease some post–root canal pain. The Advil, in turn, gave him a stomach ulcer, and that eventually made him anemic. Result? Jeff got tired easily and started taking naps and Nexium to cure the ulcer. Poor *old* Jeff.

This whole contest is driving us both crazy, but we're going to keep at it, because we're determined to outlive each other, even if it kills us.

For all of our distant-future talk, the real conundrum is the future when we're still ambulatory. According to my favorite death-clock calculations, Jeff is set to expire, hopefully painlessly and quickly, on April 9, 2036, while I'm not going anywhere until January 16, 2041. That gives us approximately 860,148,106 minutes together if we stay together that long—and the truth is the odds are against us. Many people, including futurist Alvin Toffler, have pointed to the fact that marriage as an institution doesn't make sense anymore. In his seminal and startlingly still-relevant book, *Future Shock*, written back in 1978, he predicted that in the future it will be more appropriate for us to have numerous careers and multiple marriages that will reflect the enormous personal transformations one can have given our longer life spans.* I myself had a "starter marriage," and according to Toffler's paradigm, in a very short time from now, Jeff and I should be ready to trade each other in for new spouses with whom to head off into the new directions in our lives. But I hate the thought of not being with Jeff—how else could I tell him I found something new to be mad at him about?

So I've come up with a plan as to how we can manage to extend our marriage until one of us (sadly) wins the contest. As I see it, our one hope for the future is to keep working on our level of intimacy. Experts all say that the key to a long marriage is to increase intimacy. No thanks. Give me a little mystery. Intimacy is the gateway drug to familiarity, which, as we all know, leads to contempt.

Here is a list of things I've seen recommended for building intimacy: cleaning, shopping, folding laundry, building a snowman, dancing lessons, taxidermy, going to amusement parks, gardening, badminton, Bible study, coin collecting, and model building.

Here is the list of things we don't do as a couple: cleaning, shopping, folding laundry, building a snowman, dancing lessons, taxidermy, going to amusement parks, gardening, badminton, Bible study, coin collecting, and model building.

Just living with someone can create a surfeit of closeness and transparency. If Jeff is any example, men prefer to operate on a need-to-know basis. For example, I happen to come from extremely hairless people; however, it's true that a few hairs have appeared of late. They're like those fanatical West Bank settlers: they've staked out a claim and are stubbornly making a stand on the formerly unpopulated plains of my face.

---

*Toffler and wife Heidi may have promoted the idea of serial marriage, but their marriage has spanned fifty years. "We have been arguing for fifty-six years, but we still love each other," says Mr. Toffler.

If the hair is black, you can have it lasered; but if it's blond, you can use only a certain laser, unless it has a certain thickness to it, and *if* it meets those requirements, then you have to grow it out for a few days and then *shave* it. It's so damn complicated and time-consuming that I've taken to stashing tweezers in our bedroom, the car, jacket pockets, and my wallet. It's definitely tantamount to committing social suicide and it might even be a misdemeanor to have facial hair in certain neighborhoods in Los Angeles. Meanwhile, Jeff demands confirmation from me on a biweekly basis as I sit in front of a mirror with a tweezer in my hand, "You don't have hairs, do you?" "Of course not, sweetie!" I assure him. Then I firmly close the door and go back to inspecting.

Here are some other examples of how cultivating separateness has produced an unexpected wonderfulness:

We used to take long hikes together, but after one such jaunt, Jeff became convinced he had contracted a flesh-eating virus even after it turned out to be poison oak. That was the end of hiking for Jeff. At first I was really bummed about this, but I've taken up running and am in better shape because of it.

Jeff takes baseball vacations with Ezra and his sports wife, Coach Tom, and Tom's future Hall-of-Famer son, Paris. I don't think I could survive Jeff's angry driving narration all the way to those spring training camps in Arizona, and they have a great time without me. On the other hand, I took Ezra with me on a job in Alaska. On one day trip, we were flown in by helicopter, dropped onto a glacier, and we learned to drive a dog sled. With his fear of flying, Jeff would never have accompanied us.*

---

*I informed Jeff about our adventure only when we returned home. In fact, I told Jeff that cell phones didn't work on the ship we were on, just to get a break from technology. It wasn't until a year later when he happened to call a friend traveling on the same cruise line that I was busted.

As a result of our busy work schedules, Ezra's baseball practice, and traffic in Los Angeles, Jeff and I rarely ever sit down to eat dinner together during the week. So when we do manage to grab a meal together, we have none of those so-how-was-your-day conversations followed by long, painful silences. We always have a lot to catch up on, we're really excited to see each other, and we don't argue for at least until dessert.

I never love Jeff more than when we're apart. I get so lonely for him when I travel, I call to say, "I miss you so much. You're the love of my life." To which Jeff replies, "Who is this?" And when I get back, we're very affectionate and loving and into each other for at least two to three hours.

Craving more intimacy is so much better than getting too much intimacy. We will have to be careful lest we find we've grown too distant and stop longing for each other at all. There is a difference between distance and distant. I don't pretend it will be easy. As everyone will tell you, marriage is hard work. We're both going to have to work very hard to earn enough money to afford the lack of intimacy to which we've become accustomed, but if we can keep it up, we'll retain enough mystery that we'll become our own future spouses.

Damn. That means we won't be able to stick to our mission statement of realizing our divergent futures. Wouldn't you know it? Another idea promoted by marriage experts doesn't work for us.

He Says

When I was sixteen, the future was singing in my rock band in front of adoring fans at Madison Square Garden. At twenty-six, the future was starring in, writing, and directing my own films. At forty-six, the future is now aging, illness, more aging, serious illness, and then rapid mental and physical deterioration, still more aging, followed by death. So when Annabelle insists that I talk to her about our future, I usually tell her I try not to even think about it. I'm fine right here in the present, thank you. This approach, however, does not stop her from persisting in pressuring me to make plans for our future finances and questioning what we will do and who we will be as a married couple. "If anything is certain, it is that change is certain. The world we are planning for today will not exist in this form tomorrow." So says Philip Crosby, a man I never heard of until I was looking for good quotes that agree with me about the future. The only plan I make for the future is a grocery list.

Yes, it's true that I did tell Annabelle that after she passed on I would like to meet and have one last wild ride with some young libidinous wild thing. It's also true that we both calculated our demises on death-clock Web sites. Although she found some that favored her, I found one that had me checking out on June 13, 2053, and Annabelle biting it all the way back on February 10, 2041. This was very much based on factoring in the issue of her pessimistic outlook versus my optimistic one. She denies this to no end, proclaiming that she's no more a pessimist than I am. There are many things that I am: angry, impatient, easily frustrated, cynical, and stressed out, but compared to Annabelle, I'm Deepak Chopra. On Prozac. Drinking a martini. Getting a back massage from Natalie Portman.

There are several other factors in my favor when it comes to surviving my wife. Let's be honest, is *faddist* really the right word to describe my diet of blueberries, hummus, flat bread, omega-3, and vitamin D, and avoiding red meat, pork, and dairy in favor of vegetables, seafood, and whole grains? Perhaps *culinary enlightened* might be better or *pragmatically healthy* or just plain *dietarily brilliant*! Now compare my Mediterranean/Asian/faddist nutritional regimen to Annabelle's eating grocery store sushi and downing it with her fifth café latte of the day, while simultaneously driving and texting on her BlackBerry, and I think you'll agree that it bodes a bit better for my future well-being. I also go to spinning twice a week and even though I've begged Annabelle to join me, she consistently refuses. I think she's afraid she'll have to be given emergency oxygen if she tries it and just doesn't want to embarrass herself.

OK, I admit I got an ulcer from overdoing the Advil because of severe root canal pain, but after making fun of me about my old man's teeth, Annabelle herself recently needed a double root canal. Beware the gods of irony! But most of all, I'm just a more positive person than she is and that's probably because unlike Annabelle, I'm not so fucking anxious about the future all the time.

Getting older and dying is one thing, but being and staying married is another, and Annabelle is right to question what happens to a marriage as it ages. The phrase "survival of the fittest," often attributed to Darwin and evolutionary science, actually means survival of the best at adaptation. *Fittest* makes one imagine that there is a species of frog out there pumping iron and doing wind sprints in an effort to survive the elements and predators. Darwin's actual writing describes evolution as benefiting those species that best adapt over time. I believe this adaptability paradigm holds true for marriage. If there is anything I have learned after twelve years of matrimony it's that I had better be able to adjust to whatever shifts occur in our marital ecosystem. When we first started going out, Annabelle loved how silly I was: "Oh, Jeff, who knew you were so clever and cute with all your different voices, characters, and sounds." Giggle-giggle, laugh-laugh, pants off. A year later it was: "Stop meowing at me, Jeff. I'm a person, not a cat! And if you touch me one more time with that disgusting lobster oven mitt, I'll never have sex with you again." I had to modify my behavior at least a little if I ever wanted to procreate. (I still meow a lot, way more than most cats, but the lobster oven mitt has long gone.) When we were newlyweds, she worried about our becoming one of those Hollywood couples who care only about their careers, making tons of money, and renovating their kitchens every year. Now it's, "Couldn't we redecorate our kitchen just once before we die?" Because of her change of heart about finances, Annabelle has had to adapt to what has happened to my career trajectory. When we first married, I had a much steadier and more secure income, but as time has gone by, my career has become a lot less steady and my income far less secure. So there's a very good probability that a large part of Annabelle's evolving focus on our economic situation reflects my de-evolving income. And the odds are that in the foreseeable future there will be even more changes that will require both of us to adapt if our marriage is to survive.

There are no easy answers about why some marriages last and some don't. To Annabelle, eschewing intimacy seems to be key. That is *so* her. Deny herself something everyone else in the world wants, intimacy, in order to make herself long for it—I have to admit, there is a twisted logic to it. When she's away working, Annabelle always calls to tell me how much she misses being at home with me. And when she's home, she always shoos me away, saying, "Can't you see I'm working?" Absence, however, doesn't make my heart grow fonder; it only makes my heart start wondering about how I can become intimate with someone who is not so absent. I happen to like intimacy. Don't get me wrong. I'm not talking about the kind of intimacy where you're all over each other, finishing each other's sentences, and often riding a tandem bike in the park while dressed in matching outfits, all smiley and wavy at people 'cause you're so damn happy to be married. Yet, sometimes I get the feeling that if Annabelle had her druthers intimacywise, so that she could really miss and want to be with me, I'd have to live in a separate house, in a different part of town, in a whole other time in history. Say, downtown Los Angeles circa 1949.

On the other hand, knowing Annabelle, she could completely change her mind about intimacy, just as she did about my being silly or how she felt about making money and living a less bohemian and much more mainstream middle-class lifestyle. And if that day comes, I'd best be ready to adapt. She might want us to sell our house and move into a studio apartment. That way we would save money and have our now entirely intimacy-centered life revolving around and in our bed.

For both of us, the biggest riddle remains to be solved. Why do couples stick it out until the end? Is it out of habit, fear, and just plain physical and emotional exhaustion? I think of my grandparents. Pappa Pat on the couch watching TV, eating dinner by himself while Nana Katie cleaned up the kitchen. Although she couldn't see him in the other room, she would yell at him to not eat so damn fast like a big fat slob and he would mutter under his breath between bites, "Why don't you leave me the hell alone, goddamn it!" (And they were married for fifty years!) Or is it a real and profound bond that's been made all the more rich and everlasting by the myriad of shared experiences over time, like the bonds forged by emperor penguins or Gertrude Stein and Alice B. Toklas? Perhaps is it as simple as staying together for the sake of the children. That marital martyrdom tradition of pretending to the outside world that everything's fine and dandy until the kids graduate from high school and go to college and you heave a great big sigh of divorce. What direction will our marriage take? Do we have a chance to make it together all the way into our senior years? As much as

I'm loath to think about it, I feel that it still deserves some kind of answer, however speculative and ultimately unpredictable.

All over my office there are photos and drawings of Annabelle. Some of these pictures go back to when she was a little girl, and when I see them, I feel that even when she was a child, I loved her. Not a creepy illegal arrest-me love, but the nurturing love I have for a close friend's child. The photos of Annabelle in her teenage years elicit a tender response as well, although I confess I'm starting to get a little turned on. Shots of her in her twenties during the 1980s in her Madonna/Cyndi Lauper/Boy George/downtown New York club scene phase make me laugh out loud, but I still think that if I'd met her then, I would have loved her no matter how stunningly ridiculous she looked. And by Annabelle's late twenties and thirties, we had met and I was already smitten. I like to say that I have loved all ages of Annabelle and in keeping with that spirit, I can only hope that when I'm sixty, seventy, and eighty, when I'm all gray from top to bottom and my neck flaps in the slightest breeze, I will still love all ages of Annabelle, even in her sixties, seventies, and eighties. I have always asserted that I married Annabelle because I was in love with her. And although that love was somewhat pussycentric, it was and is not solely pussy based. If I really want to experience all of Annabelle, then I have to accept and love her when she's all gray and wrinkly. If I leave her or she leaves me, then I will have missed out on truly loving her in all her ages and, worse, may have lost out on what just might be the best part of our marriage. Perhaps as we age together, our passion, agitation, frustration, even our competitive instincts toward each other, can be channeled into something more compassionate and wise. And if Annabelle and I stay married, there's even the slight chance I can achieve my lifelong dream of doing something good. Yes, I do have other much more perverted lifelong dreams, some involving me with Kate Moss in a body stocking, Anne Hathaway in a one-man submarine with lots and lots of oxygen, and Charlotte Gains-bourg in a Parisian apartment with lots and lots of good Burgundy, but I've also wondered what it feels like to be a genuinely good person—to evolve from a self-centered, vain narcissist into a man, however old and decrepit, who is able to love someone regardless of looks, social status, or sex appeal. I don't want to go all Hallmark moment here, but perhaps that is the point of marriage; it's a test to see if you're capable of not succumbing to your worst qualities and shortcomings so that in time you become the best possible ver-sion of yourself. Or perhaps you just stay together out of fear of being old and alone and end up at each other's throats, dreading every second of your spouse's company and waiting for his/her or your ultimate demise, which will finally put a humane end to your torturous relationship. What will it be for Annabelle and me? Only time will tell, but as I say, I'm an optimist.

In an increasingly disposable world where we're constantly up-grading our cell phones, computers, TVs, and cars, marriage is in-creasingly the clearest reminder that we should not discard the people we love. Annabelle and I live in LA, and in Hollywood when a person becomes very successful, he or she often buys a new and better car, a new and better house, new and better friends, and sometimes even a new and better spouse. This "success" leaves many old friends, houses, cars, and even spouses in its wake. There is a reason why famous celebrities only hang out with, date, and marry other celebrities—because they *can*. But for Annabelle and me, and the majority of other nonfamous less-celebrated mar-ried couples in the world, we can live by a more grounded creed, which is to love someone by choice and without conditions. From everyone I met and could have chosen to marry, I wanted Annabelle. I wanted to be her husband from the second I saw her. As she and

I get older, given all life's uncertainties and instabilities, doesn't she deserve to know that I will be there for her unconditionally? This seems like the only real thing I can promise her for the future: to continue to be her loving husband, "to have and to hold . . . for better, for worse, for richer, for poorer, in sickness and in health, to love and to cherish, till death us do part," until that most tragic of days when Annabelle sadly yet peacefully passes on, and after mourning her in the most heartfelt and compelling manner, I meet and take up with a twenty-two-year-old Ukrainian model who for some reason picks me to fulfill her wild and perverted fantasy for very old Jewish men.

happily ever after?

Brain scans from a 2008 SUNY–Stony Brook study suggest that while for most people strong feelings of love fade after fifteen months of being married, and are gone completely after ten years, 10 percent of couples experience the same chemical reactions in the brain when viewing pictures of their beloved as when they were in the early throes of romance.

About 65 percent of adults said they cannot live without Internet access. When asked to rate what other things they couldn't live without, the next highest response was cable television subscriptions (39 percent), dining out (20 percent), shopping for clothes (18 percent), and gym membership (10 percent). In addition, 46 percent of women and 30 percent of men said they'd give up sex before giving up Internet access, 50 percent of European men would rather watch an "important" soccer match than have sex, and a whopping 72 percent of Spanish men would rather tune in than turn on.

you can divorce, but you can't get married

Trenton, New Jersey, February 6, 2009: State Superior Court Judge Mary Jacobson ruled that New Jersey, which doesn't allow gays to marry, can grant a gay divorce. As of this printing, South Africa, Sweden, Belgium, Norway, Spain, Israel, and France, along with the state of New York, recognize legal same-sex marriages from other jurisdictions but do not perform their own.

"The very foundations of our society are in danger of being burned, the flames of hedonism are licking at the very foundation of society."
—Bob Barr, author of the Defense of Marriage Act (In 1992, while married to his third wife, he was photographed licking whipped cream from the cleavage of two women at a charity fund-raiser.)

14

. . . .

The State of Our Union

"Our nation is at war; our economy is in recession; and the civilized world faces unprecedented dangers. Yet the state of our Union has never been stronger."

—GEORGE W. BUSH

(STATE OF THE UNION ADDRESS, 2002)

The State of the Union is, of course, the progress report delivered by our presidents annually to the joint houses of Congress. It's also a 1948 Frank Capra movie about politics in which Katharine Hepburn poses as Spencer Tracy's wife in order to help him get into elected office. In real life, Hepburn and Tracy were romantically involved for twenty-seven years, a pairing that many people regard as one of the great romances of contemporary times, even though he was married to someone else, drunk for much of that time, and never acknowledged their love affair publicly. If they were alive today, their Facebook status would be "It's complicated."

She Says

I love my husband, I just don't want to be his "friend." I was on the opposite coast from my family at my friend Neena's apartment when I learned that Jeff had just "friended" her on the social networking site Facebook. "Really, Jeff?" I said, "I had no idea he was even on Facebook." I had never been on the site, so Neena signed on and showed me my husband's profile picture. It was a picture of Jeff and Ezra walking down the street together. That's so cute, I thought . . . my two guys. Then we clicked onto his photo album. There's Jeff and Ezra at Yankee Stadium. And wait, there's another shot of them, and though it's hard to tell exactly where they are, it's clearly a scene of domestic bliss. And then I glance over at Jeff's information and learn that my spouse has declined to post his marital status. That's when it occurs to me. Where am I? Is Jeff divorced? Could be. Where is the mother of his child? Who knows? Did this woman abandon the family? Maybe. Did she die a tragic death, but not so tragic that they haven't recovered enough to go to Yankee Stadium? It's very possible. It's just a dad and his motherless-moon-faced-babe-magnet child floating out there all alone in cyberspace. I pick up the phone and call him, tell him I love him and miss him (after all, I am out of town), and then I gently suggest that if he doesn't add a picture of me, I'm going to divorce him. To which he replies, "Is it going to be that easy?" Our e-mails get increasingly heated over the next two days. He gives me some crappy excuse about how he has forgotten how to upload new pictures since he made his profile and how if he changes his status now and says that's he's married, he'll be deluged with congratulatory messages, and some people will even think we got divorced and he's married someone else. We're in a stalemate, but by the time my plane touches down in Los Angeles, Neena has e-mailed me the news: Jeff has added a picture of me to his Facebook page. I had to see that for myself, which meant that I had to join the site. I promptly "friended" my husband and he turned me down. After much cajoling, Jeff agrees to "friend" me and I get to see the picture. It's of the three of us. I won. I was so excited with my victory that I wanted to learn more, so I scrolled down to the list of his friends. He has a lot of them: Caryn, Kimm, Jennifer, Holly, Leslie, Erin, Stacey, Stacie with an *ie,* Maddie, Madeline, Michelle, Marianne—80 percent of the friends of Jeff turn out to be female. Who are all these women? Some names I recognized as old girlfriends and acquaintances,* but others are a complete mystery to me. Then I casually peruse his status updates. Here are some of the highlights:

12/3: Jeff is lust in the wind.
12/10: Jeff is thinking about vaginas (plural????).
12/18: Jeff is porno in motion.
12/28: Jeff is horny for the New Year.

On some days he updates his status more times than he talks to me. I can't help but notice that there are posts from all of his "friends." Holly exclaims, "Oh, Jeff, you were always horny." Kimm chimes in with, "Love you, you little dimwit!" Wait a minute, only I can call Jeff a dimwit. Nadine writes, "Thanks for the perverted card!" Huh? What's going on here? I know that Holly was an old girlfriend who's married, Kimm sounds familiar, but who the hell is Nadine? Nadine is *gorgeous.* Is this Facebook or is this J-Date? So I'm in my home office, which is located directly upstairs above Jeff's home office, and though we're less than a hundred feet apart,

---

*See Chapter 2, "A Saab Story," page 26. Every one of the girls he writes about has friended him.

we're not talking to each other; we're fighting online. I angrily write to him: "Who the hell is Nadine and what kind of card did you send her!" He shoots off a note informing me that Nadine is an old friend from his MTV days, and as I'm writing "Listen, mister, I don't know what you're doing, but I'm not happy about this," messages start popping up on Jeff's home page; the first one is from Nadine. She says, "I'm so sorry, have I upset your wife?" Then another one on mine, "Oh, this is fun—it's like we're all in therapy together," and another, "Now, kiss and make up, you two," and then my phone rings. It's Spencer, a friend I haven't spoken to in months. "What is going on? Are you guys OK?" he says with an urgency in his voice. That's when I realize I've been writing on Jeff's "wall," which is being read by not only all of his friends but also all three hundred or so of mine. When someone feels compelled to break the cyberspace wall and reach out to you in real life, you know it's serious. It's also humiliating. It was like I had read Jeff's diary, scanned his e-mails, listened to his cell phone messages—all things I've always maintained I would never, ever do. It's the modern equivalent of rummaging through your partner's pockets for receipts. In public.

Isn't that what I have been advocating, that we give each other space, and let's face it, room to flirt? Flirting might even have some indirect health benefits. Research conducted at the University of South Alabama in 2003 showed that people who don't flirt very much have lower energy levels and rate themselves as less attractive than people who flirt a lot. Besides, the "work spouse" is now a commonly accepted phenomenon, and since Jeff works on his computer, in essence, his computer *is* his office. Facebook is Jeff's work spouse. I want Jeff to feel attractive and have energy, so if he wants to flirt on Facebook, that's fine. I just don't want to know about it. On January 30, 2009, I "unfriended" my husband.

This whole episode was completely innocuous; it didn't even rise to the level of a *Little Children*-esque discovery. Besides, I am the one with the short attention span and the bad record of fidelity, one of the reasons we are even together, and it's not like I don't have my own work spouses.

Recently I was headed to lunch with a colleague whom I was having some vague fantasies about what it would be like if I traded my man for another man. Let's call him Other Man. Other Man seemed to find me so engaging and complicated, and complicated, in this case, in a good way, meaning intriguing and witty and not my ability to simultaneously sneeze/burp/fart/and complain about people who sneeze, burp, and fart at the same time. Other Man thinks I am aging so well—he doesn't know I'm wearing Spanx and that my ass is surprisingly larger out of them. When I answer his calls, I'm friendly and warm. He gets Phonabelle, not the curtness that Jeff is subjected to. Other Man thinks I am a fairly accomplished person, but unlike Jeff, he hasn't had a front row seat to witness the really big honking opportunities I've blown. He didn't see me tank on *Hollywood Squares*, nor did he stand in the back of the studio mouthing the words *I love you* as the contestants forfeited matches to avoid playing my square. He's never seen my closets or my bank account statements, nor has he sat up with me when I tried to kick an SSRI, my one-woman live-action version of *The Exorcist*, Parts I, II, and the prequel combined. Other Man lives on the opposite coast, so he has no idea whatsoever who I am, which is great!

Other Man shows up for our lunch in acid-washed jeans. Acid-washed jeans? He's never gotten into my pants and already he's in his bad jeans. I glance down and notice he has a long black hair of surprising thickness protruding from a mole on his left arm. In that instant, it hits me that Other Man most certainly has a slew of odd habits and quirky housekeeping requirements that would begin to manifest immediately should he become My Man. I know I will find as many things that annoy me about him as I have about Jeff. It's also at that moment that I realize I am able to maintain the level of judgmentalness that I so cherish only because I have someone in my life who knows me so well and still manages to love me. Isn't that what love is? Knowing someone's life story and not using it against them? OK, maybe it's more like knowing someone's life story, using it against them, and *still* loving them.

I immediately snap back to reality, focus on the menu, and say a secular humanist prayer of gratitude that I somehow had the foresight to marry Jeff.

It's definitely "complicated." I know that this doesn't sound even remotely like the romantic fantasy Jeff was looking for, but everything we've gone through has built our history, the story of us, which is as solid a foundation as anything I've ever experienced in my life.*

Does this mean that we'll stay married forever? When asked why her marriages failed, Margaret Mead famously answered, "I've had three marriages and none of them was a failure." As much as I like to make fun of Jeff, I know that being married to him makes me be a better person. What started when we moved in together has continued. I've adopted many of Jeff's infectious qualities. I love to have houseguests. Everyone is welcome now at Chez Us. Jeff has even gotten me to use nicknames. Somewhere along the way, Sergeant Gurwitch got accompanied by "Yes, sir," and then I morphed

---

*Biological anthropologist Helen Fisher tells us that the life span of human love plays itself out every four years, just enough time to wean a child. That might have been true in our hunting and gathering days, but these days it takes more like eighteen years to raise a kid, if you're lucky. Maybe we're fighting our biology, but four years isn't very much time to create a really rich history together.

into The Sir. Then because I have so little imagination about such things, I started calling Jeff Sir also.*

Our cat Stinky is seventeen years old now; Jeff says she's retired to Florida because she spends most of her time sleeping in the warmest spot in the house, a pool of sunlight on my upstairs office desk. Jeff and I will stop whatever we're doing, even arguing, to stand and listen to her crunch her little vittles when she comes downstairs to eat during the day. And it still moves me to think of how Jeff tried to save Esme/Fraidy Cat/Freaky's life, even though he positively loathed her.

Once we added Ezra, Jeff deemed him to be a Sir, so here we are, The Three Sirs. Ezra is thriving in every way possible. That was another one of the unexpected pleasures of Cotillion. We were reunited with some of the families that were in that original Mommy & Me group. The moms can't get over how well Ezra is doing—one cried when she saw him. Being a kid, Ezra doesn't remember any of them, and just shrugs it off.

Amazingly, we've just been given yet another stunning diagnosis for Ezra's kidney. During that $22,000 staycation, Ezra had one of those new high-resolution MRIs. Purely by chance, they caught a glimpse of his kidney. His nephrologist says she can see the kidney better and it may not be dysplastic after all. We've taken him off his daily medication, and so far the kidney seems to be working up to par. Jeff swears this is a result of his positive thinking. That's fine. I'll just keep making sure our son gets monitored on a regular basis.

We're a team. Team Gurkahn. Isn't that an awful name? Almost

---

*I have heard that this is not that uncommon; we have friends who call each other Lou. Neither of their names, Peter or Yvonne, is any derivation of Lou, Louis, Louise, or Luanne, at least to my knowledge.

as bad as Gurwitch, but Jeff married me anyway. We're like a tiny unremarkable Jewish version of Kobe and Shaq when they won championships together before their egos ruined the Laker dynasty. We're like Brangelina but without all of the kids, money, fame, and high-profile philanthropy. We're a modern-day Lewis and Clark and our Oregon Trail is our marriage.

OK, I'll be honest, Jeff wrote that paragraph with me. I don't really know that much about Lewis and Clark, except that one of them was very depressed; one had a dog; and they were guided by the fabulously resilient and resourceful Native American Sacagawea, who had a baby (that presumably had an anus) along the way. I hope they made it to Oregon, though I'm not completely certain that they did. I had the idea about famous teams and Jeff filled in the details. I was worried people would think we were conflating our importance, but Jeff argued that readers would understand we mean this metaphorically. We also fought about which names to include, but that's just the kind of marriage we have, although I'm sure Jeff will disagree.

He Says

In high school I was voted by my graduating class not Class Clown, or even Most Likely to Need Rehab; no, I was Class Flirt. Twenty-nine years later, nearly thirteen of which I have been married (thirteen years—my indoor monogamy record), I still am a Class One Flirt. Only now my classroom is called Facebook and my classmates are my old friends and past dates, fuck buddies, and girlfriends. Here's an example of one of my Facebook interactions with some old girlfriend/past date/fuck buddy: "Hey, great to hear from you again. You're making jewelry now? Wow, I never knew you could make necklaces out of mice bones. That's so cool. I'm living in Los Angeles with my wife, Annabelle, and son, Ezra. He's going to be twelve! My wife and I are writing a book together about our marriage. It's so crazy. Wow, time sure flies, huh? Haven't heard from you since Chicago, summer of 1987. Those were the days: drinking beers, playing pool, smoking cigarettes by the shores of Lake Michigan at sunrise . . . So what have you been up to? You still like to 69 all the time?"

But how does all of this Facebooking bode for the State of Our Union? I believe it bodes well. Here's why: when Annabelle was first sending me threatening e-mails about putting her photo on my profile page under threat of divorce, I asked her, "Is it going to be that easy?" Then I sternly told her, "It's Facebook. It's my Face and my Book. If you want to tell me what to do with my Face and Book, then join the site and try to friend me." After our spat was displayed on the Facebook "wall," and Annabelle recanted her initial disapproving assessment, I got to thinking that this was the first, and as far as I could remember, only time that Annabelle was actually jealous. Indeed, she's never been a jealous person at all and hasn't seemed to mind how flirty I am with all her attractive friends, several attractive waitresses at our neighborhood restaurants, the extremely fit hotties in my spinning class, including the instructor, and every supercute mom at Ezra's school and baseball team. I have actually imagined that I could be sitting on our couch making out with a girl when Annabelle would come home, take one look at us, and sigh dejectedly, "I just had the worst audition," and then go upstairs without batting an eye. And here she was all bent out of shape and jealous about the girls on my Facebook page, and that made me feel really, really . . . good. After all these years, she truly cares.

This all leads me to ask, Who the hell is this acid-washed-jeans guy whom Annabelle refers to as Other Man? Should I be worried about him and his hairy mole? Personally, I could have lived very happily without knowing about acid-washed-jeans guy. I'd prefer that when it comes to that, what happens out of town stays out of town. On the other hand, I think it's a good thing that other guys find Annabelle still sexy and desirable. It's great for her ego and mine, too, because men hitting on your wife means you're lucky to have such a hot one. And besides, to be candid, I had an affair once. It happened after Annabelle was fired by Woody Allen. She was in New York working on a play he wrote and was directing. It was her lifelong dream to work for him, so understandably she was completely devastated when she got canned. However, that didn't stop her from turning lemons into lemonade by collecting hundreds of other people's stories about being fired and turning them into a book, movie, and a theatrical stage show, and even a radio show that was produced in LA by Susan Raab Simonson, the wife of one of my closest friends, Eric Simonson. Nevertheless, Woody Allen was absolutely banned from our house—and I don't mean to be didactic or facetious in any way—but every book, movie, and magazine article. I wasn't even allowed to tell a joke mimicking his voice, which is something I'm pretty good at and enjoy doing when I'm drunk enough at parties. The total Woody prohibition wasn't so terrible because this was during the time that Woody Allen movies sucked. Yet when *Match Point* came out and everyone jumped back on the Woody wagon, I tentatively asked Annabelle if she'd like to go and she kicked me. About a month later, when she was out of town working, I snuck out to see *Match Point*. Luckily, it was midafternoon and at this point in the movie's run, no one was in the theater. Minutes before the lights dimmed, I turned to see a small group enter the theater. My eyes locked on Susie Raab Simonson. As her close friend and radio show producer, Susie knew all about how Annabelle felt about Mr. Allen and her unqualified prohibition of everything Woody from our life. She quickly spotted me and was grinning from ear to ear, immediately sensing what

I was doing there. "Annabelle doesn't know, does she?" she teased. I was so busted. I lowered my head in shame and begged, "Susie, if Annabelle ever asks where I was today, please, please just tell her I was with another woman. That she may forgive me for, but not this." She cracked up, but I drew her closer and whispered, "Seriously, don't tell her." I really meant it. A tremendously sad and tragic footnote to this story: Susan died of breast cancer. And bless her dear heart, our beloved Susie never did tell Annabelle that she caught me cheating with Woody Allen.

Annabelle has also given me something so great, so awesome, so incredible, so something that no one else can, she *gives* me stories. As a writer, stories are invaluable, but also as a human being, I need stories. Who are we without our stories? I mean, without stories we would live in fragmented moments trying to balance all of the various obligations and responsibilities that are our jobs, schools, and relationships with the daily regimented essentials of eating, pooping, and driving. (In Los Angeles, it's mainly driving.) Our stories are what keep us sane and humane in a world that's often not very sane or humane. Our stories are what link us together. They are what bind us as husband to wife, parent to children, friend to friend, and all those people you used to sleep with before you got married. Isn't that what Facebook is all about? It's the millions of people around the world who are weaving the threads of their old stories into their current stories. At any rate, no one has ever given me stories like my Annabelle and our bewitched, bothered, and bewildered of a relationship, not even my days adrift at my military school. She was my muse even before we got married, and to this very moment she continues to by my muse. She inspires me, she intrigues me, and she is forever giving me great stories like this one:

We finally got to take our overdue honeymoon in Napa Valley

a year after our wedding. We spent all day playing tennis and biking so we could spend all night eating at Napa's amazing restaurants. I liked touring all the wineries, and as we passed by the
Niebaum-Coppola Estate Winery on our bikes one afternoon, I
wondered out loud why Francis Ford had Niebaum's name in front
of his. Annabelle knew the answer immediately. And I had no
reason to doubt the authenticity of the information, because she
knows things like this. Annabelle is a bona fide generalist or what I
have come to deem a "macroist." While a specialist knows a vast
amount about one specific subject—a podiatrist knows about feet;
a sommelier knows about wines (and I know all the good free porn
sites)—a macroist knows a good deal about a great many fields of
interest. Annabelle's not a certified expert in any one field, but she
has loads of pertinent information to impart on many domains.
She may not be an executive chef, but she knows a lot about food
preparation because she starred on a cooking show for almost seven
years and worked very closely with the show's chef. She has no
degree in psychology, but she is very knowledgeable when it comes
to Jungian analysis of dreams because she did a ton of research and
reading while she hosted a show about dream interpretation. After
she was fired from the Woody Allen play, Annabelle educated herself on the nation's employment and economics policies, and by
the end of that journey, she was collaborating with U.S. senators, a
former Labor secretary, and UAW members around the country. So
it sounded entirely reasonable when she told me that Francis Coppola was a notoriously bad businessman and that Niebaum, his
lawyer, had to help him keep his vineyard financially afloat after a
rocky start. As a reward, Coppola added Niebaum's name to the
winery.

Later on, when I paid a solo visit to the vineyard, I saw that in
addition to the winery and gift shop there was a museum. Inside

the Centennial Museum was the story of Gustave Niebaum, a Finnish immigrant who made his fortune in the Alaska fur trade and then in 1879 pursued his dream of establishing in the Napa Valley a great wine estate to rival the estates of France. In February 1995, Coppola purchased the massive stone Inglenook Chateau and its adjacent vineyards, reuniting the original Napa Valley estate founded by Gustave Niebaum, preserving his legacy for future generations. Annabelle's perfectly plausible story about Niebaum-Coppola turned out to be absolutely 100 percent false. Embarrassed by her completely illegitimate tale, she defended herself by stating that she had mixed up the facts about Coppola's Zoetrope Studios' financial problems with his winery. That studio part was true, but the winery part . . . My macroist-muse strikes again. And another story was born!

The thing is, for me Annabelle is a veritable jukebox of greatest-hits stories. Press FU-99 and you get "The Fuck You Lady of 1999." When Ezra was just a baby, Annabelle set herself up as the household's one-woman Standards and Practices, and she forbade cursing. She didn't want Ezra to learn how to speak from listening to me swear at my "fucking computer!" and the "piece-of-shit toaster!" One night after Ezra's colic cries finally ground to a halt at around nine o'clock, we began to hear party sounds emanating from our next-door-neighbor's house. We knew the parents were away on a vacation and had left their sixteen-and-a-half-year-old daughter alone. Clearly, she proceeded to have one of those sixteen-and-a-half-year-old-my-parents-are-out-of-town parties. I had them when I was growing up and felt that it was fine—until around one in the morning. Not only was the party still going on, it was getting *louder!*

By around two, we couldn't take it anymore. Ezra would be up in a few hours, and without sleep we'd have to start yet another day at work exhausted, irritable, and completely ineffective. The party was directly below our bedroom, and Annabelle wanted to go out on our porch and yell at the teens to shut down their party immediately. I never wanted to be one of the old fogies who yell across houses at "young folks" to stop having a good time because it's late and we're so *old* we need to sleep. So I told Annabelle that I'd go across and tell the teens in a reasonable and teen-friendly manner to keep it down.

I was on my way over when I heard screeching coming from our porch: "Shut the fuck up, you fuckers!" Guess who was cursing like Tony Soprano? Couldn't she wait one minute for me to go over there? And as in a bad teen movie, some Teen Tough Guy yelled at her to mind her business, and she totally lost it. "I am minding my fucking business and if you don't get the hell out of there, I'm calling the fucking cops, fuck face!" Teens could see from our porch that she had a phone in hand and fingers on 911. "That's right, go the fuck home before I have you all fucking arrested." As I struggled to get back to our house, I had to dodge and weave around stoned and drunken teens who, fearing Annabelle's wrath and their imminent arrest, scrambled out of our neighbor's house and into their daddy-bought teenmobiles. Annabelle was screaming at them all the way: "That's right, you better get the fuck out of here, you fuckers!" After the Fuck You Lady incident, I pretty much was given free pass to curse all I wanted to.

There's more: press jukebox number EM-08 and you get "The Edible Mission of 2008." As big a jerk as I am with Ezra playing sports, when it comes to doing homework, Annabelle has made Ezra cry more times than Simon Cowell has *American Idol* rejects. Tears were flowing when Annabelle, the czarina of schoolwork and the Stalin of everything environmentally friendly, determined that Ezra's social studies assignment, the construction of a model of the

San Juan Capistrano Mission, was the perfect opportunity to ex-periment in sustainable architecture. Thus she insisted that they build solely out of biodegradable materials. Feet were a-stomping in frustration when Ezra learned how impossible it is to Elmer's-glue graham crackers together. The green version of San Juan Capis-trano turned out more like a sad and crumby adobe hut assembled by an early version of a *Homo sapiens* still unaccustomed to manip-ulating his opposable thumbs than like a model of the "jewel" of the California missions. Instead of a historical replica of a religious site where swallows famously return each and every year, Annabelle's sticky sweet creation provided an excellent dwelling for a number of home-invading insects.

And the hits keep right on coming. I hope they never, ever stop. For at the end of the day, when I sign off from Facebook after saying good-bye to all my Facebook gal-pals, there is only one I want to be with. Only one woman I want to have a glass of wine with and talk about our days. One woman I want to hold and kiss. The one woman I want to undress and sleep with is my sexy, hot, funny, smart, macroist, one-woman story machine: Annabelle. Alas, when I get to our bedroom, she's already sound asleep. Because she just got back from New York and although it's ten here in LA, it's one o'clock in the morning her time and she's completely ex-hausted, and she'll be totally pissed off if I try to wake her up so we can fool around. So I just watch her sleep a little. It's nice when she's asleep—she looks so peaceful and it's so quiet since she's not talking. Man, I love her. Thank God she's my wife.

Acknowledgments

Many thanks to the numerous people who helped us write this book and somehow still manage to stay married. To our fearless advocate, Laura Dail and the Laura Dail Literary Agency; indefatigable manager, Andy Cohen; talented and patient editor Suzanne O'Neill; her wonderful assistant, Emily Timberlake; and, of course, the fabulous Tina Constable. Thanks also to the great team at Crown: Jenny Frost, Jill Flaxman, Annsley Rosner, Patty Berg, Laura Duffy, Elizabeth Rendfleish, Patty Shaw, Amy Boorstein, and Jill Browning.

Friends, Family and Supporters: our loving parents Shirley and Harry Gurwitch, Ilene and Bob Kahn, and Bob and Ilene's super-significant others, Pati Demont and John Tartaglia. Jeff's devoted sister, Marcy Kahn. Annie Hamburger and Big Heart Productions; Kimberly Rubin; Elyse Roth; David Borgenicht; Chris Burney and Second Stage Theater; *The Nation* magazine; Paul Glickman, news director of KPCC. Heartfelt thanks to Steve Hibbert, Sue Wolfe, and Eric Simonson, the directors of our stage show in Los Angeles. Annie Howell and the Planet Green Network. All the sports-fanatic families of the Toluca Titans baseball team as well as the parents and outstanding teachers of St. James Episcopal School, for having a great sense of humor.

Our Early Readers: Robin Shlien, Neena Beber, Gia Palladino Wise, Tonya Pinkins, Yvonne and Peter Johansen, Chris Romeo, Erika Schickel, Tom Gorham, Sybil Sage, Holter Graham, Debra Goldstein, Alicia Diaz Granados, Tamara Krinsky, Annabelle's always insightful and steadfast sister Lisa Gurwitch, and Jeff's all-time best friend, Peter Berson.

Our Live Performances: Lauren Correo; Gary Mann and Paul Stein and the Comedy Central Workspace; Romie Angelich of "Published, Produced, or On Their Way"; Lita Weisman at Borders; Jaclyn Lafer and Maggie Rowe of Sit 'n' Spin; Wendy Hammers and Tasty Words; Matt Price of *4 Stories and a Cover*; Jane Edith Wilson and Gary Lucy at Lit Up; Daniel Gallant and Nuyorican Poetry Café.

We must mention Rachael Friedan, who helped collate the manuscript and then offered this insight: "Maybe you took my grandmother Betty too seriously, Annabelle."

We owe a special debt of gratitude to the Pull-thru Network, Bonnie McElroy, Kathy Tague, Susan Elsberry, Dr. Elaine Kamil, Dr. Alan Klein and Dr. Danielpour, Dr. Harry Cynamon, Beth Harrison of the Bowel Management Clinic at Children's Hospital of Los Angeles, and Dr. Alberto Peña, who innovated the pull-through surgery.

Also our great appreciations to Ezra's sitters: Kathryn Aagesen, Jolie Franciscus, and Brady Wright.

Jeff would like to thank the Palms Thai Restaurant in Hollywood for letting him edit the book there long after lunch was eaten, and Annabelle would like to thank the Starbucks coffee company, whose grande soy lattes have just about replaced her bloodstream.

And lastly, we are forever grateful to our incredible, inspiring, and unimaginably gifted son, Ezra Kahn, for sharing his story with us.

Tragically, our beloved doctor and friend Columbus McAlpin passed away on September 3, 2004. He left a wife and children of his own, and the loss to the community was immense. All the kids whose lives he saved and whose cases he tirelessly followed were known as Columbus's kids around the hospital, and Ezra will always be part of his legacy. We were so lucky that Big Mac was on call on February 24, 1998.

Annabelle Gurwitch is an actress and writer. She first gained a comedic following during her years of cohosting *Dinner and a Movie* on TBS. Annabelle turned her experience of being canned by Woody Allen into *Fired!*, the off-Broadway play, touring show, book, and documentary film. Her film premiered on TV as a Showtime comedy special and has been screened everywhere from the Southwest Film Festival to the Department of Labor on Capitol Hill. She's been a regular commentator on *Day to Day* and *All Things Considered* on NPR and a humor columnist for *The Nation* magazine.

She has hosted television shows on ABC, VH1, Style, and HBO. Her acting credits include the TV shows *Medium, Boston Legal,* and *Seinfeld,* and the films *Shaggy Dog, Melvin Goes to Dinner,* and *Daddy Day Care.* Her work off-Broadway garnered her a place in the *New York Times Top Ten Performances in Theatre of the Year 2002.* Her essays have appeared in the *Los Angeles Times, Child,* and *Glamour,* www.freshyarn.com, and in two anthologies: *Note to Self* and *Rejected!* She currently hosts the series *Wa$ted!* on Planet Green. This is her second book and second marriage.